Governing Oneself and Others

On Xenophon of Athens

THE McDONALD
CENTER FOR
AMERICA'S FOUNDING
PRINCIPLES

M E R C E R
U N I V E R S I T Y

THE A. V. ELLIOTT CONFERENCE SERIES

Guided by James Madison's maxim that "a well-instructed people alone can be permanently a free people," the McDonald Center exists to promote the study of the great texts and ideas that have shaped our regime and fostered liberal learning.

Will R. Jordan and Charlotte C. S. Thomas, Directors

No Greater Monster nor Miracle than Myself: The Political Philosophy of Michel de Montaigne, ed. Charlotte C. S. Thomas (2014)

Of Sympathy and Selfishness: The Moral and Political Philosophy of Adam Smith, ed. Charlotte C. S. Thomas (2015)

The Most Sacred Freedom: Religious Liberty in the History of Philosophy and America's Founding, ed. Will Jordan and Charlotte C. S. Thomas (2016)

Promise and Peril: Republics and Republicanism in the History of Political Philosophy, ed. Will R. Jordan (2017)

When in the Course of Human Events: 1776 at Home, Abroad, and in American Memory, ed. Will R. Jordan (2018)

Power and the People: Thucydides' History and the American Founding, ed. Charlotte C. S. Thomas (2019)

From Reflection and Choice: The Political Philosophy of the Federalist Papers and the Ratification Debate, ed. Will R. Jordan (2020)

Liberty, Democracy, and the Temptations to Tyranny in the Dialogues of Plato, ed. Charlotte C. S. Thomas (2021)

The Beginning of Liberalism: Reexamining the Political Philosophy of John Locke, ed. Will R. Jordan (2022)

The Founding: Essential Documents, ed., Will R. Jordan (2023)

GOVERNING ONESELF

AND OTHERS:

ON XENOPHON OF ATHENS

Edited by Charlotte C. S. Thomas

MERCER UNIVERSITY PRESS
Macon, Georgia

MUP/ 693

28 27 26 25 24   5 4 3 2 1

Books published by Mercer University Press are printed on acid-free paper
that meets the requirements of the American National Standard for
Information Sciences—Permanence of Paper for Printed Library Materials.

Printed and bound in the United States.

This book is set in Adobe Caslon and Lithos Pro (display).

Cover/jacket design by Burt&Burt.

ISBN   978-0-88146-926-4

Cataloging-in-Publication Data is available
from the Library of Congress

CONTENTS

ACKNOWLEDGMENTS

This collection of essays is based on the 2022 A.V. Elliott conference for Great Books and Ideas, the 14th annual conference sponsored by the McDonald Center for America's Founding Principles, entitled "On Xenophon."

The McDonald Center for America's Founding Principles began as a small conference in the Spring of 2008. It secured initial funding that summer through Mercer University's Academic Initiatives Monetary (AIM) fund, and has grown substantially each subsequent year. Neither this volume, nor the conference it is based upon, nor any of the other important work now done by the McDonald Center would have been possible without the foresight of Mercer President, William D. Underwood, the confidence of the AIM committee, the support of then College of Liberal Arts Dean Lake Lambert, and the entrepreneurial spirit of the Center's founders. Anita Gustafson continued in this tradition and showed the McDonald Center consistent support and encouragement during her time as Dean of the College.

In the Spring of 2013, the McDonald Center received a generous endowment gift from Mr. A. V. Elliott, for whom our annual conference is now named. Also in 2013, Thomas and Ramona McDonald made an endowment gift to support all of the Center's work, and with it they gave us their name. We are, and always will be, in deep debt to the Elliotts and McDonalds for their support.

Our "On Xenophon" conference was both a virtual gathering of Xenophon scholars and also the culmination of a yearlong reading group made up of Mercer faculty and students. I would like to thank all of the participants in that group by name. Each of them contributed significantly to the excellent conversation that animated our conference and this volume of essays, which it inspired. So, thank you: Will Jordan, Kevin Honeycutt, Marc Jolley, Patrick Jolley, Joseph Payne, David Swigart, Crescent Rainwater, Papa Guerrero, Michael Hurst, Brandon Miley, Kendall Webb, Safia Tejani, Alexandra Jones, Anna Hale, Amelia Rivers, Shelby Ryals, and Matthew Shatto.

I'm sincerely thankful to Peter Ahrensdorf, Wayne Ambler, Thomas Martin, Gregory McBrayer, Carol McNamara, Paul Rahe, and Richard Ruderman for presenting their scholarly work at the Elliott Conference, for interacting so thoughtfully with each other and our students at the conference, and for submitting their revised essays for publication in this volume. It has been a great honor to learn about Xenophon from these brilliant, lovely people.

Many, many thanks are due to Marc Jolley and to the whole staff at Mercer University Press who, as always, have been a pleasure to work with.

Finally, it continues to be a great privilege to work as co-director of the McDonald Center with one of its founders, Will Jordan. For many years, now, I have enjoyed the good work of fostering important conversations about great ideas among delightful people. Without Prof. Jordan's energy and foresight, the McDonald Center would not exist. Without his thoughtfulness and good judgment, it would not be thriving. Without his friendship, my work for the Center would be much less fun. So, thanks, Will, for all you do, and for the great grace with which you do it. Everyone who benefits from the good work of the McDonald Center is deeply in your debt.

CONTRIBUTORS

PETER AHRENSDORF, James B. Duke Professor of Political Science, Affiliated Professor of Classics, Davidson College

WAYNE AMBLER, Associate Professor Emeritus, Herbst Program for Engineering, Ethics, and Society, University of Colorado Boulder

THOMAS MARTIN, Professor and Jeremiah W. O'Connor Jr. Chair in Classics, College of the Holy Cross

GREGORY MCBRAYER, Director of the Core Curriculum, Associate Professor of Political Science, Ashland University

CAROL MCNAMARA, Director, Great Hearts Institute for Classical Education

PAUL RAHE, Professor of History, Charles O. Lee and Louise K. Lee Chair in the Western Heritage, Hillsdale College

RICHARD RUDERMAN, Associate Professor of Political Science, University of North Texas

CHARLOTTE C. S. THOMAS, Professor of Philosophy, Co-Director of the McDonald Center for America's Founding Principles at Mercer University, Director of Great Books, and Executive Director of the Association for Core Texts and Courses

INTRODUCTION

Charlotte C. S. Thomas

Xenophon's reputation has waxed and waned over the millennia. For centuries, he was a central figure in classical education, and then for much of the twentieth century, he was hardly read at all. Happily, his star has been in ascendance for the last few decades, and we are the beneficiaries. Socrates' "other" student certainly warrants our careful attention, whether our interest is in fifth century BCE Athenian politics, history, or philosophy. With this volume, we hope to showcase Xenophon's breadth as well as his depth. The first five essays in the volume focus on Xenophon's *Cyropaedia*, while the last three branch out into other Xenophontic works (*The Hellenica, The Memorabilia,* and *The Symposium*). All of them attempt to deepen our understanding of Xenophon's commitments as a philosopher, politician, and historian and how his work exists in the intersection of the three.

In "On the Appeal of Xenophon's Education of Cyrus," Wayne Ambler, who is the translator of the most widely read contemporary translation of Xenophon's *Cyropaedia* into English, offers a synoptic account of Cyrus' qualities and policies that lead to his success. He begins by acknowledging two major points of contemporary scholarship on Xenophon that frame his account: (1) that he reads "the *Education* not as the history of actual events but as a general treatment of a timeless problem," and (2) that it is important to him to "step back from all-out admiration of Cyrus…and to assess his qualities carefully." Staying true to these guiding principles and looking at key moments in the *Cyropaedia* with his expert eye, Ambler draws his account to a close with several interesting and somewhat surprising conclusions about Xenophon's Cyrus.

Peter Ahrensdorf's "The Distinctive Character of Cyrus' Education in Xenophon's *Education of Cyrus*" takes up the question of what Cyrus' education really is, what constitutes it, to what extent it was a success, and what, if anything, makes it distinctive. Tracking every mention of education or teaching in the *Cyropaedia*, Ahrensdorf carefully discerns patterns and tends to key episodes that seem particularly illuminating of this defining idea. Cyrus' death bed musings become a touchstone for Ahrensdorf to draw some conclusions about whether the Great King understood his education to have been a success and what else, if anything, he might have wished for his education.

In "Freedom and Friendship in *The Education of Cyrus*," Carol McNamara focuses on the tendency of human beings to want to be absolved of "the discipline and drudgery of the ordinary rule of law," and Cyrus' exploitation of this tendency in the interest of gathering followers and expanding his rule. McNamara focuses on this tendency as a problem, and Cyrus' exploitation of it as a cautionary tale. She then looks for possible responses within the *Cyropaedia* and beyond.

Gregory McBrayer, in "Animals as Models for Rule in Xenophon's *Cyropaedia*," turns his attention to animals, one of Xenophon's favorite devices in the *Cyropaedia* and elsewhere in his corpus. Thinking of rulers as shepherds is one of the oldest political tropes in literature, and Xenophon runs with it. Thinking of those who are ruled as sheep cannot but immediately follow, and with it a myriad of questions about what it means to be human in a political context. So, herd animals feature prominently in Xenophon's works, but so do other domesticated animals and wild animals of various kinds, and McBrayer's account offers a very helpful framework for making sense of the way they function in the *Education*.

In "The *Cyropaedia* as Political Tragedy, A Speculative

Essay," the last essay in this volume that is focused mainly on the *Cyropaedia*, I offer a reading of Xenophon's *Education* that embraces the fictionalized character of Xenophon's novelistic account both in terms of the construction of Cyrus as a character and the construction of the cosmos of the work as an attempt to isolate and constrain human action in order to illuminate its boundaries and character. I consider the possibility that Xenophon constructs Cyrus to embody perfect despotism in a world in which there are no viable alternatives to despotism, and that in so doing, he isolates despotism itself from the character of the despot in order to illuminate its inherent flaws.

Paul A. Rahe moves us beyond the *Cyropaedia* and focuses on the *Hellenica* in his essay, "What Sort of Historian Was Xenophon?" Rahe brings to bear his well-known encyclopedic knowledge of ancient history on this question, comparing Xenophon to Herodotus and Thucydides and contextualizing his account in the broader context of contemporary scholarship on Classical Greece. The *Hellenica*, Rahe argues, is a unified work, despite having two parts with different concerns that were probably written at different times. It is in the stitching together of these halves into a whole that we can see Xenophon, discern his *modus operandi*, and get a sense of who he was as an historian.

In "A Socratic Middle Road Between Virtue and Vice," Richard S. Ruderman directs our attention to Xenophon's *Memorabilia*. Here, we are reminded again that Plato was not Socrates' only great student, and that Plato's account of Socrates is not the only one we have access to. In the section of the *Memorabilia* Ruderman focuses on, "continence" is what is at issue, and in particular the claim that one should cultivate continence before one considers entering political life. In predictable Socratic fashion, the nature of continence and of politics themselves must be addressed before their relationship can be considered. And, in a delightful twist, we're presented with a debate between Virtue and Vice personified. Ruderman closes with some thoughts on how all of these levels of the *Memorabilia* point to a coherent teaching on continence and the context in which one can benefit from having cultivated it.

"Sniffing out Sweet Smells of Freedom in Xenophon's *Symposium*" is the final essay of this collection, and it comes to us from the well-known classicist Thomas R. Martin. Martin's erudition is on full display in this delightful account of Xenophon's use of smells in the *Symposium*. Some of the smells of the drinking party are natural and others are artificial. All have cultural contexts and significant relationships to the topics of conversation engaged in the dialogue. What does Athenian freedom smell like to Xenophon? Martin believes he knows, and in this essay he'll tell you why.

1

ON THE APPEAL OF XENOPHON'S
EDUCATION OF CYRUS

Wayne Ambler

Part of the appeal of the *Education of Cyrus* is the engaging variety of events it features. It includes battle scenes, a love story, probing conversations, the wooing and exploitation of allies, heartfelt expressions of the most sincerely held convictions, and brutally cunning lies. It also tells a story whose broad outlines are attractive and easy to follow: a capable and charming young man gets the chance to lead the army that will defend his country and its allies against the aggression of a powerful enemy, and he succeeds beyond every expectation. Not only does he save his homeland, but he also manages to undo or avenge many of the injustices that had been perpetrated by the vast empire he defeats. He then establishes what was, or at least appeared to be, a new and improved empire of his own. More than any other major work of political philosophy, the *Education* is a riveting page-turner that responds to the kind of hopes that still affect many of us as we look with distress on a world disordered by corrupt and incompetent leaders and confused peoples.

The fast-paced readability of the *Education*—free as it is from the lofty philosophic talk such as that, for example, of Plato's Socrates' discussion of the "Ideas" or "Forms" or of "the divided line" in the *Republic*—has led some to think no serious effort is needed to understand this exciting book. Nevertheless, Xenophon helps us to pause and probe the attractive surface by, for example, slipping provocative points of view into his narrative,[1] by having his characters disagree with one another on crucial subjects,[2] by tacitly contrasting what his lead character says to one audience and what he says to another,[3] and by using his first two pages to have his narrators advance a claim of deadly seriousness, that—all evidence to the contrary notwithstanding—there is a science of ruling. This will be the main subject of this introduction, but I must first point briefly to another source of encouragement and help when it comes to probing the surface of the *Education*.

I refer to the scholars who in the last thirty years or so have established beyond every doubt that Xenophon was a worthy student of his teacher, the philosopher Socrates, and that this novel-like book is also profound. I cannot pause to review this literature here, but I must acknowledge two major points on which my introduction follows these studies. One is that I read the *Education* not as the history of actual events but as a general treatment of a timeless problem, that of how to rule, or of the political man and of his field of operation. Xenophon gives this man the name of a historical character, but he does not hesitate to shape his life in the way he finds most revealing, without regard to the accidents of history. Prime evidence includes his portrait of the Persian Republic, which has more in common with Sparta than with historical Persia;[4] his account of Cyrus'

---

[1] Cyrus' conversation with his father includes several examples, especially 1.6.27, where he shocks even his son.

[2] Cyrus' conversations with Tigranes, Cyaxares, and Araspas all raise questions deserving of careful thought (3.1.14–31; 5.1.37; 5.1.4–17 and 6.1.31–44). So do his discussions on justice with his mother (1.3.16–8) and father (1.6.27–34).

[3] I will discuss several cases below, but to begin, note his admission to Croesus that his attitude toward wealth is very different from the one he has implied throughout his rise to power (8.2.19–23).

[4] Bruell (1969) 9–10. Nadon (2001) 30–33.

boyhood in Media, which is pure invention; and most of the speeches and conversations in the book, whose actual words Xenophon could never have known. Contrasting Xenophon's accounts of Persia and Cyrus with those of the historian Herodotus suggests other ways Xenophon departed from history.[5]

A second very basic point on which I follow these relatively recent studies regards their tendency to step back from all-out admiration for Cyrus, the book's ostensible hero, and to assess his qualities carefully. This sort of reading is the only way to fully appreciate his virtues, but it also makes a critique possible. True, the general tenor of the book suggests limitless admiration for Cyrus, which begins by noting that he is celebrated in word and song by entire populations (1.2.1), but is public admiration of powerful men always a reliable measure of their excellence? Cyrus is demonstrably superior to such vicious or foolish other leaders in Xenophon's cast of characters, such as the young Assyrian King and his own uncle Cyaxares, but to say nothing of how the book ends (8.8), Xenophon indicates even in the very beginning that his Cyrus ruled in part by terror and intimidation (1.1.5). If this would not disqualify him from the admiration of a Machiavelli, it should help us explore the nature and limits of his beneficence. And how does Xenophon intend that we assess the more subtle differences that stand between Cyrus and other attractive characters in the *Education*, such as his father and Tigranes? As several studies have shown, Xenophon even invites a comparison and contrast between his other heroes and Cyrus, that is, between Cyrus and Socrates, and between Cyrus and Xenophon himself, the hero of another wonderful book, the *Anabasis of Cyrus*.[6] This is a high bar indeed, and it introduces a vantage point from which to assess what Cyrus

---

[5] Bruell (1969) 5–7; Bartlett (2015) 144; Nadon (2001) 16–19.
[6] Bruell, (1969) 39, and 125–33. Nadon (2001) 179–80.

achieved both for himself and for those he hoped or pretended his rule would benefit. Thus, the *Education* has become increasingly understood as a patient study of an impressive kind of man and of his activity, not a work of pure adulation.

I note these studies of the *Education* partly to acknowledge my debt to them and to encourage others to seek them out, but also to situate the introduction that will follow.[7] I will not treat the *Education* as comprehensively as they, because I mostly limit myself to considering a single question, the one that Xenophon raises in the first three pages of the book.

The Opening Question

Xenophon assigns this question to an unidentified "we," which he later distinguishes from himself.[8] Bluntly put, this plural narrator asks how Cyrus acquired and maintained political power, when so many others, both individuals and groups, have failed to do so. Against the backdrop of political failures like those we see all around us, Cyrus stands out as a stunning success, and Xenophon's narrator boldly proposes that the reason for his success was his knowledge or understanding (1.1.3). Thus, by telling Cyrus' story, the narrator initially makes the claim that there is a kind of political science that made it possible for Cyrus to conquer and rule the world. If this thesis is sustained, the best students of his book should be able to do likewise. If it is modified in a thoughtful way, we should come to understand why knowledge is not sufficient for political success and will not

---

[7] The three scholars to whose studies of the *Education* I am most indebted are Bruell (1969 and 1987), Nadon (2001), and Bartlett (2015).

[8] Xenophon uses the first person singular at 1.2.15, which revises the plural narrator's presentation of the Persian Regime. See Bruell (1969) 17 and 17n.1.

bring an end to the woes we suffer from political failure.[9]

Introducing Cyrus: Ambition, Benevolence, Rhetorical Excellence, and his Early Years

So how then does Cyrus succeed? I will single out three steps or policies fundamental to Cyrus' success, but let me first mention three personal qualities we see throughout. Perhaps the most fundamental is his ambition or, as the Greek word indicates, his love of honor. This is mentioned explicitly several times (1.2.1; 1.3.3; 1.4.1), and if he sometimes gracefully accepted the victories of others, these cases were minor and involved competitions that prepared him for future victories of greater weight (1.4.4–5). As a rule, he sought to be honored first and foremost.

A second quality which we see often is Cyrus' benevolence (in Greek, his "philanthropy"). This too is mentioned explicitly (1.4.1), and we see many examples of his readiness to give gifts and advance the interests of others. Indeed, his many benefactions are a main reason he has appeared so attractive to so many readers. Among other examples, Xenophon emphasizes his boyhood attentions to his grandfather and gift giving to his friends and their families in Media (1.4.2, 26), his sharing of his personal portion of the scanty rations allowed to Persian soldiers (1.5.1), his readiness to help various victims of Assyrian power and injustice,[10] and his treatment of civilian refugees (4.4.9–13). And yet we will have to ask whether his eagerness to benefit others stands up when his ambition demands a different course

---

[9] Thucydides claims that his *History* will enable readers to understand the fundamentals of political events, which are tied to human nature; he does not claim that it will enable anyone to guide the course of events (1.22).

[10] See below on Gobryas and Gadatas.

9

of action.[11]

A third quality, which may be mostly a means to his pursuit of honor and benevolence, is Cyrus' excellence as a speaker. If the *Education* includes an education in how to rule, a big part of this is how to speak. Whether speaking as a boy to his mother and grandfather or as a mature leader to his troops, he is extremely clever in expressing himself and getting what he wants through speech alone, as we will be sure to note in what follows. It is true and important that the raw power he often wields sometimes makes his words more convincing, as his father taught him it would (1.6.10), but his speaking ability also enhances his raw power. The practiced ability to speak well is of crucial importance for a ruler, and what follows will give examples to explain this more fully.

I will focus on what Cyrus does to conquer and rule, but Xenophon devotes almost half of Book I to Cyrus' boyhood and youth. He would not have done this if he only wanted to show the policies by which his ruler par excellence succeeded. What we learn from Cyrus' early years, which are divided unequally between his rearing under Persia's austere oligarchy and the adventures his grandfather allows him in Media, is his character or nature and the contrasting educations he receives from living under two very different regimes. The last chapter of Book I allows us a revealing insight into another education, that of his father Cambyses.

We see Cyrus' character or nature especially when he is in Media, where his privileged position as the grandson of the ruling despot allows him great liberty to act as he pleases. We thus see examples of his benevolence, ambition, daring, cleverness,

---

[11] For an early and playful example of a case in which Cyrus' desire to be first limits his benevolence, see 1.3.6–11, where Cyrus is generous to all his grandfather's servants except to Sakas, the servant his grandfather honors most (8).

and love of beauty, and these give us the opportunity to wonder whether and how Xenophon considers them to be essential requirements of the successful ruler. Almost always winning our admiration, Cyrus is also shown gloating over the dead bodies of enemies killed in his first military encounter (1.4.24). Must the love of victory in the truly political man go so far?

But the simplest and most important point is that Cyrus' early years show the great extent to which his nature and early education prepare him to rule well before he holds a position of any responsibility. He ruled his grandfather in Media, led his playmates in various contests and hunting expeditions, boldly led a daring and successful cavalry charge against the Assyrian enemy, cleverly overcame his mother's objections so he could stay for an extended period in Media, and won over the attentions of his playmates' parents. His boyhood successes even led his uncle to call him "king" (1.4.9), and his departure from Media is an occasion for an outpouring of affection and an exchange of gifts on a grand scale (1.4.25–26). Like those rare athletes of tremendous natural gifts who also train hard to develop them, the young Cyrus is naturally and purposefully drawn to activities that give him experience in leading others. No reader of Cyrus' early years is baffled by his success in his later ones.

More generally, the focus on Cyrus' character and close connection to rulers—his father is the king of Persia and his grandfather the despotic king of Media—make it necessary to doubt the narrator, who proposed that knowledge was the only requirement of political success: Cyrus also has other advantages. Surely, he knows a great deal about how to rule, but his example suggests he is also naturally suited to rule and has advantageous family connections to get him started and boost his authority. His knowledge is a necessary but not a sufficient condition of his success. If it is a letdown to suspect that the

Education does not teach everything the narrator claimed, there are two compensations. One is seeing that even if Cyrus cannot teach a science sufficient to bring success in every case, we nevertheless have much to learn from him; the other is seeing that Xenophon offers a broader and deeper education than one with power as its only goal.

Let me now propose a simple list of three major policies in Cyrus' rise to power. They are not the whole story, but they serve as a good foundation for other observations. Later, we will consider why he distinguishes so sharply between how to acquire power and how to use it.

(1) As soon as Cyrus is assigned to lead an army, he revolutionizes it in four ways.

(2) He steals a second army.

(3) He adds allies to increase the power, aggressivity, and moral purpose of his army.

Step One
Revolutionizing the Persian Army

When he is put in charge of an army, Cyrus revolutionizes it in four ways. His changes combine to make it more aggressive, more potent, more loyal to Cyrus himself than to the Persian homeland, and more independent of its allies.

He gets his first big break when a vast Assyrian alliance threatens an attack on Media, and Media turns to Persia for help.[12] Persia agrees to join this defensive effort and to send

---

[12] It is not said explicitly that Cyrus was excited by this opportunity, but I suspect he was. In the eyes of those who love honor, war presents great opportunities, as Alexander Hamilton, when just a teenager, realized. He confessed his ambition to be a weakness in a letter to a friend but adds that it led him to wish there were a war so he might rise from his lowly station.

Cyrus at the head of an army of 31,000 Persian soldiers. No sooner is he in command of this army than he begins to make radical changes to it.

His first change is conveyed by a speech, which, though short, profoundly critiques a fundamental Persian opinion and has far-reaching implications for the future.[13] He delivers the speech to the one thousand of his soldiers who belong to the Persian upper class, the Peers. His speech's main purpose is to make these soldiers more aggressive by giving them new and more powerful reasons to fight, and these also affect the question of when to stop fighting. If the purpose of a war is reconceived, so are the criteria of victory.

To effect this change, Cyrus assaults an idea that is held at least loosely in all societies but is at the core of the education of the Persian Peers, who have it beaten into them when they are young (1.2.2–3, 7, 14; 1.3.16). This idea is that moral excellence or virtue requires us to make personal sacrifices to do what is good for others, or for the common good, and that doing so is somehow good in itself, even if it is not entirely obvious how. Rewards may sometimes accompany virtuous actions, but they are not their purpose.

Explicitly challenging this familiar view, Cyrus' new education teaches that it makes no sense to make the sacrifices virtue requires unless such "sacrifices" pay off and bring rewards, and he openly charges that the effort and restraint demanded by the traditional Persian view did no one any good (1.5.8). He refers here to "what are believed to be the works (or deeds) of virtue," as if these works or deeds have been incorrectly identified by the Persians of the past and must now be redefined with an eye on

---

https://founders.archives.gov/documents/Hamilton/01-01-02-0002 (accessed July 5, 2022).

[13] For excellent accounts of this provocative speech, see Bruell (1969) 26–31, (1987) 97–99, and Nadon (2001) 55–60.

what brings us the good things we want.

He advances his teaching through suggestive examples of necessary means to desired ends, and these also help to clarify his view of what kinds of rewards we seek and who should get them. In Cyrus' view, people abstain from immediate pleasures to enjoy greater pleasures later, and speakers speak to persuade and thereby to achieve great goods; they don't speak just for the sake of speaking. Those who practice military matters do so to win wealth, happiness, and honor not only for their city but also for themselves. Any farmer who plants but never harvests is a fool, and so too with athletes who train and become capable of victory but never compete. In Cyrus' view, the Persians have trained hard and practiced exemplary self-denial, but now it's time to seek and enjoy the rewards they have hitherto ignored. Cyrus thus liberates his soldiers' passions for pleasure, wealth, happiness, and honor, which will fuel their ardor for profitable victories (1.5.7–10). The cost (and benefit!) of this liberation is that virtue is reduced to a mere means toward these true goods.

It will be necessary to evaluate this reform as we see its effects in action. If Cyrus' troops come to be persuaded that the guiding good is no longer virtue, which of the new guiding goods will attract most of Cyrus' troops? Will it be pleasure, wealth, or honor? Cyrus is an honor-lover through and through, and surely others are as well, but might not many turn their attention more to wealth and pleasure?[14] And is pleasure-seeking as good an incentive for soldiers as honor-loving? Falstaff, a great lover of pleasure, found it easy to come up with a "catechism" that deprived honor of all its attraction, and—an extreme case, I admit—an army of Falstaffs would not suit Cyrus'

---

[14] When Cyrus exhorts Persians and his new allies to pursue the fleeing Assyrians, he appeals to future pleasure, not honor, to stimulate them (4.2.22).

purposes.[15] But even honor-lovers come with this disadvantage for Cyrus, that all would want to obtain those high honors on which Cyrus seeks to have a monopoly.

Cyrus makes the promise of future pleasure, wealth, and honor more believable by assuring the Peers that they are the most virtuous and toughest soldiers around, and Xenophon's description of their training under the Persian regime makes this claim plausible. Cyrus thus disposes his troops to think that they deserve to be rewarded more than others, and, moreover, that it is within their power to see that they get what they deserve. This has got to excite the Peers, who have known only a hard and simple life of unending exercise and know only by hearsay of the pleasures available in Media, where Cyrus spent several years of his youth.

It follows, then, that in Cyrus' presentation, the upcoming war against Assyria is not the defensive war it had been taken to be, fought in the name of the homeland and to help their ally. It is rather a welcome opportunity for the poor, hardworking, and virtuous Persians to win for themselves the kind of life they had never even allowed themselves to dream of. But to achieve this purpose, it will not suffice to merely repel the Assyrian attack. The trail of wealth, honor, and pleasure will have to be followed down a long and possibly rewarding but dangerous road.

Cyrus' speech does not mention the difficulty that the Assyrian forces are vastly larger than those of the Persians and their allies. He speaks as if virtue is the only cause of victory. Since it is not, and for other reasons, he must follow his first revolutionary change with others.

Cyrus' second reform to the Persian army is to strengthen

---

[15] *Henry IV Part I* (V.i.129–139). Greed and ambition are both energizing but in different ways, and both come to the fore in the *Education* as Cyrus' project advances. Both will pose challenges for Cyrus, especially after his last battle has been won.

the edge of the sword by turning the Persian Commoners into heavy armed fighters.

As Xenophon indicated in his account of Persia (1.2.15), it is radically divided into two classes, the Peers and the Commoners. The Peers rule and are vastly outnumbered.[16] Not coincidentally, they possess heavy weapons and train regularly in how to use them. The Commoners, by contrast, work hard for their daily bread, are excluded from political decision-making, and do not possess the expensive armor that enables soldiers to fight successfully at close quarters.

Cyrus' army has 1,000 Peers and 30,000 Commoners, which at least roughly reflects the relative sizes of the two classes in the Persian oligarchy. By arming the Commoners, he will increase his heavy armed infantry by a factor of thirty, and this will help offset the allies' numerical inferiority.

Xenophon does not pretend that it is easy for Cyrus to execute this policy. Here are the challenges: Persia is poor, weapons are expensive. The newly drafted soldiers may not want to fight on the front lines, especially since they have not been trained to do so. Two classes long wary of one another may not get along easily if suddenly mixed together, and the Peers in particular may resent the implication that Commoners might quickly and easily acquire the virtue of the well-trained Peers.

Most importantly, the policy has revolutionary implications for the political order in Persia. Bluntly put, the new arms will empower the Commoners not only against the Assyrian enemy but also against the Persian upper class. If the reform succeeds and the Commoners become good warriors, will a large and potent army of 30,000 at the end of the war hand over their

---

[16] Taken together, the following passages suggest that the Peers were relatively few in number, but they do not offer a precise count: 1.2.15; 1.1.5; 5.5.3; 7.5.67–8.

weapons and return to the low station they used to occupy? What sort of Persia will emerge if the old oligarchy is overthrown?

Here and elsewhere, Cyrus' rhetorical adroitness is crucial for his success. To mention a feature of his speechmaking that is present in almost all of his speeches, he defends his new policy differently to the different audiences who must accept it—in this case, his uncle, the Peers, and the Commoners.

To his uncle Cyaxares, now king of the Medes, he stresses the advantages the reform will bring in the war against the larger Assyrian forces. Cyaxares is worried about the vast size of the Assyrian forces, so this qualitative reform looks like a good way of offsetting the advantage the enemy has in numbers. Cyrus also suggests that the Persian infantry will take the brunt of the attack, while the Medes will only be required to chase those who are fleeing the battle (2.1.9). To the Peers, he claims his reform grows out of his concern for their safety, for it will bring many more soldiers to the front to help protect them (10–11). To the Commoners, he downplays the need for training with such simple weapons and stresses that they will bring a new way of life and new rewards to the long-deprived Commoners (14–19). Put in the negative, he does not tell Cyaxares that the reform will strengthen the Persian contingent, which, under Cyrus' leadership, will not always serve Cyaxares' interest. He does not tell the Peers that this will bring an end to their traditional ability to rule over the Commoners. And he does not tell the Commoners that the new weapons will bring new risks by requiring them to fight on the front lines.

Cyaxares and the Commoners both agree explicitly to Cyrus' proposed reform, but he never asks the Peers for their opinion: he explains his policy as good for them, and then simply announces it to be an accomplished fact, and he does this at the last possible moment, after the weapons have been prepared and immediately before he invites the Commoners to accept them and all they imply. Similarly, he does not solicit the opinion of the Persian ruling class back home.[17] Would they have welcomed the arming of 30,000 subjects?

Cyrus tries to distract the Peers' attention from the revolutionary implications of his reform by referring to them as the "rulers" of the Commoners, which they have always been in the past but will soon cease to be, and by turning their attention to the importance of inspiriting their new comrades in arms (11). But the fact remains that the Peers' domination of Persian politics is coming to an end in Cyrus' army.

For each of the three audiences he addresses, Cyrus is also silent about the advantages his policy has for himself. Promoting the Commoners not only makes the army more potent, but since Cyrus does the promoting, it strengthens their loyalty to him (12–13; "Peers" translates a nice republican word that means "equal in honor," but Cyrus puts himself above them). He also gets his uncle to pay the cost of the expensive new weapons that, later, will help Cyrus' Persians to displace the Medes as the superior ally. Most importantly, this reform makes it impossible for the army ever to go back to Persia, at least without provoking a civil war, which combines with other evidence to suggest Cyrus has set out on a career of conquest and has no interest in going back to Persia to be merely one Peer among many.

Cyrus quickly proposes a third revolutionary measure to his army.[18] The proposal is to reward Persians based on their

---

[17] Nor did he ask for their approval for the radical speech he gave to the Peers in his army in 1.5.

[18] Nadon (2001) 67–68. It is Chrysantas who makes the proposal, but it is hard not to suspect that Cyrus prompted him to do so. Alternatively, Chrysantas is on his own quick to advance or support proposals when it helps Cyrus. See his defense of obedience (to Cyrus) in 8.1.1–5, his proposal that Cyrus take a "house" (i.e., a palace) for himself in 7.5.55; and his

individual merit, not strict equality. Both fairness and utility seem to recommend this policy (2.2.17–27).

If virtue needs rewards, then those who perform better and contribute more should be rewarded more. And in war, when everything is at stake, even those who contribute less see that they too benefit from policies that incentivize everyone to do his very best (20). Surely people will contribute more to a common effort if their greater individual contributions win greater rewards.

Cyrus also adds a less attractive flip side of this proposed innovation. He also calls for expunging the vicious from the army: worse than contributing nothing, indifferent or discontented members of a group weaken it by undermining the dedication of others (23–5). Removing them is also a warning to those who remain.

Cyrus has a further reason for this reform but does not state it publicly. The Peers, whose years of training lead them to see themselves as superior to the newly drafted Commoners, can now expect that their rewards will accordingly be greater than those of the newcomers. Even if the Commoners now enjoy an equal opportunity to be rewarded for their service, the Peers can reasonably think that their hard-won excellence will allow them to enjoy unequal results (22).

This proposal shares some of the thinking behind capitalism, but unlike Adam Smith, Cyrus does not surrender the task of distribution to the "invisible hand" of the free market: it is assigned to him, as I suspect he arranges or knows it must be (2.3.12, 16). If any soldier should seek to be rewarded for his efforts, and all will, it is clear whom he needs to please. So, in addition to adding an important motive for his soldiers to train

---

discouragement of further discussion in 2.3.6. See also 4.3.15–21 for his support of Cyrus' desire to develop a Persian cavalry.

and fight well, and reassuring the Peers that their virtues will not be overlooked, Cyrus' policy of individual rewards further enhances his own authority over the army.

Cyrus' fourth revolutionary policy comes after the first great victory over the Assyrian alliance (3.3). As he explains in a speech to his Persian captains, he wants to establish a Persian cavalry to make the Persian army more independent of the allies. The allies are currently helping him press forward his attack on the fleeing Assyrians, for which service Cyrus thanks and rewards them abundantly, but at the same time he is mapping out a plan to make it easier to disregard them in the future and less obligatory to share the fruits of victory with them. Adding a cavalry will bring speed and mobility to the Persian core of the army and allow them to do for themselves what they must now encourage the allies to do for them. After the captains hear the political advantages a cavalry will bring, Chrysantas rises to express his enthusiasm for the policy from the point of view of the individual.[19] He is silent about any possible risk from going into battle and fighting in a new and unfamiliar way.

As should by now be expected, when Cyrus explains to the allies that he would like them to give him the horses they have taken from the defeated enemy, he crafts a new set of reasons. He does not mention that he wants the horses to benefit the Persians but speaks instead of the common good (46). He suggests that a Persian cavalry will fight alongside the allies and help protect them, not that it will enable the Persians to displace them and reduce their share of the fruits of victory. He also chooses a good moment in which to make the request, for he

---

[19] See 4.1.11 for the importance of a cavalry; 4.3 for the speeches by Cyrus and Chrysantas; 4.5.45–50 for Cyrus' well-timed request for horses from the allies; and 4.5.54–55 for his use of humor to suggest that the horses are a light matter and the Persians the opposite of self-interested. The usefulness of the Persian cavalry in the largest battle is noted at 7.1.46.

has just shown himself to be the very model of generosity and trust in allowing the allies to retain possession of all the booty that has been seized from the enemy: all he would like is the horses, so he can better support and protect the allied cavalry (37–49). The allies can hardly refuse such a modest request from such a trusting man.

As a result of his reforms to the Persian army, Cyrus has made it more hungry for victory, more offensively minded, more powerful, more loyal to himself, and more independent of the allies.

Step Two
Stealing the Median Army

His second step is to steal an additional army. The stolen army both strengthens Cyrus and weakens the leader from whom it is stolen, namely Cyaxares, his ally and uncle.

In stealing an army much larger than his own, Cyrus must proceed cautiously.[20] His theft has these distinct and delicate elements:

He first gets permission to borrow a few Median troops for a limited mission (4.1).

He then stretches this permission so he gets a lot of troops, not just a few (4.1.10–24).

He changes the limited mission into an unlimited mission (4.2.5).

He makes the borrowed soldiers eager to stay with him rather than return to his uncle's command.

He finally gets his uncle's consent to the new arrangement by presenting him with a fait accompli and allowing him to

---

[20] For the size of the Median army, see 2.1.6. On the quality of the Median cavalry, see 1.6.10.

retain a faint semblance of authority (5.5). That is, he gets
his theft legitimated.

A few considerations make Cyrus' wild success plausible. One is
that he had previously borrowed some Median cavalry from
Cyaxares, and with the help of this cavalry, he brought a diso-
bedient but important tributary back under his uncle's control
(2.4.14–8; 3.1.31).[21] This experience made it easier for Cyaxares
to think that loaning an army to Cyrus would pay off. Cyrus'
fidelity to his ally is a useful prelude to his infidelity.

Cyrus seeks again to borrow a few of his uncle's troops after
they have together won a great victory and the Assyrian army is
in disordered flight. Since it takes a cavalry to pursue them, and
Cyrus lacks one, he asks to use some of his uncle's cavalrymen.
After much hesitation and specification of limits, Cyaxares
agrees, and goes off to celebrate the victory they have already
won (4.1.19–21). Cyrus, on the other hand, manages to increase
to the maximum the number of soldiers who follow him and
enlarge the scope of the mission they undertake.

Cyrus' success on both scores is greatly facilitated by the
timely defection of some of the Assyrians' allies. As the Assyrians are fleeing the scene of their great defeat, a group of their
subjects, the Hyrcanians, approach Cyrus about switching from
the Assyrian side to his. They possess a powerful cavalry and
offer to lead an attack against their former overlords (4.2.1–4).
Their addition to Cyrus' forces thus makes it even more enticing
to pursue the weakened and confused Assyrian army and to
seize plunder from them. This in turn makes it clearer to the
Median cavalry that there are advantages to be won by joining
with the Hyrcanians pursuing the fleeing Assyrians (10–11).

---

[21] And yet even in this episode, he begins to shift the control of the
Armenians from his uncle to himself, though he is careful not to make an
open break, while he also adds the Chaldaeans to his cause (3.2–3).

That is, the Hyrcanian defection makes it easier for Cyrus to show the Medes that he has presented them with a great opportunity, so that following him makes more sense than staying behind while their legitimate ruler celebrates their earlier victory by getting drunk in his tent. Thus, unbeknownst to the Median king, almost his entire army joins Cyrus' attack on the fleeing Assyrians, one that is much bolder and more aggressive than the limited operation Cyaxares had agreed to when he allowed Cyrus to borrow some of his soldiers.

It might appear that the Hyrcanian defection is just good luck, which would suggest that Cyrus' successes are more suited to a fairytale than to an account of the true nature of political life, but my suspicion is that Xenophon wishes to show that when a multinational empire is subjected to stress, its fault lines show. The Hyrcanians don't defect out of the blue; they defect because Cyrus' earlier victory showed the Assyrian king's weakness and made it possible for them to defect. Had Cyrus not been so bold and so successful in his first attack, the Hyrcanians would have had no choice but to remain loyal. Cyrus' success gave them a choice.

The last stage in his theft of the Median army is to get Cyaxares to consent to his own enfeeblement (4.5.18–45). This too requires several steps which mix delicacy with a keen awareness of the importance of raw force. He has taken the first step already, which is to make the Medes want to follow him rather than the ruler they inherited. He further confirms them in this view by praising them when they return from battle, by making sure his Persians have prepared ample dinners and tents for them, and by entrusting them and the Hyrcanians with vast quantities of captured spoils. When Cyaxares sobers up, he sends Cyrus a message protesting his violation of the terms on which he borrowed the troops and threatening him if he doesn't quickly return them. Cyrus responds with a letter that claims he has conferred great benefits on Cyaxares, accuses him of ingratitude, and warns him "not to deliver threats to large numbers" (27–34). If Cyrus fails to persuade his uncle of the rightness of his actions, the tough conclusion of his letter lets Cyaxares know there is little he can do about it.

Finally, Cyrus stages a meeting with his uncle in which he deftly wins Cyaxares' public acceptance of a merely ceremonial position in the army. Cyaxares really has no choice, but Cyrus arranges things such as to make it appear that the two men have reached a solution agreeable to them both (5.5). The several stages of this remarkable reconciliation are one of the dramatic highpoints of the entire *Education*, and it wins for Cyrus the appearance of legitimate rule over the Median army.

Having now outlined the steps by which Cyrus steals his uncle's army, I should perhaps be more explicit in saying that he had already shifted the command of the Persian army from the Persian authorities to himself, which might also be counted a theft. The Persian government really can't recall an army that includes 30,000 armed former Commoners, and if they should try, why would the army obey them, at least so long as they were winning the fruits of victory under Cyrus' leadership? This conflict of interest may be why, once Cyrus has established his empire, a certain coolness hangs over his return to Persia and his meeting with his father, the limited monarch of the Persian republic (8.5.21–27). Far from singing his son's praises, Cambyses cautions him against trying to rule Persia the way he rules others, greedily and for his own advantage (24).

Step Three
Adding Allies

Cyrus' next big step is intimately related to the previous one, his theft of the Median army from his uncle. It is to add allies. First he adds the Hyrcanians, and later he adds the troops of Gobryas,

Gadatas, Abradatas, and others. Cyrus' reforms to the Persian army have made it more formidable, but it is still relatively small, especially when compared to Cyrus' limitless ambitions. Adding allies adds power. Since some of these armies used to be allies of the Assyrian enemy, their embrace of Cyrus also subtracts power from the enemy. In the case of the Hyrcanians, the power they add is in the form of a cavalry, which Cyrus especially needs, at least until he is able get his hands on horses and help his Persians learn to ride.

All allies may wish victory, but they do not always do so for the same reasons or with the same urgency. The Hyrcanians live on the borders of Assyria and have defected from their powerful neighbor. Since Assyria can be counted on to seek to punish their defection, they want Assyria to suffer a blow from which it cannot easily recover. If Cyrus should decide to end hostilities and bring the boys home, the Hyrcanians will be left undefended and pay a heavy price for their actions, and Cyrus does not fail to remind them of their vulnerability (4.5.23; 6.1.2–3). In short, the Hyrcanians are in a more precarious position than Persia and Media, so Cyrus can count on them to want to keep the war going, and this is just what he wants, too, though he is driven not by fear but by ambition.[22]

Gobryas and Gadatas are made especially aggressive toward the Assyrian king for a different reason. Having suffered injustice at his hands, they hate him and want revenge. Their desire for vengeance makes them ready to run extreme risks and to persist until they see the Assyrian king not only defeated but also killed (5.3.10; 5.4.35; 7.5.27–31). They too help Cyrus keep the zeal for war at a fever pitch. As he did with the Hyrcanians,

---

[22] Deep fear of the Assyrian ruler also drives the Sacians and Cadusians to seek protection from Cyrus (V.3.24). Perhaps it is fear of Cyrus himself that leads the Indian king to support him (6.2.1–3).

Cyrus reminds Gadatas of his vulnerability (and perhaps enjoys doing so, 6.1.2–3).

We see a very different motive, but with similarly useful effects for Cyrus, in the alliance he strikes with Panthea and Abradatas. They act especially out of gratitude, amplified by a desire to show their nobility (6.1.45–51; 6.4.6–8, 10; 7.1.29–32).[23] Lower motives are more common, but higher motives may bring more determined action.

All of Cyrus' new allies are important because they add strength to his alliance, but they also bring aggressivity and moral purpose, and their motives include the desires for safety, liberty, wealth, vengeance, and gratitude. Their different motives affect what they want and need from the alliance.

The three main steps just discussed all enhance Cyrus' ability to make war, so we might label them "preparations for battle." Battles figure in only about six out of the forty-one chapters of the book, which is a way of indicating that Cyrus' long or, rather, constant preparation for battle is as determining as the battles themselves. Like athletic contests, battles are the relatively brief consequences of the preparations.

Cyrus' Main Battles

Now let's quickly review the four major battles that bring Cyrus his empire. Two of these are contested out on broad plains (3.3; 7.1), two others are directed against walled cities, Sardis in one case (7.2) and Babylon in the other (7.5). There are also the two preliminary and smaller battles he fights to bring Armenia back as a tributary ally of Media and to add Chaldaea to the Median-Persian alliance (3.1–2).

Each battle has different requirements, and success comes from different causes. The factors to keep an eye on include the

---

[23] See Nadon (2001), 152–60.

virtue and motivation of the troops, their numbers, their weaponry and technological assets, and deception.

Before the first main battle, the Commoners receive heavy weapons like those of the Peers and basic training in how to use them. Nevertheless, Cyrus calls special attention to the long education of the Peers as crucial for steadfastness and victory in battle (3.3.34–9; 54–5). Although he had orchestrated the promotion of the Commoners, now, in the crucial moments before the battle, he explains to the Peers that they must set a good example and do what they can to help the Commoners remain firm in the face of danger. While he may do this partly to give the Peers an additional motive to fight courageously, it is also a reasonable acknowledgment that military virtue cannot be created overnight. It is not surprising that after the battle, the narrator praises the conduct of the Persian Peers in particular (3.3.59, 70).

As if to highlight the importance of the Peers for this first victory, there is no mention of other contributing factors to the victory, no mention of any new military technology or any clever stratagem, for example.

The second big battle, the biggest of the entire *Education*, does not occur until three books later. In the interim, Cyrus is busy completing his takeover of the Median army, adding allies, designing and making new military technology, and preparing in other ways. Although this second battle is also a pitched battle fought on a broad plain, Cyrus proves victorious for new reasons. There are now no references to the Persian Peers, and the principal reference to "the Persians" is to their retreat under pressure from a compact mass of Egyptian infantry (7.1.34–6).

Three reasons help explain why the retreat of the Persians does not lead to defeat. One is that as they retreat, they come under the protection of large mobile towers Cyrus had had constructed, from which well-protected troops assault the

Egyptians from above. Thus, Cyrus' technological innovation helps defeat the Egyptians, whom Cyrus called "good" or "brave." The Persian cavalry also plays an important role in the defeat of the Egyptians, for they ride around and assault the enemy from the rear. Xenophon might then have praised their courage or skill, but in reviewing the battle, after praising the Egyptians, the narrator comments that of Cyrus' troops, the Persian cavalry "seemed best [or strongest, '*kratiston*']," and then explains this strength by reference to the way they were armed (7.1.46). There is no praise of the Peers or of the Persians in this battle such as there was after the first. In this case, in fact, light-armed troops are mentioned as helping to protect the heavy infantry from the Egyptians. They do so not because of their virtue or camaraderie but because they were compelled by the rear guard to stay in position and launch their missiles and shoot their arrows onto the massed Egyptians (7.1.34; 6.3.25, 27). Cyrus has again found a way to win, but the formula in this battle includes more compulsion and technology and relies less on the traditional education of the Persian Peers.

That the Persian Peers go unmentioned might mean only that the circumstances of battle have changed in such a way that their excellence is overshadowed by, for example, the multitude of the enemy or by Cyrus' newly developed military technology. But it might also mean that their excellence has been diminished by Cyrus' new teaching on virtue. If the Peers have now come to believe that military virtue is not good in itself but is rather the means to pleasure, honor, and wealth, their behavior in battle would be guided by these ends, not by the virtue that has been demoted from end to means. If the goal of toughness is to achieve a life of luxury and softness, will it hold up over the long run?

This effect of Cyrus' new teaching on virtue would only be increased by the soldiers' observation that good old-fashioned virtue is often not rewarded on the battlefield. Cyrus himself calls attention to this issue when, in one of his pre-battle remarks, he says, "if this [battle] turns out well, all will say in the future that nothing is more profitable than virtue" (7.1.19; see also 4.1.5). He implies both that the importance of virtue depends upon its profitability and that that its profitability is open to question. He does not say whether by "profitable" he means profitable for the individual soldier, for the army, or for the general in charge.

In this battle, the key exemplars of virtue are the Egyptians, "whom Cyrus calls "good" or "brave," and Abradatas, who risks and loses his life for Cyrus' sake (41, 29–32; recall also 4.1.8 on the fate of "the best troops"). If he was not rewarded by wealth or pleasure, did he at least win honor? Xenophon goes so far as to indicate that a tomb intended to honor his memory dilutes the message (cf. 11 with 15). For those who gradually become persuaded that devotion to virtue makes sense only if it brings pleasure, wealth, or honor, examples like those of Abradatas and the Egyptians would make one doubt that fighting stoutly on the front lines is always the best way to these ends. This might help explain why the Peers' virtue is mentioned only in the first of the four main battles, while improved technology is a leading cause of victory in the second battle, and deception is crucial to the last two (7.2.1–4; 7.5.13–31).

A further hint that the character of Cyrus' army has changed is that he speaks to his troops differently before the later battle than he did before the first. In the first, Cyrus explained to Chrysantas that a few words before a battle are not sufficient to transform men into dedicated fighters (3.3.51–5). He speaks of the virtue of the Peers as a consequence of long training: it can't be instilled overnight. Before the later battle, he no longer mentions this virtue but rides around offering pep talks (6.2.13ff; 6.4.13ff; 7.1.10 ff). He cannot believe that these few words will instill the qualities necessary to face the shock of battle, but he might think they are marginally useful. However this may be, by the end of the book, the Persians' virtues have vanished, and all prefer the soft life (8.8.20–26). Cyrus' success makes this dissipation possible, and in presenting pleasure and wealth as suitable ends of virtue his reeducation made it likely.

Ambition, Beneficence, and Duplicity

We noted above that the young Cyrus is said to be characterized by his beneficence, but of course we sometimes benefit others to be benefited in return, so it remains to be seen what accounts for Cyrus' benefactions and what limits they might have. Cyrus wants to help others and to be loved for so doing, but he also wants to rule and to be honored on a grand scale, so I hesitate to say that he always looks first to what is good for others.

Cyrus adds the Hyrcanians as allies, for example, and essentially steals the Median army so that it becomes more loyal to himself than to its official leader, his uncle. He accomplishes this by offering wealth in the form of spoils to the soldiers. He goes so far as to assign control of all the captured loot to them (4.5.37–41). When they are flabbergasted by this sign that Cyrus trusts them to this degree, he responds with a high-toned speech claiming that he does.

Cyrus, however, had previously explained to his Persian captains that he would put this captured wealth in the hands of their new allies, a move that needed further explaining, since the captains must have wanted to get their hands on the rewards they had been promised. Cyrus addressed this concern by saying that his goal in seeming to trust the allies with the booty was to win them over more securely to the Persians and thereby to make possible even larger gains in the future. He went so far as to say openly that he even hoped their new allies would steal some of the treasure, for their ill-gotten gains would bind them that much more strongly to the new alliance (4.2.42–45). As he says directly, "it does not seem to me to be a greater gain to take [the captured wealth] than, by *appearing* to be just to them, to try to make them delight in us still more than they do now" (42, emphasis added). Gain for the Persians is his goal; apparent justice and apparent trust of the Medes and Hyrcanians will help him achieve it.

Cyrus strengthens this plan by explaining to his captains that they should not allow their tired and hungry Persian troops to take a lunch break. Rather, they should show themselves to be concerned about the allied cavalry, then out seizing booty, and prepare a feast to be ready for them on their return (4.2.38–41). This plan too is governed by the gain the Persians will derive from it, for the allies will appreciate the Persians' services and may even begin to think their new allies are so austere as not even to care about wealth or ordinary pleasures.

As for the gain he has in mind, Cyrus hints at the scope of his ambitions and excites his Persian audience by referring to it as "the [source] from which wealth naturally springs" (44), which seems to mean great power. He asks his Persian captains to delay their gratification, as their education has prepared them to do, not to stifle it, and he stimulates them with the promise of vastly greater rewards in the future.

What he says to his captains shows that what he told the Hyrcanians and the Medes was false, but is he forthright even with the Persian captains? He speaks as if he and they were a closely united "we," but what follows will show that he has a special position of wealth and power in mind for himself.

He later confesses in a private conversation, for example, that notwithstanding his apparent disregard for personal wealth, he is in fact "insatiable for money" (8.2.18–23). If he attaches the allies by the allure of wealth, masked and elevated by the high tone of a seemingly greater devotion to justice and trust, does he do the same with the Persians? Rather than conclude quickly that Cyrus is guided by the goal of benefitting others, it is more cautious to conclude that he seems to be so guided. In the case of his wooing of the Medes and Hyrcanians, he used the appearance of nobility and beneficence to win allies for a grand strategy of which they had not even an inkling. The same could be true even regarding the Persians.

Cyrus' dramatic rescue of Gadatas offers another example in which he creates around himself what might be called an "aura of beneficence." Having suffered a terrible injustice at the hands of the new Assyrian king, Gadatas is looking for a chance to revolt against him. Cyrus' victory in the first great battle offers such an opportunity, but the location of the various armies is such that the revolt is still tricky business, and, in mid-revolt, Gadatas finds himself isolated and at risk of being annihilated. Unexpected, Cyrus appears on the scene with his army and saves the day, and Gadatas is overwhelmed by wonder and gratitude. In a key remark, he says,

> By the gods, Cyrus,...You don't need anything from me, nor did you promise me anything, nor have I done anything good for you, but you helped me so enthusiastically that I have been saved, thanks to you. (5.4.11)

Gadatas sees no interested motive behind Cyrus' dramatic rescue, and Cyrus does not challenge but even amplifies this view by attributing such noble enthusiasm to his entire army (13).

But all this is a misinterpretation. When he summoned his soldiers to march rapidly to Gadatas' aid, Cyrus explained the reasons for so doing in the calculating terms of "what is advantageous for ourselves" (5.3.31). To his army, he says that in fact it is imperative for them to help Gadatas, for only in this way can they seem to be noble and make many others wish to become their friends, while preventing everyone from wanting to be their enemies. It is satisfying to read that Cyrus was successful in saving Gadatas from the wicked Assyrian king, but his action was not the unselfish one Gadatas took it to be.

In another case, Cyrus gets his allied cavalry to agree to release unharmed many of the captives they bring to his camp (4.4.13). While beneficence in the form of mercy would favor such an action, Cyrus defends it in terms of the advantages it will bring to his army (4.4.1–8). After the cavalry agrees to spare the captives, it is Cyrus who gives them the good news, and in gratitude they prostrate themselves before him. His policy is beneficial for all concerned, but the reason behind it is what is advantageous for his campaign and his rule. Had his calculation of advantages been different, his action would have been different.[24]

The saddest example of Cyrus taking advantage of a mistaken appearance of beneficence is the case of Panthea and Abradatas, who think they owe Cyrus a huge favor after he protected the beautiful Panthea against insistent amorous advances from one of his soldiers. Out of gratitude for what he takes to be Cyrus' concern for his wife, Abradatas contributes as best he can to Cyrus' upcoming battle and even sacrifices himself, kamikaze-style, on the battlefield. Then, after finding fault with herself for having previously encouraged her husband to honor their debt to Cyrus, Panthea commits suicide (7.3.8–14). Cyrus had allowed himself to appear to be her noble protector, but Xenophon makes it clear that he saw her as a pawn among his many chessmen (5.1.17).

There are many other factors that help Cyrus win battles and build an empire, including his frequent actions regarding the gods, but I must hope the foregoing is sufficient to stimulate further thought about the reasons behind his actions and many speeches. My chief suggestion here is that Cyrus' ambition is

---

[24] For Cyrus calling for the opposite of mercy, see 4.2.18, 22, 24.

driving him toward empire, and—as beneficent as he would like to be, and as frequently as it is useful for him to be beneficent— he regulates his benefactions by the demands of his ambition. At the same time, his ambition will not allow anyone else to be a benefactor on a grand scale, and this too sets a limit on the ways in which he is willing to help others gratify their ruling passions (5.2.7–12). His frequent duplicity is required by the frequent gulf between his love of honor and his beneficence.

Cyrus' Imperial Rule

Once Cyrus acquires his empire, he institutes new and different policies with which to rule and maintain it. These new policies are the main subject of eight of the last nine chapters of the book, and a longer introduction would explain several of them as we have done with the policies that helped to win Cyrus his vast empire. I'll be content to suggest a bare list, which will at least indicate the general character of his rule.

After his conquest of Babylon has removed the last major obstacle to empire, Cyrus calls together his chief aides and delivers a speech whose main theme he summarizes as follows: "It is a great work to gain an empire, but it is a greater work by far to keep one safe after taking it." If anyone was expecting a big party and the opportunity to enjoy the pleasures, wealth, and honor they had long been training and fighting for, Cyrus sobers them up. They face, he explains, a major challenge, for they are intensely hated by the people they have conquered, with whose goods they have rewarded themselves and their allies. Cyrus realizes that he is "preparing to dwell in the biggest of cities and one as hostile as a city could be," so it is imperative for him to get his men to rededicate themselves to the virtues he had earlier explained to be merely the means to pleasure, wealth, and honor (7.5.58; 76–86). Cyrus is so fully aware that his message is unwelcome that he feels the need to argue that, in spite of this renewed requirement for restraint, it was still worth it to risk so much and fight so hard to acquire their empire. He defends his claim by saying that people enjoy "the good things" only if they continually "endure hunger, thirst, labor, and care," so his men must realize that their very happiness requires them to recommit to the old virtues (80–82).[25] However good "the good things" may be, he now claims we can enjoy them only after we suffer deprivation. How far and with what degree of enthusiasm his inner circle accepts this summons to restraint and toil is unclear,[26] but anticipating that not all will be persuaded, Cyrus also adopts other measures to keep the group on the straight and narrow.

The difficulty of maintaining his empire is reflected in the harsh and cunning policies Cyrus puts in place to try to do so, and any reader who has still been thinking of the *Education* as a story of unblemished successes and bright prospects should now be shaken from this view,[27] as the outlines of Cyrus' emerging

---

[25] He makes a few changes to the virtues they must practice, for those needed to rule the empire are not identical to those needed to acquire one. Cyrus says that daring may suffice to seize, but moderation, continence, and care are needed to hold, which momentarily leaves justice out of the picture (7.5.76). A little later Chrysantas stresses the importance of obedience, which Cyrus especially honors (8.1.1–5, 29). Back in old Persia, this quality was encouraged especially by the example of the elders, who faithfully obeyed the rulers (1.2.8). Cyrus obeys no one, so in this case he must demand of others what he cannot ask of himself.

[26] Compare his call for restraint with his earlier statement that people who abstain from pleasures at hand do so to enjoy greater ones in the future (1.5.9). His soldiers have so abstained, and they might think the future is now. Xenophon also has Croesus express a different view of happiness (7.7.27–28).

[27] Apparently, Walter Miller was not, however, for he sees the final collapse of Cyrus' empire in the very last chapter to be discordant with the happy story that precedes it (Miller [1914] 438–39). As I've suggested, less blatant sources and signs of trouble in Cyrus' empire have been indicated

despotism become ever more clear. After trying to persuade his inner circle to return to the practice of virtue, he creates two thick layers of bodyguards to protect him, and decides after careful consideration that the inner layer must be composed of eunuchs (7.5.58–70); he chooses to live in a secure palace to which the riches of Sardis are conveyed (7.5.57); he creates a network of spies (8.2.10–12); he begins to adorn himself, use makeup, and wear elevator shoes to enhance his majesty and authority; and it happens that everyone prostrates himself before him, even the Persian Peers, who had never before sunk to such a level (8.3.14). Another clever but troubling series of new policies concerns the ways Cyrus gets his inner circle to love him more than they love one another or, rather, how he arranges for each to resent the others to the point of wishing them to be "out of the way" (8.1.47; 2.26–28). If Xenophon does not have his Cyrus completely cast off his "aura of beneficence," the final establishment of Cyrus' empire prompts us ever more forcefully to question how deeply beneficial Cyrus' rule really is, even for Cyrus himself. To the question of the beneficence of his regime, its collapse in the final chapter adds the question of its solidity or durability (8.8).

Conclusion

The *Education* begins with the observation that human beings easily rule some lower species, such as cattle, and can do so for the ruler's profit, but widespread political turmoil suggests they are unable to rule over other human beings. The narrator then challenges this observation and claims that profitable rule over human beings is indeed possible, if only one does it with knowledge or understanding (*epistēmonōs*). The basis for this claim is the example of Cyrus, so he then becomes the subject

---

ever since Cyrus' first speech (1.5).

of a search for the knowledge of how to rule.

Although very attractive, especially on first reading, Cyrus' example fails to support the bold claim the narrator makes on its behalf. In the first place, Xenophon shows that knowledge is not the only requirement of the success Cyrus enjoys: he is also privileged by birth and perfectly suited to rule by such natural inclinations as his love of honor and eagerness to be loved by people for benefiting them. Anyone learning all that Cyrus knew but lacking his political nature or connections would not seek the idea of success that so animates him, or not achieve it, though his knowledge would still help him understand important aspects of the political world in which he lives.

Secondly, Cyrus' career proves disillusioning. His empire falls apart upon his death, a result he sought to avoid but could not, and it became clear that he could not simultaneously benefit all those he professed to want to help. Even if he achieved political stability over a vast area for several decades, his empire does not seem worthy of him: he had spies and bodyguards everywhere, and he did not even trust his "friends" at his politically motivated dinner parties (8.4.3). It is important to remember that there was no moral component to the question raised on the first pages of the *Education*: the question was merely whether some human beings could rule over others with the success they enjoy in ruling herd animals. The fact that Cyrus enslaves his subjects and treats them as beasts of burden, infants, or sheep is distressing but not inconsistent with the narrator's claim made at the outset (8.1.43–4; 2.14).

But, as we have seen, Xenophon has his Cyrus raise hopes not merely for rule that is widespread and profitable for a herdsman-like ruler but is also just and beneficial for others as well, and it is with the promise of this kind of rule that the initial appeal of the book largely lies. Whatever the narrator's interests, Xenophon's Cyrus begins his career with the intention of winning honor and love by benefiting others, as he had done so successfully as a boy in Media (1.6.24–25; 1.4.25). He sees the defects of politics as usual and is confident he can do better (1.6.7–8). We follow his career with interest and admiration, for—to use modern terms—he is clever, energetic, determined, and focused. And even though he also proves cunning, duplicitous, and extremely tough-minded, as we saw above, he hopes to become renowned by making his empire a better place. Nevertheless, he fails, as both the despotic character of his empire and its quick collapse demonstrate.

In this respect, Xenophon's presentation of Cyrus is parallel with his briefer presentation of the Persian regime. Persia first appears somewhat attractive, at least to those who can entertain the possibility that governments should be devoted to the common good and must form human beings into citizens (1.2.3–14), but then Xenophon gives us a second look and indicates that Persia is an oligarchy resting on an arbitrary division of its population into a few well-armed rulers and a vast mass of impoverished subjects (15). So too with Cyrus, who initially showed the promise of building an empire that would improve on Persia and see to it that merit be rewarded, but a second look shows he fails. The suggestion of these parallel observations is that Xenophon's true subject is not the solution to the problem of rule as advertised in the first three pages but its intractability. The enduring appeal of the book is that it is filled with insight not only about how Cyrus managed to defeat his rivals and build his defective empire, but also about why a satisfactory solution to the political problem is so elusive and will remain such.

References

Bartlett, Robert. "How to Rule the World: An Introduction to Xenophon's *The Education of Cyrus.*" *American Political Science Review*, Vol. 109, No. 1 (February 2015): 143–54.

Bruell, Christopher. *Xenophon's* Education of Cyrus. Doctoral Dissertation, Department of Political Science, the University of Chicago. July 25, 1969.

Bruell, Christopher. "Xenophon." In *History of Political Philosophy*. 3rd edition. Edited by Leo Strauss and Joseph Cropsey. Chicago: University of Chicago Press, 1987.

Miller, Walter. *Cyropaedia*. Vol. II. Cambridge: Harvard University Press, 1914.

Nadon, Christopher. *Xenophon's Prince: Republic and Empire in the Cyropaedia*. Berkeley: University of California Press, 2001.

2

THE DISTINCTIVE CHARACTER OF CYRUS' EDUCATION IN XENOPHON'S *EDUCATION OF CYRUS*

Peter J. Ahrensdorf

The *Education of Cyrus* offers both an account of the most widely famous person to appear in all of Xenophon's works—the founder of the greatest of empires known to his contemporaries—and the most extensive account of the education of a single individual in all of Xenophon's works.[1] It is true that the book does not offer any account of someone explicitly identified as a philosopher discussing education or teaching, as do Xenophon's writings on Socrates.[2] Indeed, "philosophy" is only mentioned once in the book (6.1.41). However, in contrast with the Socratic writings, which almost exclusively present isolated didactic conversations of Socrates with his lesser companions—with Euthydemuses and Critobouloses rather than Platos or Xenophons—and which never present the education of Socrates himself,[3] the *Education of Cyrus* presents the life and education of an outstanding human being from his boyhood to his death, first depicting his formal and informal education as a boy, youth, and young man and then clarifying the character of that education, over the course of his life, through his deeds and

---

[1] *Oeconomicus* 4.16. See also Plato *Alcibiades* 105c4–6.

[2] *Oeconomicus* 16.9; *Symposium* 1.5, *Memorabilia* 1.2.18–19, 1.2.31.

[3] See *Memorabilia* 1.2.1.

speeches.[4] The book, then, offers a singularly comprehensive account of the education of a great human being in the Xenophontic corpus and therefore sheds important light on Xenophon's understanding not only of Cyrus but also of education. Indeed, even though it is Socrates and not Cyrus who declares that "education" is "the greatest good for human beings,"[5] words related to the words for "education[παιδεία]" and "teacher [διδάσκαλος]" appear more frequently in the *Education of Cyrus* (37, 73)[6] than in either of the two longest Socratic works, the *Memorabilia* (25, 53)[7] and the *Oeconomicus*

---

[4] On the sense in which Cyrus' education is "lifelong," see Lorraine Pangle, "Xenophon on the Psychology of Supreme Political Ambition," *American Political Science Review*, 111, No. 2 (2017): 309; "Moral Indignation, Magnanimity, and Philosophy in the Trial of the Armenian King," in *In Search of History: Essays in Honor of Clifford Orwin*, ed. Andrea Radanasu (Lanham, MD: Lexington Books, 2015), 101. Xenophon's *Agesilaus* mentions that man's lineage (1.2–4) and discusses his life up through his death (10.3–4), but never discusses his education or even mentions words related to "education" or "teacher."

[5] *The Apology of Socrates to the Jury* 21.

[6] For words related to "education," see 1.1.5 (x2), 1.2.2 (x2), 1.2.12, 1.2.13, 1.2.15 (x2), 1.3.1 (x2), 1.4.3, 1.5.1, 1.5.11 (x2), 1.6.12, 1.6.13, 1.6.20, 1.6.29, 1.6.39, 2.2.1, 2.3.13 (x2), 2.3.15, 3.3.55 (x2), 3.3.59, 3.3.70, 4.2.45, 5.2.17, 6.2.32, 7.5.86, 8.3.37 (x2), 8.6.10, 8.7.10 (x2), 8.8.13, 8.8.15. For words related to "teacher," see 1.2.6, 1.2.8 (x4), 1.2.13, 1.2.15 (x2), 1.3.7, 1.3.16 (x2), 1.3.17 (x2), 1.3.18 (x2), 1.4.3, 1.6.2, 1.6.13 (x2), 1.6.14 (x3), 1.6.20 (x2), 1.6.28, 1.6.29, 1.6.30, 1.6.31 (x3), 1.6.32 (x2), 1.6.33 (x2), 1.6.34, 1.6.35, 1.6.40, 2.1.8, 2.1.20, 2.2.6 (x3), 2.2.14, 2.3.9, 2.3.10 (x2), 2.3.13 (x3), 2.3.21, 2.3.23, 3.1.13, 3.3.35, 3.3.39, 3.3.53 (x2), 3.3.54, 4.2.7, 4.4.12, 4.5.16, 4.5.32, 5.3.14, 6.2.29, 7.2.16, 7.5.35, 8.1.1, 8.1.15, 8.1.19, 8.3.2, 8.6.13, 8.7.24 (x2), 8.8.14.

[7] For words related to "education," see 1.2.1, 1.2.39, 1.3.5, 1.5.2, 2.1.1 (x2), 2.1.2, 2.1.3 (x2), 2.1.4, 2.1.9, 2.1.17, 2.1.27, 2.1.30, 2.1.34, 2.7.4, 3.8.8, 4.1.2, 4.1.3, 4.1.4(x2), 4.1.5, 4.2.1, 4.2.23, 4.7.1. For words related to "teacher," see 1.2.3, 1.2.10, 1.2.17(x3), 1.2.21, 1.2.27, 1.2.31, 1.2.41(x2), 1.2.49, 1.2.55, 1.2.56, 1.6.3(x2), 1.6.13, 1.6.14, 1.7.1, 2.2.6(x2), 2.6.32,

(20, 52)[8] and roughly two thirds as frequently as they do in all four of the Socratic works together (37/53, 72/117).[9]

On the very surface, through its title and its opening chapter, Xenophon's *Education of Cyrus* suggests that it was the "education" in which Cyrus was "educated" that enabled him to excel at ruling human beings, "with knowledge," and, while beginning "with a little army of Persians," to become the ruler over a vast number of nations (1.1.6, 1.1.3–4).[10] But what is the education of Cyrus according to Xenophon's *Education of Cyrus*? What is the distinctive character of the education that Cyrus receives? In contrast with the traditional education of the Greeks provided by Homer or the education provided by Plato, the education Xenophon's Cyrus receives does not consist of dramatic writings composed by a single author that focus on a single model of human excellence, such as Achilles or Socrates,

---

2.6.33, 2.6.39, 2.7.1, 3.1.1, 3.1.5, 3.1.9(x3), 3.1.11, 3.3.10(x3), 3.3.11, 3.4.4, 3.5.9, 3.5.18, 3.5.24, 3.7.15, 3.9.1, 3.10.13, 3.13.2, 4.1.3, 4.2.2, 4.2.4, 4.2.5, 4.3.12(x2), 4.4.5(x3), 4.7.1, 4.7.2.

[8] For words related to "education," see 3.14, 5.13, 5.14, 6.7, 7.4, 7.6(x2), 7.7, 7.12, 9.12, 12.3, 12.4, 12.5, 12.15, 12.17(x2), 13.4(x2), 13.9, 21.11. For words related to "teacher," see 3.11(x2), 4.1, 5.12, 7.7, 7.8, 7.9, 8.10, 9.1, 9.12, 9.14, 9.16. 9.18, 10.10, 10.13, 11.23, 12.4, 12.6, 12.9, 12.10(x2), 12.13(x2), 12.16, 12.18, 13.5, 13.9, 13.10, 13.12, 14.3(x2), 14.4, 15.3, 15.5, 15.9, 15.10(x2), 15.13, 17.3, 17.6, 17.9, 18.1, 18.9(x2), 19.15, 19.18(x3), 19.19(x2), 20.22, 20.52.

[9] In the *Symposium* words related to "education" appear four times (2.10, 4.45, 8.12, 8.23)

and words related to "teacher" appear ten times (2.4, 2.6[x2], 2.9, 2.12, 2.15, 4.23, 5.2, 8.16, 9.3). In the *Apology of Socrates to the Jury*, words related to "education" appear four times (20, 21, 29, 31) and words related to "teacher" appear twice (24, 26).

[10] All translations of the *Education of Cyrus* are based on the translation of Wayne Ambler (Ithaca: Cornell University Press, 2001), with very occasional modifications.

to be imitated.[11] Nor does Cyrus receive instruction from a primary, guiding teacher, as Achilles is said to have received from Chiron[12] (or Phoinix[13]); as followers of Socrates seem to have received from him[14]; and as Tigranes evidently received from a certain wise man or "sophist" (3.1.14, 3.1.38). Nor does Cyrus receive a single continuous education under one system of laws (which does present a single set of exemplars of the virtues of moderation, obedience, and continence—1.2.8), as such Persians as Chrysantas and Hystaspaes receive under the Persian laws and as the Spartans do under the laws of Lycurgus.[15] What is characteristic of the education of Cyrus is that he derives—indeed, chooses—his education from multiple sources: the laws of Persia which he was born under; his maternal grandfather Astyages, the king of the Medes, whom Cyrus describes three times as one who "teaches" and whom Cyrus freely and eagerly chooses to remain with from the ages of 12 to 15 or 16 (1.3.17, 1.3.18, 1.3.15); and his father Cambyses, the king of the Persians, whom Cyrus describes once as one who "teaches" and once as one who "educates" (1.6.20, 1.6.28) and who describes himself once as one who "educates" (1.6.29) and five times as

---

[11] Plato *Republic* 606e1–607a5; Xenophon *Symposium* 3.5, 4.6; Walter Burkert, *Greek Religion*, trans. John Raffan (Cambridge: Harvard University Press, 1985), 120; Homer *Iliad* 2.768–769, 22.158–159; *Odyssey* 11.469–470, 11.478–486, 11.550–551; Niccolò Machiavelli, *Prince*, 2nd ed., trans. Harvey C. Mansfield (Chicago: University of Chicago Press, 1998), chapter 14, p. 60; Plato *Phaedo* 58e3–59a1, 116c4–8, 118a15–17; Cicero *Tusculan Disputations* 1.71; Seneca *Epistulae Morales* 6.6; Friedrich Nietzsche, The Birth of Tragedy, trans. Walter Kaufmann (New York: Vintage Books, 1967), 89.

[12] Homer *Iliad* 11.830–832; Xenophon *Symposium* 8.23; *The One Skilled at Hunting with Dogs* 1.4, 1.16; Plato *Republic* 391b7–c6; Machiavelli, *Prince*, chapter 18, p. 69.

[13] Homer *Iliad* 9.438–444.

[14] See, for example, *Memorabilia* 1.6.13–14, 4.7.1–2.

[15] *Education of Cyrus* 1.2, *Regime of the Lacedaimonians* 2–4.

one who "teaches" (1.6.2, 1.6.29. 1.6.33 [x2], 1.6.34). Cyrus accepts certain lessons from each of his very different teachers, but he also revises and even rejects certain aspects of each education he receives from them, in the light of his own thoughts about how best to benefit others and himself (see, for example, 1.5.8–12). Insofar as it is Cyrus himself who determines the extent to which he follows each of the educations he receives, Cyrus is himself the ultimate author of his education. And insofar as Xenophon, at the end of the book, presents the effects of Cyrus' rule on his subjects as harmful to them and even to himself, one might conclude that Xenophon ultimately means to criticize Cyrus' attempt to devise an education for himself (8.8). On the other hand, insofar as Cyrus does not model himself on one exemplar of human excellence or accept one teacher as authoritative but revises the lessons he learns in the light of his own thinking and adapts the lessons he learns to his own circumstances and his own nature, Cyrus might seem to resemble Xenophon himself, who was a companion and admirer of Socrates but did not simply model himself on Socrates and even left Socrates to join a military expedition led by a Persian, also named Cyrus, who aspired to become the head of the empire founded by the first Cyrus.[16]

Cyrus' first education is the education in justice, gratitude, moderation, obedience, self-restraint in food and drink, and courage that he receives from the laws of Persia until he is 12 and then again from the ages of 15 or 16 to 26 or 27. Cyrus does

---

[16] *Memorabilia* 1.3.8–13; *Anabasis of Cyrus* 3.1.4–7; 5.1.5–13. Consider Christopher Bruell's statement that Xenophon "did not follow the example of Socrates, at least not in every respect" and that "he may have chosen to follow or imitate Socrates more freely, in a manner more suited to his own inclinations and abilities" ("Xenophon" in *History of Political Philosophy*, 3rd ed., eds. Leo Strauss and Joseph Cropsey [Chicago: University of Chicago Press, 1987], 111; see also 91–92).

not, of course, choose to receive this education in the first place, but he clearly embraces the virtues of self-restraint and martial courage (see, for example 1.2.8–10, 1.3.4–7, 5.2.5–20, 5.5.41–48) that it inculcates and he later appears to praise the Persian education emphatically for teaching through habit the willingness to labor and take risks for the sake of honor, an honor that is given more for the collective group rather than for the individual.[17] Cyrus also appears to value in some measure the discussion and deliberation that the Persian education in justice fosters when it compels the Persian boys to judge one another and to explain their judgments to one another and to their teacher (1.2.6–7, 1.3.17, 1.4.3). For he often explains his decisions to his friends and associates and encourages them, at times and in some measure, to share and explain their judgments as well.[18] Finally, Cyrus appears to adopt in some measure the spirit of gratitude toward fatherland and friends that the Persian education attempts to foster (1.2.7). For example, Cyrus invokes the good of the "community of the Persians" in his first speech as a general, he apparently hopes to confer on Persia "the rule of Asia," and Xenophon states emphatically that Cyrus "established his empire with a view to protecting it both for himself and for Persians" (1.5.8, 4.5.16, 8.1.7).

Cyrus, however, explicitly criticizes the Persian education on the grounds that it is ultimately beneficial neither to the Persians as a community or fatherland nor to the Persians as individual human beings (1.5.8). Even though the Persian regime

---

[17] 3.3.51–55, 1.2.11–12. Waller Newell notes that "the Persian Peers have been educated to believe that their honor is inherent in conforming to the laws and serving the common good" (*Tyranny: A New Interpretation* [Cambridge: Cambridge University Press, 2013], 201).

[18] See, for example, 2.2, 3.1.14–40, 3.3.49–55, 4.3.3–22, 5.1.1–18, 5.1.19–29, 5.2.22–36, 6.1.6–17, 6.3.17–36, 7.1.6–9, 7.2.9–28, 7.5.7–9, and even perhaps 8.4.6–27.

provides an effective education in endurance, discipline, and courage for the Persians who are able to partake of it, and even though the Persian regime ostensibly allows all Persians to receive this education and consequently to hold the political offices that the education qualifies them for, in truth the education—and hence the political offices —are available only to a tiny portion of the population, as Cyrus observes, a "few" who "easily rule the rest of the Persians, who are quite numerous"— perhaps some two or three thousand Peers out of the 120,000 Persians whose families are so wealthy as to spare their sons from laboring out of economic necessity (1.2.15, 1.3.18, 2.1.3). The ostensibly egalitarian but actually extremely oligarchic Persia is therefore militarily weak, with a small army wielding heavy arms who must constantly protect government buildings—presumably against the large disgruntled population of commoners—and therefore apparently must "never [οὐδέποτε]" leave Persia (1.2.4, 1.2.9, 1.2.12, 2.1.2);[19] it suffers from considerable overall poverty and lacks a cavalry; and it is vastly outnumbered and militarily outmatched by its enemies the Assyrians and also by its allies the Medes.[20]

In his *Histories*, Herodotus explicitly presents the Persians as "slaves" to the Medes before the rise to power of Cyrus,[21] but even Xenophon indicates in a number of ways that the Medes hold a certain sway over the Persians. In the first place, the

---

[19] When Persia later sends out a second army, it sends out only commoners—40,000—but evidently dares not send out any more Peers (5.5.3).

[20] 1.2.4, 1.2.9, 1.2.13, 7.5.67, 1.3.3, 2.1.3–8. See Christopher Nadon, *Xenophon's Prince: Republic and Empire in the Cyropaedia* (Berkeley: University of California Press, 2001), 40–41, 57–58; Wayne Ambler, "Introduction" in Xenophon, *The Education of Cyrus*, trans. Wayne Ambler (Ithaca: Cornell University Press, 2001), 5.

[21] See Herodotus 1.129 and also, more generally, 1.102, 1.107, 1.123–130. See also Machiavelli, *Prince*, chapter 6, p. 23; chapter 2, p. 102.

Median king Astyages feels free to summon and keep his grandson for three or four years without even asking permission from his son-in-law, who is the Persian king (1.3.1, 1.3.13). Furthermore, when Cyaxares succeeds his father as king of the Medes, he takes the liberty of urging Cyrus to lead a Persian army to help him rather than confine himself to requesting assistance from the Persian king Cambyses and the council of elders (1.4.25). What is more, Xenophon attributes to the king of Assyria the view that if he should subdue the Medes, who are "the strongest of those nearby," he would "easily come to rule over all those in the area," including the Persians (1.5.2). Finally, Cyrus' chagrin at the power that the cavalry confers on the Medes over the Persians and the effectiveness of his pretense of humble devotion in persuading the Medes to allow the Persians to acquire a cavalry—for example, his statement to the Medes that "whatever is left over [from Assyrian booty] after you have been nobly provided for will suffice, for we have not been raised with very much delicacy but in rustic fashion, so you would perhaps laugh at us, if we were draped in anything elegant, just as we will surely afford you a great laugh both when we are seated on our horses and, I think, when we fall on the ground"—both suggest that the Medes are more powerful than the Persians, that they are accustomed to think of the Persians as their inferiors, and that the Persians have been accustomed to defer to the superiority of the Medes (4.3.3–22, 4.5.1–4, 4.5.36–58; consider also 8.7.7).[22] The extremely oligarchic character of the Persian regime, then, renders Persia especially vulnerable to foreign domination and also conquest. The threat of the massive Assyrian forces conquering Media and Persia prompts the Persians to send not only 1000 heavy armed Peers—apparently the first time Peers have ever been sent outside of Persia (2.1.3)—

---

[22] See Bruell, "Xenophon," 95.

but also 30,000 light armed commoners, and enables Cyrus effectively to overthrow the Persian political order with ease, with hardly a word of protest even from his fellow Peers, by giving heavy arms and therefore political equality to the 30,000 commoners who accompany his force (2.1.11–12; but consider 2.2.11–16). As Xenophon notes of the Persian Peers, "They all were pleased, believing that they would enter the struggle with greater numbers" (2.1.12; see also 2.1.14–18). The end of the book (8.8) highlights the tremendous harm that Cyrus' imperial rule ultimately inflicts on the Persians, but the virtually unanimous acceptance of the overthrow of the old Persian regime demonstrates how fragile it was.[23]

The Persian regime is fragile not only because it is vulnerable to foreign domination and conquest but also because the education on which it rests is at odds with important aspects of human nature. In his maiden address as commander of the Persian army, Cyrus contends that the education is not beneficial to the Persians as individuals, for it requires them to suppress to a considerable extent their natural desires for "much wealth, much happiness, and great honors both for themselves and for their city" (1.5.9).[24] Even as a boy, Cyrus senses that the Persian education's strict identification of justice with lawfulness blinds the Persian regime to the natural differences between human beings and consequently imposes with violence a harmful equality in the name of justice.[25] For when Cyrus deems it just, as judge, that a big boy with a little tunic take the big tunic of a little boy and replace it with his own, since Cyrus "recognized

---

[23] See Nadon, *Xenophon's Prince*, 62–63.

[24] Bruell, "Xenophon," 97, 99; Robert C. Bartlett, "How to Rule the World: An Introduction to Xenophon's *Education of Cyrus*," *American Political Science Review*, 109, no. 1 (2015), 145–146.

[25] Waller Newell, "Tyranny and the Science of Ruling in Xenophon's *Education of Cyrus*," *Journal of Politics*, 45, No. 4 (1983), 893–894.

that it was better for both that each have the fitting tunic," Cyrus was beaten by his teacher on the grounds that "the lawful is just" and that one must "always cast his vote in conformity with the law" (1.3.17).

Cyrus' awareness of the tensions between the Persian laws and his own nature is brought to the fore by his years in Media. For Cyrus is happy in Media, so happy that he weeps when he fears that his grandfather, his host and benefactor, is mortally ill and weeps when he leaves Media—the only time in the book that he weeps for himself rather than out of pity for another, such as Cyaxares or Panthea and Abradatas (1.4.2, 1.4.26–28, 5.5.10, 7.3.8–11). And he is happy because, paradoxically, in despotic Media, he is freer than he was in Persia. In Media, as the beloved grandson of the absolute monarch—and hence, as his uncle remarks, as "our king" (1.4.9)—Cyrus is free to ride horses, to hunt, and even to engage in military combat, at the age of 15 or 16, well before the laws of Persia would allow him to do so (see 1.2.9–13, 1.4.18–25). Due to the absence of restrictive laws, Cyrus is also free in Media to witness the expression of a variety of natural passions and dispositions not so clearly visible in lawful, self-restrained, conventional Persia: the drunkenness, the general passion for pleasure, and the "liberty of speech" of Astyages and his courtiers (1.3.4–11); the erotic passion of Artabazus (for Cyrus himself);[26] and even the philosophic dispositions of Tigranes and his teacher and perhaps the sophisticated thoughtfulness of Araspas.[27] In Media Cyrus is free to make full use of his outstanding talent for horsemanship,

---

[26] 1.4.27–28, 4.1.22–24, 6.1.9–10, 7.5.48–54, 8.4.26–27. It may be Cyrus' thoughtful observation of Artabazus that enables him to recognize more clearly the power of erotic passion than does his Median friend Araspas, who seems paradoxically to cherish a Persian confidence in the power of law over eros (5.1.7–17, especially 5.1.10–11).

[27] 3.1.7, 3.1.14, 3.1.38–40, 1.4.26, 5.1.2–17, 6.1.41.

courage and skill on the battlefield, and prudence (1.4.18–24).[28] As Xenophon makes it clear, it is entirely due to the young Cyrus that the Medes win a smashing cavalry victory against the Assyrians: "not only did everyone else have Cyrus on his lips, both in speech and in song, but Astyages, who had honored him even before, was then quite astonished by him" (1.4.25). Cyrus in Media, unlike in Persia, is free to seek and to win individual praise and even glory, through his practice of generosity, through his feats while hunting on horseback, and especially through his deeds in battle.[29] It is no small wonder that Cyrus weeps at the prospect of leaving such a fulfilling and glorious life behind to return to spend one more year in Persia in the education of mere boys and then ten years among the youths who guard government buildings and hunt with the king, apparently on foot, since "among the Persians it is rare even to see a horse" (1.5.1, 1.5.4, 1.2.9–10, 1.3.3). The rest of Cyrus' career would seem to be animated by the ambition to live fully the life he first experiences in Media.

Cyrus praises his grandfather for being "more clever" than his own father "at teaching one to have less than to have more," since the despotic Astyages "has taught all the Medes to have less than himself" (1.3.18). What does Cyrus learn from Astyages during his stay in Media for three or four years? On the one hand, Astyages presents Cyrus with the spectacle of a man whose measure is not the law but his own soul, of an absolute ruler, possibly a self-made despot who, according to Cyrus' mother Mandane, somehow "made himself the master of everything" (1.3.18).[30] Astyages would therefore seem to provide a

---

[28] See Nadon, *Xenophon's Prince*, 51.

[29] 1.3.7, 1.4.1, 1.4.4–15, 1.4.18–25.

[30] But consider 1.2.1, where Xenophon describes Astyages as one "who became king of the Medes," a formulation that allows for the possibility that he inherited rather than acquired his rule. Herodotus presents Asytages as a

certain model for Cyrus, who goes on to make himself the master of a vast empire and who is addressed as "master" by his Assyrian allies Gobryas and Gadatas as well as his Lydian captive Croesus (4.6.2, 5.3.28, 7.2.9). Indeed, Cyrus goes on to imitate the Median garb and the cosmetics of Astyages that so impressed him when he first saw his "handsome" grandfather (8.1.40–41, 1.3.2). On the other hand, Cyrus' experience with the atmosphere of fear that surrounds the despotic court of Astyages, whose rule has evidently inspired such hatred that he must fear being poisoned even by his most trusted servant, teaches him a certain discretion (1.3.9–10).[31] When the twelve-year-old Cyrus first arrives in Media, he expresses himself in a forward manner, "rashly, as would a boy not yet afraid" or intimidated (1.3.8). For example, he openly expresses the intense jealousy and hatred he feels for the cupbearer Sakas and openly seeks to take his place at the court (1.3.8–9). Such a talkative (πολυλογώτερος) disposition and "liberty of speech" have in some measure been encouraged and even required of him in Persia, especially in his education in justice, "because he was compelled by his teacher both to give an account of what he was doing when he issued judgments and to obtain an account from others" (1.4.3). During his years in Media, however, Cyrus comes to learn a certain reserve. Specifically, he comes to learn how to mask his ambition and to downplay his competitive spirit with his friendly rivals in horsemanship by laughing at himself when he loses to them (even though he quickly renews his determination to surpass them and quickly succeeds— 1.4.4–5). This capacity to hide his ambition with grace and with

---

hereditary ruler (1.102).

[31] Herodotus portrays Astyages as an exceedingly cruel ruler. See 1.108–130. The harsh and even "savage" temper of Astyages' son and heir Cyaxares in Xenophon's account may also possibly hint at the temper of his father (4.5.9–12, 4.5.18–19).

self-deprecating humor proves to be invaluable to Cyrus, most immediately during his eleven years back in Persia when he must return to the dreary and egalitarian education there, but also, for example, when he seeks to persuade his dominant Median allies to allow the Persians to acquire a cavalry (and thereby lose their dominance—4.2.32–4.3.23, 4.5.15–16, 4.5.36–55). Such prudent discretion also seems to distinguish Cyrus from his grandfather.

Astyages tries to introduce Cyrus to the pleasures of high Median cuisine, but Cyrus steadfastly rejects those pleasures, as well as those of drink and women, pleasures that both his grandfather and his uncle evidently relish (1.3.4–11, 4.1.18, 4.5.8, 4.5.51–52, 5.5.41–44). The hedonism of both Astyages and Cyaxares leads them to lose their focus on the goal of victory in the harsh arenas of war and politics, as one can see most spectacularly when Cyrus outmaneuvers and effectively usurps his uncle as ruler of the Medes but also when the fifteen or sixteen year old Cyrus surpasses his grandfather in military prudence (4.1.19–24, 4.5.18–33, 5.5, 1.4.18–20). Furthermore, and more importantly, while Astyages appears to teach his subjects to have less than himself by inspiring fear in them in "the tyrannical" way (1.3.18), Cyrus, even when young, instinctively seeks to win honor and deference through generosity toward others, for example by giving them meat he has been given, doing favors for them, giving them game he has hunted, and giving them gifts he has been given (1.3.6–7, 1.4.1–2, 1.4.10, 1.4.12, 1.4.26). Later in his career, Cyrus will generously bestow on his friends and followers prosperity, honor, and even vengeance undertaken on their behalf or facilitated by him (for example, 2.3.1–15, 3.2.14–16, 3.3.2–5, 7.5.24–32; see also 1.6.8). In all these ways, Cyrus seeks to teach his subjects to have less power and honor than he has, not primarily by inspiring fear, but by actively and visibly seeking to benefit them, as his own father Cambyses also, in some measure, instructed him to do (1.6.21–25).

Surprisingly, the role Cyrus' own father plays in his education seems less visible than that played by either the Persian laws or his Median grandfather. Xenophon offers detailed and vivid accounts of Cyrus' interaction with Astyages for the three or four years he spends in Media, from the ages of 12 to 15 or 16. We witness them conversing on five separate occasions over the span of three or four years.[32] We learn that Astyages took great pleasure and delight in Cyrus, that "he loved him," and also that he came to recognize and admire his prudence, alertness, and even, in some measure, his daring.[33] We also learn that the twelve year old Cyrus eagerly sought to stay with his grandfather in Media rather than return to his father in Persia, that Cyrus wept when he thought his grandfather was mortally ill, and that he, along with his grandfather and all others present, wept when he departed Media to return to Persia.[34] There seems to be a considerable mutual affection, affinity, and admiration between Cyrus and Astyages in Xenophon's account. In contrast, Xenophon presents no similarly detailed and vivid account of Cambyses' feelings for his son or Cyrus' feelings for his father. Xenophon presents Cyrus conversing only once,[35] when Cyrus is 26 or 27, after Cyrus has been named the head of the army of 1000 Persian Peers and 30,000 commoners sent to Media, after he has publicly criticized the Persian education that he and his fellow Peers have received for failing to benefit Persia and themselves, and after he has indicated that the goal of this military expedition to Media is not merely to defend Persia and Media against this particular Assyrian attack but, more broadly, to

---

[32] 1.3.4–11, 1.3.13–18, 1.4.10, 1.4.13, 1.4.19–20.
[33] 1.4.10, 1.4.15, 1.4.20, 1.4.24–25.
[34] 1.3.13–18, 1.4.2, 1.4.25–26.
[35] Consider also 8.5.22–28. See as well 6.1.4–6.

"secure much wealth, much happiness, and great honors," presumably by expanding the power of Persia and his own power as well (1.5.9, 4.5.16, 8.7.6). And it is Cambyses, not Cyrus, who initiates that conversation (1.6.1–2).[36]

On the other hand, the conversation between Cambyses and Cyrus is the longest conversation in the book, both father and son refer to Cambyses as an educator or teacher of his son,[37] and they refer to a number of conversations about education Cyrus and Cambyses have previously had, evidently since Cyrus has returned from Media.[38] Indeed, the theme of education is especially prominent in this section of the book. Almost one seventh (5/37) of all the appearances of words related to the word for "education [παιδεία]" in the entire book[39] and more than one fourth (21/72) of all the appearances of words related to word for "teacher [διδάσκαλος]" occur in this single conversation.[40] Moreover, almost one fourth (3/13) of all the times Cyrus in particular uses words related to the word for "education"

---

[36] See Robert Faulkner, *The Case for Greatness: Honorable Ambition and its Problems* (New Haven: Yale University Press, 2007), 142.

[37] 1.6.20, 1.6.29, 1.6.2, 1.6.14, 1.6.28, 1.6.29, 1.6.30, 1.6.33 (x2), 1.6.34, 1.6.35.

[38] See, for example, 1.6.2, 1.6.5–8, 1.6.12–14, 1.6.20, 1.6.28–29.

[39] Words related to "education" appear five times in 1.6 (1.6.12, 1.6.13, 1.6.20, 1.6.29, 1.6.39) and 32 times in the rest of the book (1.1.5 [x2], 1.2.2 [x2], 1.2.12, 1.2.13, 1.2.15 [x2], 1.3.1 [x2], 1.4.3, 1.5.1, 1.5.11 [x2], 2.2.1, 2.3.13 [x2], 2.3.15, 3.3.55 [x2], 3.3.59, 3.3.70, 4.2.45, 5.2.17, 6.2.32, 7.5.86, 8.3.37 [x2], 8.6.10, 8.7.10 [x2], 8.8.13, 8.8.15).

[40] Words related to "teacher" appear 21 times in 1.6 (1.6.2, 1.6.13 [x2], 1.6.14 [x3], 1.6.20 [x2], 1.6.28, 1.6.29, 1.6.30, 1.6.31 [x3], 1.6.32 [x2], 1.6.33 [x2], 1.6.34, 1.6.35, 1.6.40) and 51 times in the rest of the book (1.2.6, 1.2.8 [x4], 1.2.13, 1.2.15 [x2], 1.3.7, 1.3.16 [x2], 1.3.17 [x2], 1.3.18 [x2], 1.4.3, 2.1.8, 2.1.20, 2.2.6 [x3], 2.2.14, 2.3.9, 2.3.10 [x2], 2.3.13 [x3], 2.3.21, 2.3.23, 3.1.13, 3.3.35, 3.3.39, 3.3.53 [x2], 3.3.54, 4.2.7, 4.4.12, 4.5.16, 4.5.32, 5.3.14, 6.2.29, 7.2.16, 7.5.35, 8.1.1, 8.1.15, 8.1.19, 8.3.2, 8.7.24 [x2], 8.8.14).

in the entire book[41] and almost one third (10/33) of all the times he uses words related to the word for "teacher" occur in this single conversation.[42]

What has been Cambyses' overall goal in teaching his son and what is his didactic purpose in having this particular conversation with Cyrus? Cambyses has evidently been aware of Cyrus' soaring political ambition for some time, for he knows that Cyrus has taken what would seem to be the extraordinary measure of obtaining private instruction in generalship; he has presumably heard that Cyrus has just offered a bold criticism of the Persians of the past for failing to use their armed forces to "secure much wealth, much happiness, and much honor for themselves and for their city"; and he must reasonably infer that Cyrus is now setting out to benefit, in his judgment, both Persia and himself by becoming a great ruler over the Persian army and other lands as well (1.6.12–15, 1.5.9). Cambyses appears to respond to his son's ambition in two ways. On the one hand, Cambyses seeks to educate his ambition by offering what would seem to be politically astute but at times shockingly harsh and candid advice: never simply trust prophets, allies, and even your own soldiers lest they deceive and betray you (1.6.2, 1.6.9–10); always attend to the provisions and health of your soldiers lest "your rule…dissolve at once" and always try to persuade them that you are "more prudent about their own advantage than they

---

[41] See 1.6.12, 1.6.13, 1.6.20 and 1.5.11 (x2), 2.2.1, 3.3.55 (x2), 4.2.45, 6.2.32, 7.5.86, 8.7.10 (x2). See also 8.6.10 where Xenophon presents Cyrus as using a word related to the word "education" in indirect discourse.

[42] See 1.6.13 (x2), 1.6.14 (x3), 1.6.20 (x2), 1.6.28, 1.6.30, 1.6.35 and 1.3.7, 1.3.16, 1.3.17 (x2), 1.3.18 (x2), 2.3.23, 3.3.35, 3.3.39, 3.3.53 (x2), 3.3.54, 4.2.7, 4.4.12, 4.5.16, 4.5.32, 5.3.14, 6.2.29, 7.2.16, 8.1.1, 8.3.2, 8.7.24 (x2). See also 7.5.35 where Xenophon presents Cyrus as using a word related to the word for "teacher" in indirect discourse.

are themselves" (1.6.9–10, 1.6.13, 1.6.15–16, 1.6.21); and "be a plotter, dissembler, wily, a cheat, a thief, rapacious, and the sort who takes advantage of his enemies in everything" by deceiving them and, if need be, by deceiving one's friends as well (1.6.27–34). Indeed, Cambyses urges Cyrus to become a veritable "poet of stratagems" (1.6.38). In all these ways, Cambyses apparently strives to teach his ambitious son how to become a successful general by fair means or foul.[43] And Cyrus accepts that teaching throughout his career, most immediately by lying to his uncle Cyaxares, the Median king, in order to induce him to supply heavy arms for the 30,000 Persian Commoners (2.1.2; see 1.5.5, 2.1.9–10).[44]

On the other hand, Cambyses also seems to attempt to divert Cyrus from his political ambition in three ways. First he emphasizes the importance of self-betterment, of becoming "truly noble and good" and prudent (φρόνιμος), not only as a means to becoming a successful general but also and even especially as an end in itself: "it is a sufficient and noble work for a man, if he should be able to take care that he himself become truly noble and good" (1.6.6); "There is no shorter road…to seeming to be prudent about such things [that is, what is advantageous for human beings] as you wish than becoming prudent about them" (1.6.21–22).[45] Secondly, Cambyses repeatedly emphasizes the tremendous difficulties of presiding "over other human beings so that they will have all provisions in abundance and so that they will all be as they must" (1.6.7); of securing

---

[43] See Nadon, *Xenophon's Prince*, 166.

[44] See, for example, regarding the importance of provisions for and the health of his soldiers, 2.4.9–14, 3.3.28–30, 4.2.34, 6.1.14–15, 6.1.23, 6.2.25–39; regarding the importance of inventing stratagems, 6.1.28–30, 6.1.50–55, 6.2.16–18, 6.4.18; and regarding the importance of deception, 5.3.9–14, 6.1.38–40, 6.3.15, 8.1.40–41, 8.3.14.

[45] See Bruell 1987, 102.

sufficient provisions for one's soldiers so as to avoid the immediate dissolution of "your rule" (1.6.9; see also 1.6.12); of providing for their health and strength (1.6.14, 1.6.16–18); of instilling them with martial zeal (1.6.19); of rendering them reliably obedient (1.6.14, 1.6.42); of defeating one's enemies (1.6.27–29); and, which seems to be of especially great importance to Cyrus, of being loved by his subjects (1.6.24–25).[46] Finally, in the concluding portion of his conversation with Cyrus, Cambyses emphasizes to him how precarious, given the weakness of human wisdom and the indifference of the gods, all military and political achievements are and therefore how important it is to be content with one's share rather than to seek happiness through conquest: "To many it has not been acceptable to live pleasantly with their share; yet because they desired to be lords over all, they lost even what they had" (1.6.45).[47] In all these ways, Cambyses seems to teach his son to follow his own example as a constitutional monarch who accepts and defers to the Persian regime, with all of its evident imperfections; who accepts his subservience to the Medians by, for example, agreeing to what is apparently a political marriage for himself with the daughter of the Median king and by allowing the Median king to keep his son for a number of years; but who somehow finds his happiness by making himself as noble, good, and prudent as possible.

Now, it is not altogether clear how these two aspects of Cambyses' education of his son—his shrewd but shockingly harsh advice as to how to succeed as a general by all means necessary and his advice to focus on perfecting oneself apart from politics and living pleasantly with one's share—fit together.

---

[46] See Faulkner 2007, 142–143.

[47] See also 4.1.14–7; Nadon, *Xenophon's Prince*, 89–90. Consider as well Bartlett, "How to Rule," 148.

Perhaps Cambyses hopes that the very harshness of his account of how to succeed as general— especially with its emphasis on the need to become "a plotter, a dissembler, wily, a cheat, a thief, rapacious" (1.6.27); to perform "evil deeds" (1.6.28); and to deceive enemies but also friends (1.6.28–34)—might undercut the appeal of the popular love and honor Cyrus seeks from the military and political life (1.6.24–25; see 1.2.1, 3.2.31). For if one wins such love and honor largely by deception—if they do not signify a true recognition of one's true excellence but rather the gullibility of those who love and honor—are such love and honor truly worth having? Are they truly deserving of being "among the greatest things," as Cyrus emphatically believes?[48] Perhaps Cambyses also urges Cyrus to be a successful general only when necessary, in order, for example, to defend Persia from conquest, but still to focus his life on the private fulfilment of perfecting one's character and mind.[49] Evidently, as we have seen, Cyrus accepts the political advice his father gives him, but rejects the advice to curb his passion to live a successful and glorious political life. Cyrus may find the alternative to the vivid and fulfilling life of winning power and honor through political and military excellence that his father offers—to become "truly noble and good" in one's private life—too nebulous to be compelling (though consider 3.1.38–39).[50] But furthermore, Cyrus

---

[48] 1.6.18; see also 1.2.1, 3.2.31, 5.2.8–11.

[49] See Nadon, *Xenophon's Prince*, 167–168.

[50] A number of scholars point out similarities between Xenophon's Cambyses and Xenophon's Socrates and suggest that Cambyses may quietly challenge his son's active, political life in the name of a contemplative life. See Bruell, "Xenophon," 102–104; Pangle, "On the Psychology," 314, 320. See also Nadon, *Xenophon's Prince*, 177–178; Bartlett, "How to Rule," 148, 153. Newell stresses that the "quasi-theological education" that Cyrus receives from Cambyses is "partly Socratic but not explicitly philosophic…. it does not stimulate an openness to the contemplative life" (*Tyranny*, 203).

evidently rejects his father's advice to curb his ambition as unacceptable and even untenable. It is unacceptable because it requires Cyrus to accept the subservience of Persia to Media and also perhaps ultimately to Assyria, if the Assyrians successfully conquer Media and Persia. It therefore requires him to live at the mercy of other powers. After all, Tigranes, who of all the characters in the book seems to resemble Cambyses most in his interest in perfecting himself apart from political and military life,[51] proves incapable of defending the very lives of those he loves most: his teacher, who is slain by his father, and his wife, who is entirely at the mercy of Cyrus (3.1.7, 3.1.36–41). But how, Cyrus may wonder, can it be reasonable to follow a life that leaves one so defenseless before one's enemies, actual or potential?[52] Cambyses' advice may also be untenable, in Cyrus' judgment, because, even if Cyrus were to embrace a purely defensive goal in coming to the assistance of Media, in order to have any hope of thwarting the Assyrian conquest of Media and Persia, it would seem that he would have to lead 1,000 Persian Peers out of Persia for the first time, give heavy arms to the 30,000 commoners, and also seek, as he goes on to do, additional allies. Indeed, one crucial omission in the political advice Cambyses offers to Cyrus is the importance of sheer numbers of soldiers to defeat a numerous enemy. Cambyses speaks on the assumption that Cyrus will confront his enemy on "an even field [ἰσοπέδῳ]" (1.6.41), without having to fear being overwhelmed by massive enemy forces. Cyrus, however, recognizes the

---

[51] Consider Ambler's suggestion that Cambyses and Tigranes are the "quiet heroes" of the book ("Introduction," 18; see also Pangle, "Moral Indignation," 112–113). Consider as well Nadon's description of Tigranes as Xenophon's "alter ego in the book" (*Xenophon's Prince*, 179: see also 79–80, 158; see as well Bruell, "Xenophon," 103; Faulkner, *Case for Greatness*, 168).

[52] For a crucial contrast on this point between Cyrus and Xenophon, consider *Anabasis of Cyrus* 6.6.8–16, 7.1.25–31.

imperative to add to the number of his forces to even the odds against his foes, first by giving heavy arms to the commoners, thereby effectively increasing his forces thirtyfold, but also by repeatedly adding allied forces.[53] And once Cyrus gives heavy arms to the commoners, the narrowly oligarchic order in the army and in Persia as a whole must inevitably be overthrown, and either Cyrus must establish and rule a new, expansionary or imperial, order or the ensuing chaos will leave Persia again vulnerable to a foreign attack and conquest.[54] Even Cambyses later acknowledges that Cyrus, purportedly with the help of the gods, "made you, Persians, famous among all human beings, and honored in all Asia" as well as wealthier and militarily stronger (8.5.23).[55] Cyrus appears to conclude, then, that, in order to benefit Persia, by securing it against foreign conquest and domination, and to benefit himself, by securing himself from actual and potential enemies, gaining the satisfaction of benefitting Persia and perhaps other subjects, and winning the glory he craves, he must reject his father's advice to curb or even forswear his political ambitions.

As the end of the book indicates, Cyrus does not ultimately benefit Persia or even himself. As a consequence of ruling Persia and even Asia as a whole so effectively and so completely, as though they were his own children, Cyrus renders his subjects incapable of ruling, restraining, or defending themselves (8.8.1, 8.8.6–7, 8.8.20–21). Through becoming the Father and Benefactor and Shepherd of his subjects, he infantilizes and even

---

[53] See 2.1.2–9, 3.1.30–32, 3.3.25–26, 5.2.25–36, 5.4.29–32, 5.5.44–45, 6.2.14–15. See Nadon 2001, 62.

[54] As Faulkner puts it, "The alternative to Cyrus' Persian empire was an Assyrian empire" (*Case for Greatness*, 148–149).

[55] But, as Faulkner notes, Cambyses, though apparently praising of Cyrus here, may also be "responding to a fait accompli," with Cyrus' "imperial army" at his borders (*Case for Greatness*, 143).

emasculates them, as his uncle accused Cyrus of emasculating him through his benefactions.[56] Indeed, Xenophon appears to predict that the infantilized Persians themselves, along with their associates, may be conquered by the self-governing Greeks in the not so distant future (8.8.7, 8.8.20–26). Moreover, Cyrus does not clearly benefit himself, for even though he attains the summit of power and glory, he is evidently haunted by a gnawing and poisonous fear of death by assassination from even his seemingly most trustworthy subjects (8.1.45–48, 8.4.3). As he remarks to his sons on his deathbed: "And throughout the past, I fared just as I prayed I would, yet a fear accompanied me that in the time ahead I might see, hear, or suffer something harsh and it did not allow me to think too highly of myself or to take extravagant delight" (8.7.7). Addressing his younger son, who according to Cyrus' wishes will not be king as Cyrus was, he affirms "to you I bequeath a happiness more free from pain…for being anxious over many things, for being unable to be at peace because you are goaded to compete against my deeds, for plotting and for being plotted against, these things must of necessity accompany the king more than you" (8.8.11–12). Finally, in almost his final words, the dying Cyrus claims to feel "pleasure…since I cannot suffer evil any longer" (8.8.27). Throughout his life as emperor, Cyrus apparently lives in fear for his safety––as he remarks to Croesus, he now seeks to "harvest safety and glory" (8.2.22)—and devises ever more elaborate methods of protecting himself from the deadly envy of those around him.[57] As Tigranes earlier remarked, "of all terrible things, fear especially subjugates souls" and Cyrus' abiding fear of threats to his life, power, and glory evidently deprives him of the happiness he

---

[56] 5.5.25–34; see also 3.1.41, 3.2.2–4, 7.2.26–29, 8.1.1, 8.1.25, 8.1.43–44, 8.2.7–9, 8.2.14, 8.5.58–65. See Newell, "Tyranny," 892.

[57] 7.5.37–70, 8.1.16–29, 8.1.40–47, 8.2.1–14, 8.2.24–28, 8.4.3–5, 8.5.1–16, 8.6.7–14. Consider Nadon, *Xenophon's Prince*, 110–120, 126–127.

hoped to acquire therefrom (3.1.23–25; cf. 3.1.38). Accordingly, even though Cyrus repeatedly claims to be happy, Xenophon never affirms in his own name that Cyrus was happy (8.1.23–24, 8.7.6–9, 8.7.27; cf. *Memorabilia* 1.6.14, 4.8.11).

The ending of the book suggests, then, that Cyrus' particular attempt to devise an education for himself was a failure, and that he should have heeded his father so as to devote his life to bettering himself through the private pursuit of excellence rather than to seeking happiness through ruling over others. Xenophon may even suggest that, rather than seek out those who might educate him in generalship and political prudence, as he evidently did at some point after returning from Media, Cyrus should have sought out while in Media the wise teacher of Tigranes, as he evidently did not, but as Xenophon himself evidently did in Athens in the person of Socrates (1.6.12–15, 3.1.7, 3.1.14, 3.1.38–39). Nevertheless, in his disinclination simply to follow any of his teachers, including his father and teacher Cambyses, and in his inclination to devise an education for himself that suits his particular nature and circumstances, Cyrus does bear a certain resemblance to Xenophon himself. For when his teacher Socrates apparently attempts to curb Xenophon's political ambition, Xenophon does not simply and immediately follow his advice, but takes most seriously the model of political life that "Cyrus" represents and indeed proves himself to be a most excellent practioner of that way of life, even though he does, in his own way and following his own path, ultimately ascend from "Cyrus."[58] Indeed, insofar as Xenophon himself, through his writings as a whole, offers an education for us, his readers, perhaps he presents us, not with one model of excellence, as Homer or Plato do in their writings, but multiple models of excellence—such as Socrates, Cyrus, and Xenophon

---

[58] *Anabasis of Cyrus* 3.1.4–7, 5.1.5–13.

himself—so as to encourage us, rather than simply and without due reflection to embrace one individual character as a model of excellence to be imitated, to ponder for ourselves the lessons to be learned from and through each of the very different, exemplary characters he presents and to think through for ourselves how to apply those lessons to our own circumstances and to our own nature.

3

FREEDOM AND FRIENDSHIP IN
THE EDUCATION OF CYRUS

Carol McNamara

Introduction

The Education of Cyrus famously begins with a statement of Xenophon's identification of *the* most persistent political problem: human passion and ambition make political stability elusive. This restless longing among human beings for honor and power, or for freedom from oppression, causes recurring turmoil in political life, with democrats overthrowing oligarchies, monarchies, and tyrannies, and ambitious or avaricious men subjecting free people. Xenophon notes that while herd animals willingly submit to those who manage them, human beings often resist political rule (1.1.2).[1] Xenophon's observation appears to be neutral with a view to the regime: his judgment seems to be that political rebellion or change, whether it involves the subversion of democracy or insurrection against a tyrant, is inherently problematic. Instead of despairing of a solution to the apparent causes and dangers of political turmoil he identifies, however, Xenophon proposes the rule of Cyrus, the great founder of the Persian empire, as an answer to the challenge of political instability. Cyrus "acquired very many people, very many cities, and very many nations, all obedient to himself," which suggests to

---

[1] All references are to Xenophon, *The Education of Cyrus*, Translated by Wayne Ambler (Ithaca: Cornell University Press, 2001).

Xenophon "that ruling human beings does not belong among those tasks that are impossible, or even among those that are difficult, if one does it with knowledge" (1.1.3). Xenophon does not elaborate immediately here his understanding of the exact knowledge required for effective rule. Instead, we must read the *Education of Cyrus* for an account of how Cyrus came to excel "in ruling human beings" (1.2.6). Our initial expectation, then, is that Xenophon will provide a universal blueprint education for ruling well.[2] But Xenophon also implies early on that there might be something idiosyncratic about Cyrus' seemingly technocratic imperial form of rule, as his ability to satisfy and pacify populations was based upon "fear of himself" and the "desire of gratifying him" (1.1.5).

In fact, Xenophon sows doubt about the viability of Cyrus' despotic rule as a universally replicable model, if we reconsider his early observation that "human beings unite most of all against those whom they perceive attempting to rule them" (1.1.2). Xenophon's apparent suggestion here is that the desire to live freely is fundamental to human nature. And yet, we are faced with the seeming paradox of Xenophon's contention that Cyrus was able to rule over human beings as easily as shepherds manage beasts. This apparent contradiction points to at least two possibilities: first, to succeed in ruling over willing human beings in a way that deprives them of their freedom, either it is necessary to establish absolute rule somehow imperceptibly, without the notice of the ruled; or, second, rule will inevitably face the challenge of the tenacious human desire and perpetual

---

[2] See Christopher Nadon, *Xenophon's Prince: Republic and Empire in the Cyropaedia*, for discussion of Xenophon's presentation of "his model of a 'perfect king'" in the *Cyropaedia*, as a universal model for "a technical art or science" for political rule that transcends artificial boundaries of time and place for replication (Berkeley and Los Angeles: University of California Press, 2001) 27.

hope for freedom with which Xenophon begins "The Education of Cyrus." My proposition in this essay is that both possibilities characterize the Persian empire Cyrus founds. Cyrus' drive to rule over the known world has a surreptitious character, the full nature and true purpose of which escapes both his countrymen, the Persians in the army fighting with him from the start, and those who join his enterprise along the way. They are carried away with the exhilaration of engagement in what the charismatic Cyrus presents as a defensive expedition, the promise of reward, both material and in terms of honor, and Cyrus' persuasive rhetorical ability to construct consensus for his plans and innovations. When the expedition reaches its end with Cyrus' defeat of the Assyrians and his acquisition of the Babylonian palace, the reality of Cyrus' full design to manage the needs and expectations of the empire through a universal administrative state from above, without the political consent and participation of its inhabitants, becomes apparent. In the place of citizens, there will only be subjects. Even those who believed they were friends and partners in Cyrus' enterprise find they are subordinates, in fact, caught in his manipulative web of complete subjugation.

If the second proposition is also true, the stability and integrity of the empire will eventually wane as a result of the personalization of Cyrus' power and the human restlessness to be free from the heavy hand of despotic rule. In fact, Xenophon makes clear that this agitation begins with the end of Cyrus' personal rule first among Cyrus' heirs as soon as Cyrus closes his eyes for the final time. He reports that after Cyrus' death, his sons "immediately fell into dissension, cities and nations immediately revolted and everything took a turn for the worse" (8.8.1). With Cyrus' death, political ambition and the natural human desire for freedom immediately reemerge, which suggests that Cyrus' model of rule did not provide a permanent solution to the problem of political instability. This observation requires us to raise the question why Xenophon would present Cyrus' rise to and exercise of power as an example worthy of contention as a solution to the human political problem he identifies?

Freedom From Virtue and the Rule of Law

The argument of this essay is that it is Xenophon's project from the beginning to demonstrate the susceptibility of human beings to the hope of liberation from the discipline and drudgery of the ordinary rule of law as a means to living well. In the *Cyropaedia*, Xenophon shows us that Cyrus' project satisfies two forms of human longing simultaneously. He is able to lull the Persians into the temporary belief that material comfort and safety will suffice to satisfy their desire to live well, while he also presents the most honor loving and ambitious with the expectation that in his meritocracy their superior ability will receive notice, praise, honor, and reward. In the end, however, Xenophon teaches us that politics, understood as the desire to rule and participate in ruling, that is, the desire to be free and self-governing, is a persistent principle of the human condition and that it cannot be suppressed indefinitely, especially when its suppression becomes apparent to the ruled. Perhaps, then, Xenophon's teaching is that the very effort to find a solution to the problem of political instability is fraught with the danger of looking for one human being to answer the call for a new order, a perfect leader who will bring about a perfectly satisfactory political order.[3] Cyrus is a model of ambition that the young and

---

[3] Christopher Bruell contends that: "In the *Cyropaedia*, Xenophon presents his thoughts on the character of the perfect ruler and the on the political way of life at its peak." *History of Political Philosophy*, Third Edition,

ambitious, like Alcibiades,[4] admire and seek to emulate. Xenophon seeks to demonstrate how a Cyrus might seduce an army and a people with false promise as a warning against the seductive siren call of an enigmatic despotism that presents itself as a free and peaceful solution for world order.

Xenophon prepares us for his account of Cyrus' project by explaining how, together with his royal birth, his nature and his education are the foundation of his success in captivating everyone with whom he interacts. Xenophon recounts Cyrus' celebration in word and song by the barbarians "as having been most beautiful in form and most benevolent in soul, most eager to learn, and ambitious, with the result that he endured every labor and faced every risk for the sake of being praised" (1.2.1). Xenophon's historically fictional account of Cyrus' perfection is the stuff of exaggerated legend and it implies his own skepticism of the mythical narrative surrounding Cyrus' legacy as a great founder. It is the reputation of a man who held the absolute fascination of and power over the political imagination of the people he governed, but who also stands as a nostalgic memory or totem of an earlier idyllic Persian era of power, prosperity, and stability, an image Xenophon seeks to contest.[5]

Xenophon's presentation of Old Persia is intriguing. Initially, we are impressed with the idea of a small city state that

---

edited by Leo Strauss and Joseph Cropsey (Chicago: University of Chicago Press, 1987), 92.

[4] Socrates lures a young Alcibiades into a discussion of justice by appealing to his greatest ambitions and demonstrating that it is only by conversing with Socrates that he will acquire the self-knowledge he needs to compete with the Persian kings and become renowned among the Greeks. *The Roots of Political Philosophy*, edited by Thomas L. Pangle (Ithaca: Cornell University Press, 1987), 198–203.

[5] Nadon also indicates that Cyrus' reputation among Greek youth served to make him a model of a cautionary tale for Xenophon, as I also argue above, *Xenophon's Prince: Republic and Empire in the Republic* 28.

dedicates itself to the education and character formation of the young to prepare them to be noble and good leaders for the future, who will maintain the rule of law that preserves the just Persian way of life.[6] But Xenophon also seeks to prevent us from indulgence in nostalgia for the small republic, that sustains itself through a self-deception. Xenophon recounts that during his Persian education, Cyrus demonstrably "surpassed all his age-mates both in quickly learning what was necessary and in doing everything in a noble and manly way" (1.3.1). Xenophon implies that Cyrus' natural superiority was apparent to him even as a child, and yet, despite his clearly greater ability, Cyrus received recognition similar to that of his peers. The infamous cloak story Cyrus recounts to his mother in Media to prove his knowledge of Persian justice suggests what Cyrus learned from observation of his superiority. Cyrus is punished by his teacher for his presumption of superior knowledge to the Persian laws protecting private property because he proposed the redistribution of coats, a small coat to a small boy, and the transfer of the small boy's large coat to a large boy (1.4.16–17). This story reveals two insights that inform Cyrus' project for the future: first, that the Persian law inflicts artificial restraints on the satisfaction of natural need and reward for the exercise of independent judgment; and second, that the law imposes a uniform, apparently impartial but also impersonal solution on each situation, whereas a human being with superior knowledge and insight into the needs of each human being can adapt his judgment to the particular requirements of each circumstance. It is this insight that guides Cyrus' redistribution of the boys' property according to his understanding of their apparent needs, but he acts without regard for the laws governing the preservation of wealth that maintain the ruling class of Persia. Cyrus' ruling reflects his

---

[6] Christopher Bruell, *History of Political Philosophy*, 93.

70

perception that the Persian laws are neither entirely rational nor always just. The Persian ruling class make a virtue of necessity: their moderation with a view to wealth is a necessity born of Persia's resource poor geography, but it also justifies the exile of economic activity, which it considers vulgar, to the outer reaches of the city, in favor of "the good order of the educated," which takes place in the center of the city (1.2.3). But those who lack the marginally superior wealth sufficient to support the leisure necessary for this education of the young "in the laws of the Persians," even if they possess the requisite talent, are unable to participate. Xenophon reveals that "those who are not able...to raise their children without putting them to work" cannot afford to send them to "the common schools of justice" (1.2.15). Because there is no ostentatious wealth in the city, the Persian peers can deceive themselves that the education in virtue is available to all who choose it (1.2.15). But Cyrus understands early on that there is little necessary natural difference between the peers and the commoners who lack the economic resources to participate, except the chance of birth into the class of commoners. The Persian republic understands itself as free, egalitarian, virtuous, and merit-based, but it subjects the many commoners to the few peers by denying them the chance for equal opportunity to receive the education that would habituate them in the virtue required to win them honor in old Persia. Xenophon reveals that although Persia understands itself as an aristocracy, it is an oligarchy in practice, sustaining itself by denying the opportunity for virtue and political participation to the commoners.

We are left to wonder whether Xenophon believes there was anything truly good and noble about the Persian republic, especially after his presentation of Cyrus' public critique of the principle of practicing virtue simply for the sake of being good men, without the expectation of any external reward, upon his departure with his army from old Persia (1.5.8–9). And yet, once Cyrus liberates the peers—and the commoners—from the idea at the heart of Persian law that it is praiseworthy to dedicate one's life to the procurement and practice of individual and civic virtue for the sake of the common good, it is unclear what will replace it. Xenophon also makes clear that although the young Persian peers learn continence, obedience, and military skill, they have recourse to no argument they can articulate as to why their republican virtue is choice-worthy, except that the habitual practice of moderation and justice enables them to avoid the inevitable public shame of departing from it. The Persian education in justice aims chiefly at the avoidance of injustice, in particular, the shame of ingratitude (1.2.6–8). Practice teaches the young peers that moderation and obedience are a noble and good way of life without explanatory justification.

When Cyrus' uncle, Cyaxares, requests his assistance in a defensive war against the Assyrian king, Cyrus exploits his traditional role as general, which gives him leadership of the Persian army in war, to raise doubts about the Persian way of life and the laws that support it. He uses his freedom as military leader to create the conditions for expansion of his leadership and his military assignment. Cyrus begins his transformation of the Persian army in a speech in which he questions the code and achievements of the Persian education. Bruell tells us that Cyrus immediately seeks to tempt his Persian comrades with the "opportunities for wealth and distinction" he first observed in Media.[7] He accomplishes this by releasing the young peers from their obedience to their immediate elders and from their reverence for their ancient ancestors by questioning the use to which they put their virtue. A consideration of the past and the future

---

[7] Christopher Bruell, "Xenophon," *The History of Political Philosophy*, 94.

leaves Cyrus at a loss as to what material good either the ancient ancestors or the current peers have gained from their abstention "from the pleasures at hand" and the practice of virtue (1.5.7–9). Cyrus does not seek to undo the Persian education in continence, but instead, to explain to the young peers that their self-control should serve as a preparation for "much more enjoyment in the future" (1.5.9). Cyrus equates the practice of justice and virtue to the practice of other arts: rhetoric or clever speech is for the sake of "speaking well to persuade human beings and thereby to accomplish many and great goods." Similarly, the practice of "military affairs" serves not to engage perpetually in fighting, but so that "by becoming good in military affairs they shall secure much wealth, much happiness, and great honors both for themselves and for their city." Cyrus seeks to liberate the Persian peers from their understanding that a life dedicated to the practice of virtue is its own reward, resulting in a life well lived. Cyrus argues that such virtue should serve as the utilitarian foundation, the necessary preparation, for achieving the ends he defines as success, and the proper recompense for what they deserve: "much wealth, much happiness, and great honors" (1.5.9). The Persians should understand their virtue as a means to a practical and material end that will make them far happier than did the austere, abstinent old Persian way of life.

The fact that the Persian education in justice involves argumentation and habituation but not the study of "letters," the more liberal education, which Xenophon explains that the Greek youth receive, deprives the Persian peers of the ability to reflect seriously on their training with a view to justice and offer arguments with which to test or refute Cyrus' challenge to their way of life. Instead, Cyrus' rhetoric, the clever speaking to which he refers earlier, quickly persuades the peers to join him in pursuit of victory against a lazy enemy (1.5.11–13). Cyrus treads a fine line here: to encourage the Persians to leave behind their way of life and, although they do not know it yet, follow him beyond the military task at hand, he must promise them rewards for their efforts beyond the Persian practice; but to succeed in these endeavors, he will rely on their continued, habitual dedication to the pursuit of virtue as a source of pride, a practice he can reward with the honor they most crave. So, in the end, Cyrus concludes his speech with the promise not of wealth and pleasure to reward their "noble and warlike" virtue, but instead the praise most valued by the lovers of honor who "must of necessity take on with pleasure every labor and every risk" (1.5.12). Ultimately, Cyrus replaces the approval of the Persian elders with his own praise for the displays of labor and virtue against the enemy he knows the Persian peers will demonstrate as a result of their education. Xenophon shows us here what supersedes the dedication to the common good at which the virtue produced by the Persian education and practice aims. The peers essentially trade their freedom under the self-governing adherence to the rule of law for subjection to Cyrus through the honor he dispenses in the service of his pursuit of absolute rule over the entire army and eventually the Persian empire as a whole.

Subjection to the Personalization of Power

Cyrus' early disposition to believe in his superior judgment in providing for the needs of others is reinforced for him by his exposure to the despotic rule of his Median grandfather. There, he learns how to win affection and honor from those whom he benefits with the goods of others. When his grandfather provides him with gifts and opportunities, Cyrus, whose habitual self-control limits his taste for lavish food and luxury, and even his need for material comfort, distributes the gifts to grateful friends and associates. The example of the fancy side dishes and meats with which his grandfather furnishes him during dinner in Media illustrates the point. Instead of gorging himself, Cyrus distributes the meat to each of his grandfather's servants as a reward for the way in which each has benefited him, by teaching him to ride, throw a javelin, or for honoring and serving his mother and grandfather (1.3.4–7). Here, we see how Cyrus acquired and perfected the art of manipulation through the apparent virtue of generosity. Without real personal sacrifice, Cyrus learns to benefit others in a way that pleases and indebts them to him personally, in most cases significantly beyond their ability to reciprocate. It is perhaps no surprise that the Persians judged ingratitude as the most shameful of vices because it was a sign of impiety and disrespect of the elders, the sources of traditional Persian authority, and hence deserving of the severest punishment. As a result, the effect of Cyrus' generosity on the Persians in particular, but also on others who would subsequently join Cyrus' ranks in pursuit of some sort of benefit or salvation he could provide, is to create a series of seemingly benevolent obligations that bind individuals and groups to Cyrus and on which he capitalizes to further his imperial project.

Cyrus brings together his apparent liberation of the ambition and desire of the Persian peers from the limits imposed by Persian law and custom with his peculiar practice of generosity to unite the army of Persian peers and commoners in a collective military pursuit under his exclusive leadership. To facilitate his pursuit of victory, honor and absolute power, Cyrus revolutionizes the Persian military in two important ways that make the path forward possible and the return to old Persia impossible. The return to old Persia, the Persian republic, becomes impossible as soon as Cyrus disassociates the teaching of justice and virtue from the Persian self- understanding that the education serves the pursuit of a just and moderate common good. From our external perspective, the education serves the ends of the ruling class in old Persia: the maintenance of their rule over the common people. Once the commoners join the ranks of the peers in armaments and fighting equally, they cannot return to a degraded status in old Persia. We have discussed Xenophon's revelation of the means by which the peers excluded the commoners from the education and thus the means to participate in ruling. And yet, we know that there is still something self-sufficient and beneficial to the minimalist order the general and judicious subjection to the rule of law sustains and that limits excess in old Persia, a restraint that Cyrus' reform seeks to manipulate for the sake of what he promises is future gain.

But how does Cyrus lay the groundwork for the elimination of political life and the fulfilment of his imperial ambitions? Xenophon shows us first that Cyrus accomplishes his revolution not by force or open imposition from above, but surreptitiously through his persuasive ability to engineer his preferred answer to any question or proposal he introduces. The effect of Cyrus' rhetorical leadership is to leave the impression that those he rules, in this case, the army, have freely chosen the path he proposes. In other words, Cyrus never poses a question the outcome of which is uncertain to him. To expand the size of his fighting force, Cyrus proposes the distribution of heavy armor to the Persian commoners. His strategy is to persuade the peers to accept this effectual democratization of the army by arguing that all the Persians will be safer if the peers agree to an expansion of their ranks. Interestingly, an unidentified peer rises next to encourage the peers to allow Cyrus to invite the commoners to take up the heavy arms and fight with them. He leads the peers to see that with their leadership, the commoners will "become better" (2.1.11–12). Whether Cyrus has arranged for the unidentified peer to speak ahead of time, or he speaks spontaneously, the result is the same. The peers are persuaded that Cyrus has the best interests of the army in mind when he proposes its expansion. Similarly, Cyrus makes the commoners aware that by extending the responsibility of fighting with heavy armor to them, he is freeing them from their lower status and elevating them to equal opportunity with the peers, a challenge and an opportunity they are more than prepared to seize (2.1.14–19).

Cyrus' second revolutionary proposal for debate is whether to maintain the principle of equal shares or introduce merit—distinction and success on the battlefield by soldiers—as the principle to govern the distribution of goods won through battle. Again, instead of announcing the new principle, Cyrus proposes it as a question up for discussion and decision by the army itself (2.2.17). And again, both the peers and the commoners agree to the new meritocratic principle. The peers agree, as Cyrus tells Chrysantas, "partly because we advise it, and partly because it is shameful to deny that he who works hardest and especially benefits the community is deserving of the greatest things" (2.2.20). Here, Cyrus relies on the education of the peers to value honor and avoid ingratitude and shame. In fact, Chrysantas argues when the matter is before the entire army that it would be shameful for "the bad" to have "the thought of sharing equally in what others achieve by virtue, even though he does nothing noble and good" (2.3.5). Chrysantas, Xenophon tells us, was a man distinguished by his "prudence" rather than his strength or height. Clearly, his prudence dictates the moral authority of Cyrus' argument that even if the strongest and swiftest gain the most, the slower and weaker will gain more on the whole through the superior capacity of the strong and swift than through a system of equal distribution that fails to reward ambitious effort. In fact, the competition to exhibit virtue in Cyrus' presence begins at the moment of the debate, so that it is no surprise that Cyrus' proposal not only wins the day, but that it was also "decided that each be honored in accord with his worth and that Cyrus be the judge" (2.3.16). The Persian soldiers vote not only to reward treasure on the basis of worth on the battle-field, but they also voluntarily and unanimously decide to elevate Cyrus to the position of supreme judge of all merit and worth in the army. It is the first full step towards satisfying Cyrus' voracious desire for the power to be the source of every good and honorable benefit to everyone in Persia and beyond. And he achieves this absolute authority through voluntary submission. That the commoners jump at the chance for advancement and elevation is no surprise. The Persian peers as a whole, however, voluntarily relinquish their relative freedom under the law to subject themselves to Cyrus' sole judgment and rule over them in order to receive his praise. They trade political friendship and a form of self-governance for the promise of honor bestowed by Cyrus.

The End of Politics and Friendship
under Cyrus' Rule

There is much more to say about how the flaws in the old Persian education left the peers susceptible to Cyrus' corruption. In the end, however, the Persian peers find that they have somehow assented to a golden cage, in which they are captive of Cyrus' power and his suspicion of his most talented men. As emperor, Cyrus rules by the adage of keeping your enemies close, perhaps as he does the defeated Lydian king, Croesus, but your friends closer. The Persian peers and those among his closest advisers contend with one another around the Babylonian palace dinner table for a seat closest to Cyrus as a sign that he honors one of them more than another on any given day. For example, Cyrus explains when asked that he honors Chrysantas over Hystaspas, because "Chrysantas here did not wait for our call; he instead reported before he was called, for the sake of our affairs." While we knew that Chrystantas was prudent, here, we also find out that in fact Cyrus valued Chrysantas for his counsel about his affairs with allies and the army. Chrysantas was willing to say from among the assembled army what Cyrus could not say but needed to be said to ensure that Cyrus' position won the day's debate (8.4.11). It is thus noteworthy that Chrysantas is among the friends of Cyrus who seeks to go out into the empire to rule as a satrap. We wonder whether it is Chrysantas who seeks escape from Cyrus' constant company, or if he volunteers to travel in the empire to serve as a means of external surveillance (8.6.6–7).

In Babylon, each day all of Cyrus' friends were required to appear at court to train and then to dine with him. Whether one can call the subservient "friends" is a vital question because the lives of those closest to Cyrus were not their own; they belonged to Cyrus. In fact, Cyrus particularly asks his friends to report to him "whenever someone seems to ask for what is just" so that they could deliberate about the request and accomplish it for them (8.3.20). Perhaps, Cyrus wanted to keep track of the just concerns of his friends, or wished to track any mention of the just or the political among the wise and talented. Cyrus managed their contributions as allies just as he managed the administration of his empire in every facet through a system of stations through which riders on horseback would pass information from one rider to another to ensure the swiftest system of communication from the outer provinces (8.6.17). In every case, information reached Cyrus through a configuration of communication designed to ensure he was always fully cognizant of every kind of activity in the empire and among his associates.

Our sense of the rupture and tension between old and new Persia is reinforced by the manner in which Cyrus returns to ancestral Persia after his final capture of Babylon and his full defeat of the Assyrians (8.15.27). Cyrus very intentionally leaves his army at the "borders of Persia," aware that the old

Persian peers would consider a great show of force unseemly and boastful. Instead, he marches

> into the city with his friends, bringing sufficient sacred victims for all Persians to offer in sacrifice and feast on. He brought such gifts as were fitting for his father, his mother, and his friends; and such as were fitting for magistrates, elders and all the Peers. He gave [gifts] also to all the Persian men and Persian women, as many as the king still now gives whenever he arrives in Persia. (8.5.21)

Xenophon makes clear that just as he judged what was fitting when he redistributed the coats between the small and large boys as a child under instruction, Cyrus considers carefully the gifts that are appropriate or "fitting" for a king to distribute to each of the Persians: family, leaders, Peers and all the people.

This distribution of gifts and goods, prompts Cambyses, Cyrus' father, to call together, not the whole city, that is, not the commoners who might be particularly susceptible to corruption by Cyrus' gifts, but "the Persian elders and magistrates...those who presided over the greatest matters" to express his concerns about the compatibility of Cyrus' new Persia with the traditional Persian way of life (8.5.22). Cambyses cautions both sides against unification. He begins by warning Cyrus against endeavoring to corrupt the Persian way of life by trying to rule Persia as he does others, "with a view to your own special advantage" (8.5.24). Cambyses, thus, identifies the manner in which Cyrus has revolutionized Persia outside the walls of the city. He recognizes that Cyrus has established a tyranny, which is dedicated to the "special" advantage of Cyrus, the one man who rules all of new Persia's imperial possessions. And he is clearly alarmed at the ease with which Cyrus has accomplished his corruption of the Persians and their education outside the city's borders.

In light of Cambyses' insight into Cyrus' tyrannical form of imperial rule, he seeks to preserve the Persian republican way of life for as long as possible, during his lifetime in any case, knowing that Cyrus will remain his heir. So, he cautions the Persian elders against the temptation posed by Cyrus' newly acquired wealth and power, all that his "fitting" gifts to the Persians represent, and against the usurpation of Cyrus' power that their envy might inspire. He reminds them that Cyrus led an army from old Persia, with their permission, and, "with the [help of the] gods," made the "Persians famous among all human beings, and honored in all Asia." In so doing, he enriched and provided work and support for all those who campaigned with him. Cambyses also notes that Cyrus has formed a cavalry, which creates "for the Persians a tie to the plains" (8.5.23). His speech has the intention of sternly warning the Persian leadership and Cyrus that the way of life in old Persia is incompatible with that of Cyrus' new Persia. He reminds the leaders that Cyrus has made the return of his Persian army to old Persia impossible, by enriching them beyond the standards of old Persian life and by creating a cavalry that cannot function in the rocky mountain terrain of his ancestral home. Politically, he has transformed the politics of Persia from a self-governing republic, subject to the rule of law, to a despotism. In light of these differences, Cambyses proposes a defensive compact between the two Persias. Cambyses seeks a means to protecting the Persian republic, which, despite its flaws, he clearly prefers to Cyrus' imperial rule. Even with the limitations on the advancement of the commoners, the republic exhibits greater freedom to participate in the political life of the city as citizens under the rule of law for at least a certain portion of the population, while Cyrus' imperial rule leaves room for only one to rule.

While Cyrus was able to maintain absolute authority over this universal system of technological administration, it is clear that no one person commanded the allegiance of or generated fear among the people in the empire as Cyrus had. The result was that political ambition even within his own house arose and the desire in the wide empire for freedom from the rule of a man they had never seen irrupted (8.8.1–2). The Armenian king had once explained to Cyrus, when he saw an opportunity to free himself from the oppressive rule of the Medians: "I desired freedom, for it seemed to me to be noble both that I be free myself and that I leave freedom for my children" (3.1.10). The Armenian is grateful that Cyrus allows him to remain on the throne if he resumes his tribute payments and joins the campaign against the Assyrians on the Persian side, but would the Armenians remain faithful to the Persians in the case of the death of Cyrus—whom they feared sufficiently to remain subservient within the empire? Xenophon's answer is clearly no—at some point, we inevitably regret our loss of freedom and long to reclaim it.

This observation of the ultimately irrepressible human desire for freedom and self-government leads us back to the question of the justice or continued viability of old Persia or a similar republican government. If neither a small republic, nor a vast universal empire provide solutions to the political problem with which Xenophon introduced the *Education of Cyrus*, would Xenophon be forced to concede defeat in his search for a solution to the challenge of political instability? Many suggest that Xenophon sends us back to Socratic philosophy. With that diagnosis I agree. But Xenophon was also a practical man. Does he suggest a political solution? In Xenophon's *Memorabilia of Socrates*, he recommends that the rule of good laws to which the governed consent is the best way to persuade the ruled to accept some degree of wisdom embodied in the laws (3.8). Such a form of rule seeks to avoid injustice, even if it cannot achieve the elusive perfectly stable political arrangement or rule for which Xenophon seems to search at the beginning of the *Education of Cyrus*.

4

ANIMALS AS MODELS FOR RULE IN XENOPHON'S *CYROPAEDIA*

Gregory A. McBrayer

I. Introduction

Xenophon's works abound with depictions of animals. Three of his works have animals embedded in their titles: *Peri Hippikēs* (*On the Skill of Horesmanship*), *Hipparchikos* (*The Skilled Commander of Horse Cavalry*), and *Kynegetikos* (*The One Skilled at Leading Dogs*). For centuries, his treatises on horses and hunting with dogs have been read by enthusiasts and celebrated for the accuracy of their description of animals and their helpful advice regarding their care. Xenophon's interest in animals seems to be guided, in part, by a desire to understand animals in their own right, but he also seems to be led to study animals partly by a desire to understand human things. Xenophon's characters liken students to puppies, soldiers to horses, and subjects to sheep. Further, his only account of Socrates' course of education occurs in a bridle shop.[1] Xenophon's *Cyropaedia*, or *The Education of Cyrus*, discloses what is distinctly human—but vulnerable to destruction—by portraying a ruler who rises to emperor of almost the entire known world, but who is able to do so only by reducing his subjects to sub-human, beastlike status.

In the introduction to the work, Xenophon presents Cyrus as possessing extraordinary insight into human affairs. We are

---

[1] Mem. IV.2.1. See Bonette (2018)

told that he alone possesses a science or knowledge of human affairs. Understanding humans well implies that one understands human beings and can distinguish what is uniquely human from what humans have in common with other animals. In particular, Xenophon's introduction indicates we can learn a great deal about human beings by comparing how human beings are ruled with how other animals are ruled. The introduction begins from the tentative judgment that it is easier, given his nature, "for a human being to rule all other kinds of animals than to rule human beings" (I.1.3). However, after reflecting on Cyrus, "we were compelled to change our mind to the view that ruling human beings does not belong among those tasks that are impossible, or even among those that are difficult," provided one rules knowingly (or scientifically, *epistamenōs* I.1.3). One might be inclined to the view, on the basis of the introduction, that Cyrus understands human nature, and this understanding enables him to rule well. However, nothing could be further from the account that follows.

The remainder of the *Cyropaedia* develops and calls into question the hypothesis Xenophon offers in the introduction. Humans are indeed very difficult to rule, and Cyrus' enormous political success is the result not of a knowledge of human affairs, but rather, at least in part, from his supposed insight that humans are easier to rule to the extent that they can be tamed like animals.[2] As a consequence of Cyrus' taking control of an enormous empire and improving the material conditions of everyone who submits to him, Cyrus dehumanizes everyone under his rule, reducing them to their basic, animal remnant of human nature. While the subjects in his empire remain biological human beings, Cyrus figuratively reduces everyone in his empire

---

[2] There are, of course, other reasons for Cyrus' success, not least of which are his ancestry on both sides and other natural capacities (I.2.1–2).

to the status of an animal. Cyrus' mastery over his subjects contrasts sharply and negatively with *political* rule over free and equal persons.[3]

The *Cyropaedia* opens with a reflection on a principal distinction between human beings and animals, namely that it is much harder to rule human beings than it is to rule other kinds of animals. To be more precise, Xenophon begins by contrasting humans to herd animals, who, Xenophon contends, are more willing to obey their keepers than are humans their rulers.[4] They go where led, they feed on whatever their keepers drive them to, and they allow their keepers to use any profits that arise from them (Xenophon is silent regarding the diet of the keeper). Further, Xenophon has never seen a herd unite against its keeper, and herd animals do not rebel, he suggests, because they are kept safe and fed. From this discussion of herd animals, Xenophon draws the dubious conclusion that it is easier for a human to rule *"all* other kinds of animals than to rule human beings" (I.1.3, emphasis mine). In any event, by making this explicitly political comparison between human beings and non-human animals, Xenophon encourages readers to reflect on what kind of an animal a human being is. If rule is an essential part of politics, and if human beings resist rule to a greater degree than any other animal, including the wildest and solitary, non-gregarious animals, Xenophon's introduction challenges the notion, championed later by Aristotle, that humans are political by nature.[5] The introduction suggests humans become political as a

---

[3] Cf. Aristotle *Politics* I.7 1255b17–19

[4] The Greek for "herd" is derived from the verb "to lead" (*agō*), so herd animals are "led" animals.

[5] Of course, Aristotle may not be as sanguine as he lets on. See his two references to the Cyclopes in *Politics* I.2 1252b10–1253a40. Compare also what he has to say about bees and herd animals at 1153a8 with what he says

result of something analogous to domestication.

Xenophon's account of herd animals seems pollyannaish. He claims never to have perceived a herd of horses or cattle unite against its keeper, but we later learn that individual horses and cattle disobey, resist, and attempt to strike their keepers.[6] To be precise, Xenophon does not claim never to have seen a herd animal disobey; he only says he has never seen them unite in rebellion. But the failure of herd animals to unite against keepers may be less the result of willingness to obey, and more the result of an inability on the part of animals to unite due to limitations with regard to communication. Their rebellions are isolated, impotent, and ineffectual—but not non-existent. Moreover, by referring to cattle and horses as "herd" animals, Xenophon obscures the possibility that even these animals must have become domesticated at a particular point in time, a Herculean task if ever there were one.[7]

By drawing the comparison between humans and tame animals, Xenophon prompts one to inquire what kind of an animal the human being is. He nudges the reader to ask whether humans are akin to tame animals. Further, if humans are tame, gregarious animals like horses and sheep, we may have, like those animals, become tame at a particular moment. For the

---

about them in *History of Animals* I.1 487b34 and following. Aristotle also distinguishes gregarious or "herd" animals from political animals in this passage, and the distinction may help us to see more clearly what Cyrus aims to do by transforming humans from political into (merely) gregarious or herd animals.

[6] Pheraulus reports having seen oxen and horses strike (II.3.9).

[7] One of Hercules' labors was in fact stealing the mares of Diomedes. Poseidon created horses and tamed them (*Iliad* XIII.24–29), and Bellerophon, Poseidon's son, knows how to tame them like his father. See (Burkert and Raffan 1985, 136 and ff). Two epithets for Poseidon are "horse tamer" (*damaios*) at Corinth Pind. Ol. 13, 66. and horse caretaker (*hippokourios*) at Sparta Paus. 3.14.2. Consider Genesis 1:23–24.

introduction denies that humans are gregarious herd animals in the way pigeons, cranes, and swans are gregarious. There must have been a master tamer.

Xenophon suggests that Cyrus might be one such unique ruler, insofar as he advances the thesis that Cyrus alone figured out a science of ruling human beings in the way that other human beings figured out how to rule animals. Indeed, Cyrus' understanding of humans is central to the amazing scope of his political project. Alternatively, though the introduction denies man's political nature, Cyrus' attempt to reduce human beings to the status of a herd animal could reveal that man is, in fact, deeply political in the last analysis.

In any event, Xenophon recounts Cyrus' enormous political success, and he traces Cyrus' life from beginning to end. Cyrus' empire was limited on one side by the sea, another by the mountains, to the North by cold, and the South by heat. Cyrus became the ruler of an empire that extended to the natural limits of the known earth. He brought peace to a world rife with conflict; he tolerated great variety in ways of life, mostly leaving local customs in place. Xenophon connects Cyrus' amazing success to his understanding of human nature, and Cyrus' understanding of human nature is shaped in part by what he comes to understand about non-human animals and how humans are like and unlike them.

II. What kind of animal is a human being?

What kind of an animal is the human being, according to the *Cyropaedia*? To use language evocative of Rousseau, has man been de-natured? Perhaps humans have been tamed and broken, or perhaps the attempt to "tame" or domesticate humans has only been partly successful. One cannot help but think of the alternative accounts of human nature posited by other political philosophers. Thomas Hobbes, for example, says that humans are solitary, nasty beasts by nature.[8] We only come together because we are afraid, and reason dictates pursuing society. Hobbes likens human beings to wolves, but wolves are not in fact perfectly solitary animals.[9] Rather, wolves are gregarious animals, though their social groups, packs, are quite small. It is in fact quite rare to find the "lone wolf."[10] Strictly solitary mammals are difficult to find in general, and even those come together for the purpose of procreation.

Aristotle, on the other hand, likens human beings to bees, which would imply that human beings are highly gregarious by nature, and that our social arrangements are more spontaneous than Hobbes would allow.[11] The alternative of lone wolf and bee seems insufficient. Humans do not seem to have the spontaneous associative tendencies of bees, nor do we live like lone wolves. But if we think of wolves as living in small, social, hierarchical units, that description of original man seems plausible. Being carnivorous by nature, humans have more in common with wolves than with bees.[12] It seems to be the case that small group animals tend to be carnivorous (lions, wolves), whereas larger scale associative animals tend to be herbivores (sheep, cattle). And it seems to be the case that these small, carnivorous groups are hierarchical, whereas herbivores tend to be more egalitarian. Some schools of fish and flocks of birds display an

---

[8] Hobbes is most empahtic on this point in *De Cive* (I.2). See also *Leviathan*, Ch. XIII.

[9] "Man to man is an arrant wolf" Hobbes, *De Cive* Dedicatory Letter.

[10] Aristotle, *History of Animals* VIII.5 594a30

[11] However, Aristotle recognizes there was someone who founded the first city, *Politics* I.2 1253a30. Further, he claims elsewhere that man is both a gregarious *and* a solitary animal (*History of Animals* I.1 488a6).

[12] But humans can be gentle or tame, whereas wolves are *always* wild. Aristotle, *History of Animals* I.1 488a27. Cf. Locke, §25

amazing order, seemingly without hierarchy, others have a hierarchy (pecking order), while others still, taloned birds, for example, are not gregarious animals at all.[13] If humans are like wolves or lions, that would imply that humans are hierarchical animals (unlike sheep, cattle, birds, and fish) that originally dwelt in small social groups, and any attempt to render humans equal, to end that hierarchy, would require effort. Furthermore, it would render quite questionable the tenability of a large-scale human organization (like an empire) with a single leader at the top. Humans would have to be changed significantly to become members of a world community, and an enormous inequality would be required between ruler and ruled. Perhaps in accord with this, Xenophon exaggerates the extent of Cyrus' rule in order to give the impression that Cyrus' empire spans the whole world; Cyrus' empire has no neighbors, it spans the ends of the earth.[14]

Xenophon does not show that world empire is impossible, but, through Cyrus, he shows us how such a large-scale empire might be directed by a single individual. The ruler of a large human community on the scale of an empire would have to be, or appear to be, a member of a different species than the humans he rules. He can do this by pursuing one of two goals, or pursuing both simultaneously: elevating himself to a position to where he appears greater than human and diminishing the ruled to sub-human status.[15] In the *Cyropaedia*, Cyrus achieves world

---

[13] Aristotle, *History of Animals* I.1 488a4–5.

[14] "[Cyrus] acquired nearly every (*pampolus*) human being, nearly every city, and nearly every nation." (I.1.3)

[15] Alternatively, perhaps Xenophon leads us to see that the people in Cyrus' empire have been reduced to their merely human status (*anthropoi*), their biologically human status, and that men and women (*andres* and *gunaikes*, respectively) lead more fully human lives than mere human beings.

peace by dehumanizing his subjects, on one hand, and by making himself appear to be superhuman, or even divine, on the other.

III. Cyrus' Education in Dehumanization

Cyrus learns the lesson of dehumanization, the lesson that it can be advantageous to treat humans like animals, when he is still a young man, although the point of the lessons escapes his notice. His Persian education lays the groundwork for treating humans as non-humans, but this fact is not revealed to him until he is a young adult. Upon accepting his first official military role, as leader of an army preparing to defend Media from an Assyrian attack, Cyrus departs for Media with his father, Cambyses, the King of Persia, who accompanies him to the Median border. Eager to prepare his son to be able to lead his army successfully, Cambyses attempts to educate his son about the difficulty of ruling human beings, especially while on military campaign. No doubt, Cambyses is guided in part by a strong paternal desire to ensure his son survives this military campaign. To that end, Cambyses exhorts his son to take many common-sense measures, like paying attention to supply chains, ensuring his troops have enough to eat, exercising them, and he also discourages Cyrus from relying on others for provisions, including even

---

Cyrus, Xenophon says, rules over nearly all human beings (*anthropoi*). References to "human being" in the *Cyropaedia* are often derogatory, and, according to the Liddell Scott lexicon, "*anthropos*" is frequently used in a contemptuous sense in Attic Greek. Cf. *Regime of the Lacedaemonians*, where Xenophon refers to Spartan women as "females" (1.4). According to Strauss, "By using that expression [females] [Xenophon] refers, I assume, to the fact that Spartan women were left to their animal natures much more than were Spartan men, because they were much less disciplined" (Strauss 1939, 505 and fn3).

his own uncle.

Cyrus is surprised to learn that he should not rely on his uncle, an ally, but his father offers even darker advice Cyrus is initially stunned to receive. Cambyses exhorts his son to become, in Cyrus' words, "a plotter, a dissembler, wily, a cheat, a thief, rapacious, and the sort who takes advantage of his enemy in everything" (I.6.27). Cyrus understandably asks his father how he is supposed to become so nasty at the snap of his fingers, having been educated in virtue since childhood. His father responds that the Persians surreptitiously teach their young to be able to do many evil deeds (I.6.28). The Persians taught their young to commit evil deeds—but not on human beings; they had them practice on animals, specifically in hunting. The conversation with his father marks the beginning of Cyrus' intentional use of humans as animals—although there are slight hints that he recognizes the value of food in motivating others during his boyhood trip to Media (I.3.6–7). Cambyses reminds Cryus that he has been taught to make snares for birds, to lie in ambush for them, and even train birds as spies to trap other birds. He has trained dogs to pursue hares, learned how to pursue them, and learned their paths if they escape. If Cyrus can translate the skills he learned in hunting into how he deals with enemies, Cambyses says he does not know how Cyrus could fail (I.6.41). Dehumanizing his enemies allows Cyrus to commit great evil deeds against them. Curiously, although enemies are represented by wild animals, Cambyses focuses on relatively harmless wild animals. He refrains from discussing animals elsewhere described as wild and dangerous, like bears, boars, lions, and leopards. Again, the Persians only teach this double lesson surreptitiously. They do not instruct the young that they are allowed to do evil to fellow human beings; rather, they teach them "simply" to tell the truth, not to deceive, not to steal, and not to take advantage, so that the boys might grow up to be "tamer" citizens.

In any event, his father focuses on the way Cyrus' education has prepared him to treat his enemies as animals, but once, almost in passing, he also conveys to Cyrus that he ought to treat his friends as such as well (I.6.19). Cambyses likens Cyrus' soldiers to dogs, with whom one cannot always use the same call, arousing their desires and falsely raising their hopes. We will see Cyrus learned this lesson well, as he regularly speaks of his soldiers as dogs.

IV. Species Separation and Successful Rule

Cyrus pursues a two-fold strategy for securing his rule: first, he reduces those under his rule to the status of an animal, and he also raises himself to the level of a god.[16] We see early hints that Cyrus dehumanizes those around him early in his career, when he likens his troops to animals (I.2.28–29), but his efforts do not really get into full swing until after he captures Babylon. Once he captures the crown, he quickly establishes bodyguards as a new class of people whom he dehumanizes, and, finally, Cyrus begins to dehumanize all his subjects—both the weak ones and the strong. Again, after the conquest of Babylon, Cyrus begins to wear the trappings of royalty and embellish his appearance and reputation so as to leave the impression in some of his subjects that he not only descends from the gods, but is in fact divine himself.

Cyrus likens his troops to horses and dogs. He feeds his troops and exercises them together so that they become tame with one another because he has also found, among animals

---

[16] Cyrus' name means something like "Lord," so the title of the work would be "The Education of the Lord," and Xenophon's other work on Cyrus would be "The Rise of the Lord."

generally, a terrible yearning for one another among those who have been fed together. Further, he held that his troops would be tamer toward one another if they have been exercised together, just as he had observed in horses.[17] Further, his army is able to expand because he is willing to incorporate foreign arms from wherever he can find them—this, after all, is how those who are interested in attaining the best horses conduct themselves (II.2.26).[18] Cyrus clearly finds the animal side of human nature, and tends to it in order to further his rule.

A similar case occurs when Cyrus first establishes a cavalry among his army. The cavalry officers will appear to others (including their own troops, not just their enemies) as winged human beings—almost as members of another species (IV.3.15).[19] Here we see a preview of the other side of species separation conduces to ruling well—elevating rulers to a greater than human status.

These examples probably do not raise any hackles, and we are probably more accepting of treating military men like animals guided by the judgment that military discipline requires something like it. Much more problematic is Cyrus' treatment of his eunuchs and the way he views the subjects of his empire.

When Cyrus becomes King, or emperor, he realizes that he needs bodyguards, and so he makes those who serve near his person eunuchs.[20] I imagine we already see the horror of

---

[17] II.1.29. "Tame" (*praos*) also occurs at I.6.33, II.2.8, and VI.1.37.

[18] "You seek whatever horses may be best, not those from your fatherland, so also take from all [sources] such human beings as you think will most contribute to your strength and good order."

[19] Chrysantas makes the remark about winged human beings, not Cyrus, but consider VIII.4.11.

[20] Xenophon's ambiguous phrasing leaves opens two possibilities: Cyrus finds eunuchs and establishes them as bodyguards, or Cyrus castrates a

castration—but why does Cyrus castrate them, or why does he use castrated humans as bodyguards? The answer is that they are universally despised, no one loves them. They have no wives or children. But he noticed that other animals, when castrated, retain their strength but are much easier to rule.

> From other animals he took it as evidence that unruly horses when castrated cease biting and being unruly, but they become no less warlike; and bulls when castrated give up their big thoughts and disobedience, but they are not deprived of their strength and energy; and dogs, similarly, cease to abandon their masters when they are castrated, but they become no worse at guarding and for the hunt (VII.5.62).[21]

There are no "manly men"—no bulls or horses or dogs under Cyrus' rule. These three "strong" types match on to human types. Bulls are said to have "big thoughts" (*mega phronein*), like some among his strongest subjects who had the high thought (*phronēma*) that they were competent to rule. Horses, by contrast, correspond to the human type who does not want to be ruled. Only Cyrus' bodyguards are the victims of literal castration, but Cyrus' troops and subjects have all been metaphorically neutered.

We see this clearly in the praise heaped upon Cyrus by one of his strongest, earliest supporters, Artabazus. In a speech meant to persuade Cyrus' army to continue campaigning against the Assyrians, Artabazus—who is unnamed at this point—says that Cyrus seems to have been born a king by nature, "no less than is the naturally born leader of the bees in the hive, for the bees obey him voluntarily" (V.1.24). Now, Xenophon was aware

---

multitude of men and makes them his bodyguards.

[21] Note that the first two animals mentioned in this passage are also mentioned in the introduction as being easy to rule (I.1.2).

that the leader of the bees was a queen (*Oeconomicus*, 7.32), and this mistake thus sheds light on what Artabazus, wittingly or not, is saying about Cyrus and his troops by reversing the gender roles. Artabazus suggests that Cyrus is the only man in his army; everyone in the army has been turned into a woman or a drone.

Cyrus does not stop at dehumanizing his troops and his bodyguards; rather, he debases all the subjects over whom he rules. Cyrus divides his subjects into two principal categories: those whom he subdued and perceives to be weak, and those whom he holds to be strongest (VIII.1.45–46). Because he perceives these classes to have different characters, Cyrus rules them differently. Cyrus treats the former like herd animals, specifically like sheep, and the latter he aims to break or domesticate like horses, bulls, and dogs. The former group consists of ordinary subjects of his empire, and the second comes principally from the army.

To be fair, Cyrus improves the lives of his subjects markedly in some sense. On the one hand, there is now peace, and the goodness of peace should not be diminished. But on the other hand, there are few outlets to demonstrate one's virtue or to do anything "big"—big thoughts are squashed. Most telling is Cyrus' description of the people in a long chapter where Xenophon says he will recount how Cyrus made himself "beloved." In this long chapter, Xenophon boils down the ways in which Cyrus makes himself beloved by his subjects to five. Cyrus makes himself loved by providing his subjects with food, by giving gifts, and by maintaining a secret police. Xenophon then repeats the centrality of gift giving, and finally he says Cyrus makes himself loved by providing free medical care to his subjects. Cyrus fed his subjects, showered them with gifts, and provided them with medical care so that they would be happy, just like a shepherd ought to make use of his flocks while making them happy *in the happiness of sheep* (VIII.2.14). The subjects of Cyrus' vast empire are turned into docile sheep.

To return to the supposedly strong, even his chief military allies have been neutered—and in many cases the imagery is quite vivid. Croesus, by his own account, has been turned into a woman by Cyrus, Gadatas was already literally a eunuch, and Gobryas, since his son was killed by the Assyrian King, is figuratively castrated.

Cyrus' dehumanizing project expands in scope as his empire expands, and it also grows in cruelty. At the beginning it's just his troops, but it becomes especially amplified as the empire grows to include eunuchs and subjects. Everyone under Cyrus' rule has become either an animal: some have been reduced to the status of sheep, others drones, others horses and dogs, and some castrated animals.

But Cyrus does not stop at trying to reduce his subjects to the status of animals; he also aims to deify himself in the eyes of the vast majority of his subjects, those he subdued and whom he perceives to be weak.[22] In the first place, he sets himself up over the priests (*magoi*), and, judging the piety of his subjects to be good for himself (VIII.1.25), makes public displays of his own piety. Further, Cyrus tricks his subjects into believing that he, their ruler, is categorically different from them: Cyrus cultivates the perception that he was no ordinary human. Once he has captured Babylon, Cyrus takes great pains to make himself appear more beautiful than he really is by wearing robes, rouge, and tanner (VIII.1.41), and to make himself appear taller than he is, both by wearing platform shoes and by strategically positioning tall subjects beneath him (VIII.1.41, VIII.3.14). Further, he aims to present himself as free entirely of bodily

---

[22] With regard to those whom he held to be strongest, and therefore feared, Cyrus pursued different tactics (VIII.1.45–46, VIII.2).

96

defect—the very way Cyrus describes the gods to be (VIII.7.22). He also seeks to leave the impression in his subjects' minds that he is not subject to natural bodily functions (VIII.1.42), and to give the appearance that he wonders at nothing, that nothing surprises him. That is, he aims to give off the appearance of omniscience, like the all-knowing gods (see I.6.46). Of course, we cannot forget Cyrus' alleged ancestry that traces back through Perseus to Zeus (I.2.1), and that he begins using a royal standard reserved for members of his family. Cyrus' subjects worshipped him (*sebomai*, VIII.8.1).[23] And they also prostrate themselves before him, an act previously associated with worship of the divine (VIII.3.24, cf. VII.5.32, IV.5.29). Just as Cyrus seems to render the schools of justice obsolete by instituting himself as a "Seeing Law," Cyrus' apotheosis similarly arrogates the honor and obedience accorded to the traditional gods. The results are the same: once the divine emperor dies, the subjects no longer have him to worship. Cyrus' role as Seeing Law is connected to his attempt to appear divine. To the extent Cyrus is worshipped, that cannot but undermine traditional piety.

V. Conclusion

The Education of Cyrus opens with the suggestion that humans have a strong innate desire not to be ruled, that humans have a natural longing to be free, and, as a result, politics is rife with conflict.[24] Cyrus' great empire holds out a great promise that there can be a solution to the political problem. The *Cyropaedia* prods readers to take seriously the possibility that Cyrus is the model ruler, and the introduction, at least, inclines readers to the

---

[23] Cf. *Mem.* I.1.14, IV.3.13; *Ages.* 3.2, 11.1; *Hell.* 3.4.18 and VII.3.12.
[24] See III.1.10–11.

view that knowledge is the necessary and sufficient requirement for successful political rule. The man who, alone among all other rulers, possesses the knowledge or science of ruling, and is able to rule the whole world, is Cyrus the Great. Cyrus manages to rule over an enormous empire, bringing peace and prosperity to all who are within his empire.

But that peace must be purchased at great cost. What Cyrus appears to "know" is that humans are harder to rule than other animals, so if one wants to rule over human beings, one must transform them into horses and cattle. The political animal has to be degraded into another herd animal: citizens must be transformed into subjects, and humans must be made into brutes. The enormous success of Cyrus' tyrannical empire requires not only the killing of myriad human beings who are enemies, but it also requires the violent dehumanization of his subjects, troops, and allies.

Xenophon's masterpiece, *The Education of Cyrus*, has a lot to teach us about politics and how to rule. It gives full voice to our longing for a solution to the problem of political instability, to our hopes that someone of outstanding virtue can bring about peace and prosperity. But it shows us the cost of achieving this noble goal. Cyrus' success is the result not only of reducing human subjects to the status of non-human animals but also of elevating human rulers to the status of gods or demi-gods. Under world peace, the vast majority of human beings would live lives no better than sheep, and their superiors would become like so many herding dogs. And, of course, there would be one quasi divine shepherd at the top, doling out benefits, food, and entertainment, robbing anyone else of the opportunity to demonstrate his or her excellence.

Bibliography

Aristotle. *Generation of Animals & History of Animals I, Parts of*

Animals I. Translated and edited by C. D. C. Reeve. Indianapolis: Hackett, 2019.

———. *Politics.* Translated by Carnes Lord. Chicago: University of Chicago Press, 1984.

———. *The Complete Works of Aristotle.* Translated and edited by Jonathan Barnes. Vol. One. Princeton: Princeton University Press, 1984.

Bonette, Amy L. "An Introduction to *On Horsemanship.*" In Xenophon, *Xenophon's Shorter Writings*, 277–293. Edited by Gregory A. McBrayer. Ithaca: Cornell University Press, 2018.

Burkert, Walter, and John Trans Raffan. *Greek Religion: Archaic and Classical.* Malden, MA: Blackwell, 1985.

Hobbes, Thomas. "De Cive." In *Man and Citizen*, 87–388. Edited by Bernard Gert Indianpolis: Hackett, 1991.

———. *Leviathan.* Edited by Edwin Curley. Indianapolis: Hackett, 1994.

Homer. *The Iliad.* Translated by Richmond Lattimore. Chicago: University of Chicago, 2011.

Liddell, Henry George, and Robert Scott. *A Greek-English Lexicon.* Oxford: Clarendon Press, 1996.

Locke, John. *Two Treatises of Government.* Edited by Peter Caslett. Cambridge: Cambridge University Press, 1988.

Strauss, Leo. "The Spirit of Sparta or the Taste of Xenophon." *Social Research* 6, no. 4 (1939): 502–536.

Xenophon. *Education of Cyrus.* Edited by Wayne Ambler. Ithaca: Cornell University Press, 2001.

———. *Memorabilia.* Translated by Amy C. Bonnette. Ithaca: Cornell University Press, 1994.

———. "Regime of the Lacedaemonians." In *Xenophon: The Shorter Writings*, by Xenophon, edited by Gregory A. McBrayer, translated by Susan D. Collins and Catherine S. Kuiper. 107–125. Ithaca, NY: Cornell University Press, 2018.

5

THE *CYROPAEDIA* AS POLITICAL TRAGEDY, A SPECULATIVE ESSAY

Charlotte C. S. Thomas

I. Cyrus' Virtue

In the *Cyropaedia*, Xenophon presents a fictionalized account of Cyrus' education as an ascent to the heights of despotic power. One might reasonably expect a student of Socrates to frame his account of such an ascent with a concurrent descent into moral depravity, but that is not what Xenophon gives us. Instead, Xenophon's Cyrus seems to make the best choice of every alternative that is presented to him throughout this ancient novel, both for his own sake, but also importantly for material improvements to the lives of those who submit to him. The salient aspects of his character and their effects on his relationships with others seem to be consistent from his boyhood through the height of his conquests. Cyrus garners power because of his ingenuity and ambition, but also because he makes good on his promises to make people's lives better.

> Cyrus was willingly obeyed by some, even though they were distant from him by a journey of many days; by others, distant by a journey even of months; by others who had never yet seen him and by others who know quite well that they would never see him. Nevertheless, they were willing to submit to him, for so far did he excel other kings both those

who inherited rule from their forefathers and those who acquired it through their own efforts (1.1.3–4)[1]

From the beginning to end of the *Cyropaedia*, even in his boyhood, Cyrus is shown to be an excellent leader, and because of that, people want to be led, and then ruled, by him. Cyrus' ever-expanding reputation as an excellent ruler is key to what Xenophon announces early as his central question. How is it, he muses, that one man could so easily control other men when that task seems so difficult? Why is it generally so much harder for men to herd men than to herd animals, and why does this general rule not seem to apply to Cyrus? (1.1.3)

Xenophon's framing of the question should raise an eyebrow. To liken government to herding and political leadership to shepherding is straight-forwardly to deny the autonomy of the individual and to construct a model of politics that immediately acts in opposition to self-determination. Presumably, the reason it is more difficult to herd men than sheep is that men have a better developed sense of their own ends. It may not be unjust to subordinate the ends of a sheep to those of a shepherd, but it is clearly unjust to enthrall a free man. The *Cyropaedia* presents this political ideal that seems to devalue self-determination not because Xenophon thought that despotism was the only plausible political order, but because he wanted to construct a fictional cosmos in which the essential character of despotism could be shown in the clearest possible relief.

Cyrus perfectly embodies the shepherd of men Xenophon sets up as the political ideal in his introduction. From redistributing large and small tunics as a boy to putting on the eyeliner in Babylon, Cyrus knows how to herd people. In neither case,

---

[1] All citations to Xenophon's *Cyropaedia* refer to Wayne Ambler (trans.), Xenophon. *Education of Cyrus* (Ithaca: Cornell University Press), 2001.

nor in the myriad episodes that occur between them in the narrative, does Cyrus take seriously the individual interests of those who are subject to him. He treats populations like herds, and he does so brilliantly. People almost universally come to believe that Cyrus' decisions for them are superior to their own decisions for themselves, and they happily outsource their life-choices to him. Cyrus may be corrupt, and his corrupt character may be displayed in his willingness to subjugate everyone around him, but since his subjects perceive their goods (as well as Cyrus') aggrandized by his rule, his is not a simple case of developing despotism or devolving moral character.

This consistency in Cyrus' character over time also serves to isolate the character of despotism in the *Cyropaedia*. Not only are there no apparently preferable alternatives to Cyrus' rule in the narrative, there is also no way to confuse the nature of despotism with the character of the despot. If Cyrus were corrupted by despotism, the evils of the Persian regime after having secured Babylon could be seen as a reflection of the evils of Cyrus' corrupted character. But since Cyrus' character is not altered in any essential way by his despotic rule, the effects of despotism can themselves emerge more clearly. That is, insofar as Cyrus continues to make good decisions for himself, his empire, and his subjects (insofar as their good is understood collectively), his despotism appears to be the best of all possible despotisms. Any flaw in Cyrus' despotism is a flaw in despotism, per se.

Within a cosmos where despotism appears to be the only viable option, one cannot blame the character of the best possible despot for the evils of despotism. Nor can one, in Cyrus' case, attribute the evils of despotism to political gaffs, since he makes none. He acts perfectly and apparently in perfect compliance with the gods. If living in the cosmos of the *Cyropaedia* is not choice-worthy, it can only be because despotism itself (and the best possible despotism) is incompatible with a shapely human life.

In his wonderful introduction to his translation of the *Cyropaedia*, Wayne Ambler argues that the just decisions Cyrus is often credited with are hollow. They are only apparently just. More careful consideration—according to Ambler—reveals that Cyrus' decisions are always motivated by his desire to increase his power. It is impossible to argue with the claim that Cyrus' decisions constantly and intentionally move toward more power and more security for his regime- but it does not necessarily follow that because his political decisions arc self-serving that they are not also in the interests of his subjects. It is not clear that just because Cyrus moves himself toward more power that he does not also move his subjects toward a better life, perhaps even towards a more just regime.

In order to consider whether or not Cyrus acts justly, one must ask how justice is defined in the *Cyropaedia* and what reference points we might use to judge whether a decision or action conforms to that definition. If the standard for political justice is political stability, peace, prosperity, equity, a just distribution of goods, approbation of the tactics involved, or comparison to alternative possibilities—it would be difficult to argue that Cyrus did not meet each of those standards. Cyrus' interventions improve the lives of those who give themselves to him, and those who persist in opposing him all eventually die. The stark absence of plausible regimes of free and self-determining citizens suggests not that Cyrus' sense of justice is hollow, but instead that Xenophon has carefully crafted a world in which despotism is a good man's best hope.

II. The Armenians and the Chaldeans

In order for this interpretation to be plausible, it must be clear that Cyrus' judgments are, from beginning to end, both just within their context and most fitting for each occasion. The Armenian Expedition, Cyrus' first military campaign, is a perfect example of the pattern Xenophon continues throughout the *Cyropaedia*. Cyaxares, king of Media and Cyrus' uncle, calls Cyrus to lead the Persian army in the defense against an immanent attack of the huge and powerful Assyrian army. Completely outmanned and overmatched, Cyrus argues that Cyaxares should allow him to rein in the Armenians first, who have stopped paying their rightful tribute to the Medes and have failed to send an army to aid in the defense against the Assyrians. Cyrus promises to bring back money and an Armenian army if Cyaxares will send with him some cavalry units. Cyaxares agrees.

Using strategies derived from his experiences as a hunter, Cyrus manages to pin the helpless Armenian king, capture his family, and take control of his treasure without engaging in battle. Then he calls the Armenian to stand trial. The Armenian asks the right question of Cyrus: "Who," he asks, "will be the judge." Cyrus' reply is perfectly direct: "Clearly he to whom god granted to treat you as he wishes even without a trial." (3.1.6) The judicial structure of this episode seems to be a perfect example of Ambler's claim that Cyrus only metes out apparent justice. There will be a trial, but the judge will have the right to do with the Armenian what he wishes regardless of the outcome of the trial. The image of due process is Cyrus' gift to the Armenian, which is to say it is apparently hollow.

The involvement of the Armenian's son, Tigranes, in the legal proceeding is complicated and interesting, especially since we learn that he was the student of a teacher who sounds a great deal like Socrates. But, unfortunately, delving into that exchange of speeches would take us away from this essay's focus. Suffice it to say, Cyrus establishes that it would be well within his rights to have the Armenian killed, even given his decision to honor the trial that he chooses to conduct. But he knows that if he decides to spare the Armenian instead, it will be possible for him to keep his promise to his uncle to return with money and an Armenian army. Sparing the Armenian and honoring Tigranes' arguments also win the loyalty of both.

Is the Armenian's trial a sham because it is conducted at Cyrus' whim rather than according to the rule of law? Perhaps. Does the outcome serve Cyrus' ends independent of the good of the Armenians? Yes. But, are Cyrus' judgments necessarily unjust because of this context? What are the alternatives, and are they better? The Armenians have stopped paying tribute and are fortifying themselves, so affirming the status quo is against the interests of Cyaxares and the Medes, independent of Cyrus' ambitions for empire. Cyrus spares the Armenian, treats his family with respect, returns his fortune, and welcomes his son as a trusted advisor. Is this only apparent justice? It clearly serves to increase Cyrus' power and to move him one step closer to wearing high heels and eyeliner in Babylon, but does it also not secure some version of justice for the Armenians and for the Medes to whom they owe tribute?

As if to ensure that we understand the arrangement with the Armenians not just to be a fleeting and superficial success, Xenophon's narrative goes on to describe Cyrus' successful campaign to resolve a long-standing military conflict between the Armenians and the neighboring Chaldeans (3.2.12). Seeing that skirmishes with the Chaldeans began when Armenians were seen approaching the border by Chaldeans posted at a mountain top outpost, Cyrus organizes his armies to race up to that outpost and secure it before the Chaldeans have time to call for reinforcements. Using to his advantage even the Armenian's uncontrollable desire to flee from the Chaldeans, Cyrus again achieves his objectives with very little bloodshed. Having secured the outpost, he brokers a treaty between the Armenians and the Chaldeans and stations some of his men there permanently to enforce it.

This episode is particularly hard to understand as Cyrus' invocation of apparent justice for the sake of private aggrandizement. It is obvious that Cyrus benefits from peace between the Armenians and the Chaldeans, since in peace they will be more productive, and their tributes will be larger and more reliable. But it is equally obvious that the Chaldeans and Armenians benefit from their new arrangement. Insofar as Cyrus took control of the military, political, and economic landscape, no one in this episode emerges as self-governing or independent. That possibility is consistently absent in the *Cyropaedia*. But, bracketing that, Cyrus makes the perfect deal. Everyone is happy. Everyone's material situation has improved. Some real form of political justice has been introduced where before there was only violence and disorder.

III. Cyaxares

The *Cyropaedia* proceeds episodically to show example after example of Cyrus securing his position and increasing his power while at the same time improving the material conditions of those who yield to him or whom he conquers. One of the most poignant occurs when he is reunited with his uncle, Cyaxares, and they debate the question of whether or not to disband Cyrus' army (5.5). Cyaxares listens to Cyrus' claims that all of his campaigning has been pursued in loyalty to Cyaxares, but Cyaxares wisely explains that Cyrus has successfully transferred to himself all of the loyalty and deference once shown to himself. Using the analogies of dogs, attendants, and women, Cyaxares makes a case to which Cyrus has no response.

> If I seem to you to lack judgment in the way I take these things to heart, put yourself in my situation, and then see how they appear to you. If you were raising dogs to guard yourself and what belongs to you, and if someone were attentive to them and thereby made them more familiar to

himself than to you, would he delight you by this attention?...if someone should so dispose your attendants,
whom you maintain for the sake of your protection and military expeditions such that they wish to be his rather than
yours, would you owe him gratitude in return for this good
deed?...if someone so attentive to your wife that he makes
her love himself rather than you, would he delight you by
this good deed? Far from it, I think, and I know well that
in acting like this, he would be unjust to you in the highest
degree. (5.5.28)

In Cyaxares' case, the fact that Cyrus has improved his material
conditions is far less important than the fact that he has dis-
placed him as the ruler of his army and the benefactor of his
people.

Cyaxares does not limit himself to analogies, however, in
his response to Cyrus. After laying out his compelling case, he
elaborates on it in terms that leave no room for misunderstand-
ing.

When I said to lead those who were willing to go, you took
my entire power and left, leaving me deserted. And what
you took with my power, now, of course you bring to me
and my country and you enlarge my power. Since I am in
no way responsible for these blessings, I seem to offer myself up to be treated well, like a woman, and both to other
beings and to these my subordinates you appear a man and
I unworthy of rule. (5.5.33)

Cyrus' only response to Cyaxares' argument is to ask his uncle
to stop blaming him. He does not dispute the facts. He does not
offer an alternate account. He does not offer to amend his ways.
He just asks Cyaxares to give him some time to prove himself.

When Cyaxares grants Cyrus the extension he requests,
Cyrus moves immediately to make sure that all the men of rank
in his camp are loyal to him and will oppose Cyaxares' proposal

to disband the army. The next day at the council meeting, each man in turn argues the merits of keeping the army together, and Cyaxares has no alternative but to try somehow to contribute to the campaign that he cannot interrupt. When Cyrus mentions the need to build siege engines, Cyaxares immediately offers to build one for the army. Cyrus, apparently unable to allow Cyaxares to enjoy a moment of largess, immediately promises to build two. Cyaxares' position is hopeless.

Assessing the justice of Cyrus' actions in this episode is tricky. Cyaxares' argument is airtight. Cyrus took more than Cyaxares meant to give and continued to take more than he could afford to lose. The only possible response to Cyaxares' complaint is to look at what likely would have ensued if Cyrus had yielded to it. Do we have any evidence that the Medes and Persians under Cyaxares' command could have withstood the Assyrian threat? Do we have any evidence that if the army disbanded that Cyaxares would be able to protect any of the nations that Cyrus had subjugated? Do we have any reason to believe that Cyaxares could manage the empire that Cyrus had created? To all these questions, the answer has to be no. Unlike many other characters in the *Cyropaedia*, Cyaxares understands the cost of submitting to Cyrus, but by the time the situation is clear to him, he has no power to oppose him and no viable alternatives to pursue. To disband the army would be to allow the world that Cyrus has begun to order to fall back into disorder. In our cosmos, such chaos might be precisely what was needed and desired by those who wish to be self-determining; but, in this cosmos there is no promise of peace without order, and no promise of order without a political shepherd.

IV. Babylon

In the final book of the *Cyropaedia*, Xenophon takes us back to the original question posed in Book One and dispels any possible lingering doubts about the dark political ideal presented in the narrative.

> ...an argument of [Cyrus] is remembered that says the functions of a good shepherd and a good king are similar, for he said that just as the shepherd ought to make use of his flocks while making them happy (in the happiness of sheep of course), so a king similarly ought to make use of cities and human beings while making them happy. So it is not to be wondered at, if in fact he was of this judgment, that he competed to be superior to all human beings in his service (8.2.14).

Cyrus is a shepherd of men and cities; he knows how to use them while making them happy. Sheep, Xenophon reminds us, can only enjoy the "happiness of sheep," whatever that might be.

Men and cities apparently can also be happy under the control of the shepherd, but one must ask what sort of happiness is open to them. How can cities be happy at all, unless happiness means, in this circumstance, being well ordered by the despot and peaceful? The happiness of human beings within Cyrus' rule cannot include self-determination any more than can the happiness of a sheep within the herd. The ideal is externally imposed order, comfort, and peace. In the cosmos of the *Cyropaedia*, the only alternative to despotism seems to be vulnerability.

Because there is no politically viable alternative to despotism in the *Cyropaedia*, it may be that Cyrus is both a despot and a man of uncorrupted judgment. This possibility seems least plausible at the end of the narrative when we are shown Cyrus donning the Median robes that he refused to wear as a young general, concealing below them high-heeled shoes to make him

110

appear taller to his Babylonian subjects, and even advocating the wearing of eyeliner and rouge. Beyond these superficial measures, we also see Cyrus develop the conventions of despotism, using fear, ritual, and redistribution of property to control his subjects. Although these measures seem to be signs of corruption, a closer look makes clear the political necessities that motivated these despotic measures. Xenophon is careful to account for the origin and purpose of each of the despotic conventions, and he carefully puts them into a context that should invert the obvious criticism of Cyrus' judgment and character.

Xenophon lets us enter into Cyrus' consideration of how to present himself to the Babylonians by giving us a conversation between Cyrus and his most down to earth adviser, Pheraulas.

> Cyrus believed that Pheraulas, who was from the class of Commoners was intelligent, a lover of beauty, good at putting things in order, and not unconcerned with gratifying him....So he called him in and deliberated with him about how he could make his procession most noble for those of goodwill to see, and most frightening for those who harbored ill will. After the two of them considered it and reached the same conclusions, he bade Pheraulas take care that the procession on the next day turn out in just the way they decided would be noble. (8.3.5)

Cyrus and Pheraulas' version of what was most noble turns out to be opulence so overwhelming that people unaccustomed to prostrating themselves to anyone found themselves on the ground when confronted with the new and improved Cyrus. Faced with the daunting tasks of making peace in a hostile city and integrating subjects from cultures with a long-standing history of violence, Cyrus does what is required of him; and that is to look and act like an oriental despot.

V. Cyrus' Backstory

If Cyrus makes the best possible decision in each episode, and if his choices lead him inexorably towards becoming the greatest despot in history, one must ask how Cyrus came to be in a situation where necessity drove him and, through him, drove the world to vassalage. Does Cyrus make a deal at the crossroads in his early life? Are there moments of real choice in the narrative before all of the circumstances of the universe push him and the world toward despotism? I believe one must go back to the very beginning of the *Cyropaedia* to answer this question. As early as the Armenian expedition, Cyrus' first military campaign, necessity seems to guide him toward absolute power, so one must look earlier than that if one hopes to find Cyrus' entry point.

Cyrus is called to lead the Persian forces by his uncle, Cyaxares, when it seems that the Assyrian threat to Persia and Media requires immediate action. The source of this threat is that Assyria has convinced the nations neighboring Persia and Media that Persia and Media are likely to unite and threaten the region. Xenophon gives us no indication that the Medes and the Persians have any interest in a military alliance before they find they have to defend themselves, and the Persians and Medes are portrayed as cultures committed to very different versions of peaceful life—not as expansionist or war mongering. So, how does the Assyrian make plausible the idea that they are likely to become a military threat? He tells the world that since there has been intermarriage between Media and Persia, a military union is the next natural step (1.5.3). This rumor, as Xenophon presents it, is what made it possible for the evil, imperialistic Assyrian to garner support for an attack on Persia and Media.

What makes this circumstance remarkable is that the intermarriage between Media and Persia is the marriage of Cyrus' parents. Cyrus is, himself, the embodiment of the intermarriage of Media and Persia. As such, it is his existence that triggers

112

Persia and Media's vulnerability. This echoes Achilles' existence in the *Iliad* as the embodiment of the marriage of Thetis and Peleus that occasioned the judgment of Paris and the genesis of the Trojan war. Like Achilles, Cyrus' birth created the war that defined him.

Why would Xenophon craft a cosmos in which one man's birth moved the world to upheaval? I think the question may helpfully be reframed, "why would anyone write a tragedy?" Xenophon has offered us a political tragedy. He has created a cosmos within which the boundaries of human freedom and responsibility are more apparent to us. He has made a world fit only for despotism and populated it with people who could have been free. Cyrus, in particular, displays the virtues of a great politician, but in the *Cyropaedia* he can only be a great shepherd because his birth reset the boundaries of possibility.

Herodotus offers an account of Cyrus' birth which supports this reading. In that account, Astyages has a dream that his daughter's child will pose an existential threat to his existence, and he orders a slave to murder him in his infancy (*Histories*, 1.108–110). Using the trope that Sophocles would later use in *Oedipus Tyrannus*, the slave gives the infant Cyrus to a shepherd rather than carrying out the order to kill him, opening the door for Astyages' nightmare to come true.

In the *Cyropaedia*, the essence of despotism is visible because it has been isolated from all of the accidents generally associated with it, much like in Sophocles' *Oedipus Tyrannus*, Tiresias' knowledge is isolated from the power and benefits usually associated with knowledge. Cyrus' despotism is not the cult of a selfish, grasping personality. It is not the context for the conventional punishment of virtue or reward for vice. It is not a regime ordered without concern for the good of its citizens. Instead, in the cosmos of the *Cyropaedia*, despotism is the best hope for peace, prosperity, and civil society. Just as Tiresias stands as the

113

test of whether we actually love knowledge or only think we do because we love what we think it brings, Cyrus' despotism stands as a test of whether we really love self-determination or only think we do because we think we love the life it makes possible. In the *Cyropaedia*, all of the material effects of self-determination are generated by despotism. Like the challenges of Glaucon's statues in Book II of the *Republic*, Xenophon has constructed Cyrus' rule such that self-determination and slavery can be divorced from their outward appearances and considered in themselves. Thus, Xenophon asks, in the most pointed possible way, whether we love self-determination indeed, and what our love of freedom might mean if we were faced with a perfect despotism in a world where more just regimes seemed doomed to fail.

VI. Conclusion

In the end, of course, living in Cyrus' Babylon does not look at all choice worthy. Cyrus himself seems to know the restrictive laws in Babylon are problematic, albeit necessary and he lives outside the city as much as possible. Despotism itself is dissolute. but not the despot. This ending seems also to have a didactic function. If, along the way, the reader cannot help but have sympathy for Cyrus if despite one's apparent commitment to self-determination cannot help but want to be ruled by his steady hand and unwavering practical wisdom, the ending provides a fitting chastisement. Those who are closest to Cyrus are required to appear in court regularly and follow his rules precisely. Everyone, despite one's rank, knows that the city is full of spies: "the eyes and ears of the king." Everyone knows that everything they have really belongs to Cyrus and everything they do depends on his pleasure. When you give up self-determination, Xenophon seems to say, this is what you get, and it has nothing to do with who you give up your freedom to. Even the angelic Cyrus and his perfect despotism—his benevolent dicta-torship—cannot avoid turning men to sheep if those men turn him into their shepherd.

So, finally, Xenophon's *Cyropaedia* also operates as response, of sorts, to Thucydides' Melian dialogue. Why might the Me-lians choose death and destruction instead of peacefully capitu-lating to an inevitable defeat to an Athenian empire that will likely leave them alone for the most part? Because losing one's freedom is too high a price for peace and apparent prosperity. Because humans ought not willingly become sheep, regardless of the consequences—regardless of how attractive the entice-ments of the shepherd might appear.

6

WHAT SORT OF HISTORIAN
WAS XENOPHON?

Paul A. Rahe

Scholars who study the history of ancient Greece frequently express frustration when the narrative supplied by Thucydides son of Olorus abruptly comes to an end and Xenophon son of Gryllus takes up the tale. For, as a source of information for the course of events in what Strabo in the time of Augustus called the Peloponnesian War,[1] the latter is far inferior to his predecessor.

One might, of course, wish to argue that the comparison is unjust—that the son of Gryllus was not an historian. But Xenophon himself invites such a comparison. His *Hellenica* is, after all, a continuation of Thucydides' narrative. That is the way in which he presents it himself. His first words are "*Metà dè taûta*"—after "these things." And the *taûta* that he has in mind—the "things" that come before "the things" that he relates—are "the things" that Thucydides related. Moreover, in the early chapters of his narrative—which is to say, in the chapters that complete the story that Thucydides intended to tell in his *War between the Peloponnesians and the Athenians*—Xenophon follows Thucydides' practice of marking out the years by signaling the beginning of each new campaigning season in the spring.[2] So, if one wants to understand what sort of historian

---

[1] Peloponnesian War: Strabo 14.2.9. All translations are my own.

[2] *Metà de taûta*: Xen. *Hell.* 1.1.1. Beginning of campaigning seasons: 1.2.1, 3.1, 4.1–2, 6.1, 2.1.10, 3.1.

Xenophon is, one must imitate him and juxtapose his brand of story-telling with that of the predecessor whom he honored by finishing off his history.[3]

Thucydides' Program

Thucydides had a program, and he made no bones about it. With regard to his account of "the deeds done by those active in the war," the historian denies that he thought it proper to write on the basis of chance reports or his own transient impressions. Regarding the deeds "which I witnessed and those I learned about from others," he asserts, "I checked out each insofar as was possible with scrupulous exactitude [*akríbeia*]," adding that "these investigations required a great deal of labor because those present at particular events were at odds with one another as a consequence of favoritism or a failure of memory."[4]

What we know from other sources (including contemporary inscriptions) suggests that, in striving for accuracy, Thucydides was as good as his word. On rare occasions, of course, he falls short of the *akríbeia* he advertises, and he tells us considerably less about domestic politics in the various cities than we would like to know. But his description of the events of the late 430s and thereafter is highly accurate and chronologically precise.[5]

---

[3] In this connection, see Nino Luraghi, "Xenophon's Place in Fourth-Century Greek Historiography," John Marincola, "Xenophon's *Anabasis* and *Hellenica*," and Michael A. Flower, "Xenophon as a Historian," in *The Cambridge Companion to Xenophon*, ed. Michael A. Flower (Cambridge: Cambridge University Press, 2016), 84–100, 103–18, 301–22.

[4] Thucydides on his endeavor to report of events accurately: 1.22.2–3.

[5] Example illustrating Thucydides' capacity for error: cf. the list of *stratēgoí* provided at Thuc. 1.51.4 with the list supplied in *IG* I³ 364 = *ML* 61 = *O&R* no. 148, lines 19–21, and see Arnold W. Gomme, Anthony Andrewes, and Kenneth J. Dover, *A Historical Commentary on Thucydides*

With regard to the speeches that adorn his narrative, Thucydides takes a different tack. He begins by acknowledging that both he and his informants "found it difficult to remember or otherwise preserve [*diamnēmoneûsai*] with precise accuracy [*akríbeia*] that which was said," and he admits that to some degree he was forced to rely on his own impressions. Then, in explaining the procedure he will follow in his book, he advances a cryptic—and some would say, a self-contradictory—claim: "When, in my judgment, each of those speaking most fully expressed what was demanded by the situation then at hand [*perì tôn aieì paróntōn tà déonta*], this I had him say, sticking as closely as possible to the overall gist [*xumpásē gnómē*] of what was actually said."

In reporting what was said at the time, Thucydides was highly selective, as all historians are. For the most part he ignored idle chatter, inane comments, and other inconsequential utterances, as all historians try to do. His aim was to relate the arguments of importance that were articulated at the time; and, as is evident from the literary character of the speeches that he provides us with, he did so generally in dense prose, to a considerable degree in words of his own choosing, arranging the material with an eye both to its dramatic impact and to the light, he believed, contemporary commentary (when accurate, when in error, and also when deliberately deceptive) could cast on the thinking and argumentation that informed and illuminated the deeds of men.

In pursuit of this aim, Thucydides may on occasion have done something that modern historians scrupulously avoid: he may have exercised something verging on poetic license. Where he had no precise knowledge what was actually said, he may for

---

(Oxford: Clarendon Press, 1991–2008), I 95–96, and Simon Hornblower, *A Commentary on Thucydides* (Oxford: Clarendon Press, 1991–2008).

dramatic purposes or for the purpose of illumination have supplied what was, he thought, apt to have been uttered because appropriate to the occasion.

Where, however, he had a pretty good idea of what was said, he simply selected out the argumentation that he thought especially revealing or otherwise apt. If the arguments made by different men on opposed sides at different gatherings sometimes seem to respond to one another, it is not, as some suppose, because the speeches in Thucydides are a species of historical fiction. It is because the historian thought these particular arguments, when and where they were in fact articulated, especially apt and worthy of being highlighted and because he took delight in their juxtaposition.[6]

---

[6] Thucydides on his reporting of the speeches delivered: 1.22.1 with Gomme, *A Historical Commentary on Thucydides*, I 140–48, and Hornblower, *A Commentary on Thucydides*, 59–60, who cite selectively from the vast secondary literature on this passage, and with Paula Debnar, *Speaking the Same Language: Speech and Audience in Thucydides' Spartan Debates* (Ann Arbor: University of Michigan Press, 2001), passim (esp. 14–23, 221–34), whose discussion is especially apt. In translating *diamnēmoneûsai*, I have kept in mind the possibility that Thucydides may have composed for himself and secured from others written memoranda summarizing the more memorable of the speeches he and they had heard: Mark Munn, *The School of History: Athens in the Age of Socrates* (Berkeley: University of California Press, 2000), 292–307. What George Cawkwell, "Thucydides' Judgment of Periclean Strategy," *YClS* 24 (1975): 53–70 (at 65–68), reprinted in Cawkwell, *Cyrene to Chaeronea: Selected Essays on Ancient Greek History* (Oxford: Oxford University Press, 2011), 134–50 (at 146–48), says about the speeches in Thucydides' first book—that there is nothing in them that was "unthinkable in 432/1"—could be extended to all of the speeches in Thucydides' work. No figure is reported to have said anything that was unthinkable at the time he putatively said it. Cf. Jon E. Lendon, *Song of Wrath: The Peloponnesian War Begins* (New York: Basic Books, 2010), 417–25 (esp. 420–22), for a cogent— if, I think, ultimately unpersuasive—argument in favor of the view that the speeches were "of the author's free composition," and Virginia J. Hunter *Thucydides the Artful Reporter* (Toronto: Hakkert, 1973), who appears to think

There is one additional matter of vital importance for understanding what sort of historian Thucydides wanted to be—and that is the fact that he greatly admired foresight. Some men, he knew, needed no instruction in this regard. Themistocles achieved what he achieved "by his own native intelligence, without the help of study before or after." If, "in a future as yet obscure he could in a preeminent fashion foresee both better and worse" even "when there was little time to take thought," it was solely because of "the power of his nature." Such was Thucydides' conviction.

Most men, he knew, were not so blessed. But among these, he believed, there were some who possessed a capacity to profit not only from study but also from reflecting on their own experience and from weighing that of others. Pericles was, in his estimation, such a man. Of him, he wrote:

> When the war broke out, in this…he appears to have foreknown the city's power. He lived on thereafter for two years and six months; and, when he died, his foreknowledge with regard to the war [*pronoía…es tòn polémon*] became still more evident. For he told them that they would win through [*periésesthai*] if they remained at rest [*hēsucházontas*] and looked after the fleet and if, during the war, they made no attempt to extend their dominion and refrained from placing the city at risk.

If we compare the two passages, we can infer from Thucydides' silence what we would in any case be inclined to suspect after examining the conduct of policy in Athens from 461 on—that the *pronoía* possessed by the son of Xanthippus was less a matter

---

that the artistry on Thucydides' part that she documents rules out objectivity. For a helpful corrective to the claims presented by the latter, see Hans-Peter Stahl, "Narrative Unity and Consistency of Thought: Composition of Event Sequences in Thucydides," in *Brill's Companion to Thucydides*, ed. Antonios Rengakos and Antonis Tsakmakis (Leiden: Brill, 2006), 301–34.

of "native intelligence" than something acquired from experience. If Pericles told the Athenians that they would "win through" if and only if they restrained themselves, maintained their fleet, avoided unnecessary risk, and put off all ventures aimed solely at increasing their empire, it was because he had been among Athens' leaders when, in the midst of their first war with the Peloponnesians, they had persuaded their compatriots to dispatch a great armada to Egypt on an ill-fated mission to help wrest the Nile valley from Persian control and because he had learned something about the dangers associated with overreaching from having to cope with the fallout from that catastrophic campaign.

Thucydides composed his book for men with Pericles' potential. It was his aim to engage their imaginations and supply them with a substitute for personal experience—a knowledge of "the things" that had happened in a particular slice of the past. The "great war" on which he focused his attention he considered a revealing event of world-historical importance.

In a justly famous passage, which helps explain the immense effort he put into achieving *akribeía*, the historian tells us that he composed his account of the war not as "a contest piece to be heard straightaway" but as "a possession for all times [*ktêmá te es aieí*]." He was aware that the absence within his book of "the mythic" or "fabulous [*tò muthôdes*]" would render it "less delightful [*aterpésteron*]" to some than the work of Homer and Herodotus. But he did not care. It would, he confesses, satisfy his purpose if his work were "judged useful by those who want to observe clearly the events which happened in the past and which in accord with the character of the human predicament [*katà tò anthrôpinon*] will again come to pass hereafter in quite similar ways." In short, Thucydides saw himself as a political scientist intent on discerning patterns and as an educator of use to prospective statesmen.[7]

Xenophon's Response

Nowhere in the pages of Xenophon's *Hellenica* will one find a similar programmatic statement. Given what his immediate predecessor had done, that itself is telling. Even more telling, however, is the fashion in which he begins his narrative—*Metà dè taûta*. For he concludes that narrative with a sentence suggesting that someone else will come after him to pick up the story and he begins that sentence with the same phrase: *Metà dè taûta*.[8]

Our dependence on the son of Gryllus is for the modern historians of antiquity a source of exasperation, as I have said. Thucydides devoted thirty or more years of his life to the research underpinning his history and to its composition. Xenophon, who wrote a host of books, did nothing of the sort. To be sure, Thucydides focused his attention primarily on Athens and fell short in his account of Lacedaemon, especially where he found "the secretiveness inherent in the regime [*tês politeías tò krúpton*]" an insuperable obstacle, while Xenophon, who was intimately familiar with Sparta, paid close attention to what she

---

[7] Contrast Thucydides' eulogy of Themistocles (1.138.3) with that of Pericles (2.65), and compare his statement of his own aim (1.22.4) with the comparable passage in Herodotus (Proem); then, note Dion. Hal. *Thuc.* 7–8; and see Paul A. Rahe, "Thucydides as Educator," in *The Past as Prologue: The Importance of History to the Military Profession*, ed. Williamson Murray and Richard Hart Sinnreich (Cambridge: Cambridge University Press, 2006), 95–110. I doubt that Thucydides' prime concern was the instruction of historians—though this was surely a byproduct of his effort: cf. Lisa Kallet, "Thucydides' Workshop of History and Utility Outside the Text," with Peter Hunt, "Warfare," in *Brill's Companion to Thucydides*, 335–68, 385–413.

[8] Cf. Xen. *Hell.* 1.1.1 with 7.5.27. and see Christopher J. Tuplin, "Continuous Histories (*Hellenica*)," in *A Companion to Greek and Roman Historiography*, ed. John Marincola (Malden, MA: Blackwell, 2009), 159–70.

did, to her leading personalities, and to her institutions and propensities—which is at times, for us, a boon.[9] Moreover, we can
profit from the latter's subtlety as a writer, his discernment, and
his incisive judgment. Much appreciated in antiquity, the Renaissance, and the early modern period and largely ignored or
flatly denied throughout the nineteenth and much of the twentieth century, these qualities are now, finally, once again being
given their due, and this development promises in some measure to allay scholarly aggravation.[10]

Sixty years ago, Xenophon was held in contempt. Today,
next to no one would endorse, as nearly everyone did then, the
negative assessment of his acumen voiced by the influential
German scholar Barthold Georg Niebuhr in 1827, and next to
no one would echo the words that Lord Macaulay published a
year later:

> The Life of Cyrus, whether we look upon it as a history or
> as a romance, seems to us a very wretched performance. The
> expedition of the Ten Thousand, and the History of Gre-
> cian Affairs, are certainly pleasant reading; but they indicate
> no great power of mind. In truth, Xenophon, though his
> taste was elegant, his disposition amiable, and his inter-
> course with the world extensive, had, we suspect, rather a

---

[9] Spartan secretiveness: Thuc. 5.68.2. Xenophon and Sparta: Gerald
Proietti, *Xenophon's Sparta: An Introduction* (Leiden: Brill, 1987); Christopher J. Tuplin, *The Failings of Empire: A Reading of Xenophon Hellenica
2.3.11–7.5.27* (Stuttgart: Franz Steiner Verlag, 1993); Flower, "Xenophon as
a Historian," 301–22, and Paul Christesen, "Xenophon's Views on Sparta,"
in *The Cambridge Companion to Xenophon*, 376–99; and Noreen Humble,
Xenophon of Athens: A Socratic on Sparta (Cambridge: Cambridge University
Press, 2021).

[10] Xenophon's reputation: Tim Rood, "Redeeming Xenophon: Historiographical Reception and the Transhistorical," *Classical Receptions Journal* 5
(2013): 199–211, and "Xenophon's Changing Fortunes in the Modern
World," in *The Cambridge Companion to Xenophon*, 435–48.

weak head....Even the lawless habits of a captain of merce- nary troops could not change the tendency which the char- acter of Xenophon early acquired. To the last, he seems to have retained a sort of heathen Puritanism. The sentiments of piety and virtue which abound in his works are those of a well-meaning man, somewhat timid and narrow-minded, devout from constitution rather than from rational convic- tion. He was as superstitious as Herodotus, but in a way far more offensive. The very peculiarities which charm us in an infant, the toothless mumbling, the stammering, the totter- ing, the helplessness, the causeless tears and laughter, are disgusting in old age. In the same manner, the absurdity which precedes a period of general intelligence is often pleasing; that which follows it is contemptible. The non- sense of Herodotus is that of a baby. The nonsense of Xen- ophon is that of a dotard.[11]

Moreover, fewer and fewer scholars now share the conviction— expressed in passing by Niebuhr, vigorously defended at length by Eduard Schwartz in 1889, and once almost universally held—that Gryllus' son hated the Athenian democracy and was an unabashed admirer of Lacedaemon.[12]

---

[11] See Barthold Georg. Niebuhr, "Über Xenophons Hellenik," *RhM* 1 (1827): 194–98, reprinted in an expanded form in Niebuhr, *Kleine historische und philologische Schriften* (Bonn: E. Weber, 1828–43), 464–82, and Thomas Babington Macaulay, "History," *Edinburgh Review* 47:94 (May 1828): 331–67 (at 342–43), reprinted in Macaulay, *Critical, Historical and Miscellaneous Essays* (New York: Hurd & Houghton, 1860), I 376–432 (at 393–94).

[12] Cf. Eduard Schwartz, "Quellenuntersuchungen zur griechischen Geschichte," *RhM* n.f. 44 (1889): 161–93, reprinted in Schwartz, *Gesammelte Schriften II: Zur Geschichte und Literatur der Hellenen und Römer* (Berlin: Wal- ter de Gruyter, 1956), 136–74, with Leo Strauss, "The Spirit of Sparta or the Taste of Xenophon," *Social Research* 6:4 (November 1939): 502–36, who was the first to challenge the scholarly consensus in this particular; and see Wil- liam E. Higgins, *Xenophon the Athenian: The Problem of the Individual and the Society of the Polis* (Albany: State University of New York Press, 1977), 99–

There is, in fact, a growing and salutary willingness within the scholarly world to entertain the possibility that figures like Herodotus, Aristophanes, Thucydides, Plato, Xenophon, and Aristotle were detached observers inclined to stand apart from the fray, to regard all political regimes as flawed in one way or another, to puzzle over the virtues and defects of the various alternative modes of governance, and to consider the

---

127, and Christopher J. Tuplin, *The Failings of Empire*; "Xenophon, Sparta and the *Cyropaedia*," in *The Shadow of Sparta*, ed. Anton Powell and Stephen Hodkinson (New York: Routledge, 1994), 127–81; and "Xenophon and Athens," in *The Cambridge Companion to Xenophon*, 338–59. Then, consider Noreen Humble, "*Sophrosyne* and the Spartans in Xenophon," in *Sparta: New Perspectives*, ed. Stephen Hodkinson and Anton Powell (Swansea: Classical Press of Wales, 1999), 339–53, in light of Noreen Humble, "Was Sōphrosynē Ever a Spartan Virtue?" in *Sparta: Beyond the Mirage*, ed. Anton Powell and Stephen Hodkinson (Swansea: The Classical Press of Wales, 2002), 85–109, and see Noreen Humble, "The Author, Date and Purpose of Chapter 14 in the *Lakedaimoniōn Politeia*," in *Xenophon and his World*, ed. Christopher J. Tuplin (Stuttgart: Franz Steiner Verlag, 2004), 215–28; "Why the Spartans Fight So Well...Even in Disorder: Xenophon's View," in *Sparta and War*, ed. Stephen Hodkinson and Anton Powell (Swansea: Classical Press of Wales, 2006), 219–33; "The Renaissance Reception of Xenophon's *Spartan Constitution*: Preliminary Observations," in *Xenophon: Ethical Principles and Historical Enquiry*, ed. Fiona Hobden and Christopher Tuplin (Leiden: Brill, 2012), 63–88; "True History: Xenophon's *Agesilaus* and the Encomiastic Genre," in *Xenophon and Sparta*, ed. Anton Powell and Nicolas Richer (Swansea: Classical Press of Wales, 2020), 291–318; and *Xenophon of Athens*, as well as Christesen, "Xenophon's Views on Sparta," 376–99. For exemplary expositions of the view once in vogue, see E. M. Soulis, *Xenophon and Thucydides: A Study on the Historical Methods of Xenophon in the Hellenica with Special Reference to the Influence of Thucydides* (Athens: s. n., 1972), and George Cawkwell, "Introduction," in Xenophon, *A History of My Times (Hellenica)*, tr. Rex Warner (Harmondsworth: Penguin Books, 1978), 7–46, as well as the annotations Cawkwell added to the text. In my opinion, Ernst Badian, "Xenophon the Athenian," in *Xenophon and his World*, 33–55, errs when he goes to the opposite extreme and contends that Xenophon distorts the historical record to make his fatherland look good.

circumstances in which each could be sustained and was, in fact, the best for which one could hope. It is, as scholars are beginning to realize, a mistake to project on the distant past the propensity for regime partisanship that has now characterized political life for well over two centuries and to suppose that anyone who is critical of Athens must be a laconophile and that anyone who is not an out-and-out admirer of direct democracy must, therefore, be a passionate partisan of oligarchy.[13]

In consequence, Xenophon's penetration and his understanding of institutional dynamics, of character, leadership, and combat on land tends now to be for modern historians a spur to

---

[13] Cf. Arnold Hugh Martin Jones, "The Athenian Democracy and its Critics," *Cambridge Historical Journal* 11:1 (1953): 1–26, reprinted in Jones, *Athenian Democracy* (Baltimore, MD: Johns Hopkins University Press, 1957), 41–72; Moses I. Finley, *Democracy Ancient and Modern* (Brunswick, NJ: Rutgers University Press, 1973); and Josiah Ober, *Political Dissent in Ancient Athens: Intellectual Critics of Popular Rule* (Princeton, NJ: Princeton University Press, 1998), who treat these figures as partisans whose criticism of the Athenian democracy is unworthy of serious consideration, with Edward M. Harris, "Was All Criticism of Athenian Democracy Necessarily Anti-Democratic?" in *Democrazia e antidemocrazia nel mondo greco*, ed. Umberto Bultrighini (Alessandria: Edizioni dell'Orso, 2005), 11–23. For exceptions to the new rule, who are still inclined to sniff out partisanship where others now discern honest criticism worthy of consideration, but who nonetheless acknowledge Xenophon's keen intelligence, see Frances Pownall, *Lessons from the Past: The Moral Use of History in Fourth-Century Prose* (Ann Arbor: University of Michigan Press, 2004), 65–112; Vincent Azoulay, *Xenophon and the Graces of Power: A Greek Guide to Political Manipulation*, tr. Angela Krieger (Swansea: Classical Press of Wales, 2018); Vivienne J. Gray, *Xenophon on Government* (Cambridge: Cambridge University Press, 2007), passim (esp. 217–21); and Anton Powell, "'One Little *Skytale*': Xenophon, Truth-Telling in his Major Works, and Spartan Imperialism," in *Xenophon and Sparta*, 1–63, whose attempt to restore and amplify the thesis of Schwartz makes no mention of the secondary literature, critical of that thesis, cited in note 12, above.

reflection.[14] All of this notwithstanding, however, no one would

---

[14] On Xenophon's skill, on his subtlety as a writer, and on his political and moral discernment, see the secondary literature cited in note 12, above, and consider the later work of Leo Strauss: *On Tyranny: An Interpretation of Xenophon's Hiero* (New York: Mansfield Centre Martino Publishing, 1948), *Xenophon's Socratic Discourse:An Interpretation of the Oeconomicus* (Ithaca, NY: Cornell University Press, 1970), and *Xenophon's Socrates* (Ithaca, NY: Cornell University Press, 1972), who was the pioneer in the treatment of Xenophon as a thinker worthy of study. Then, see William P. Henry, *Greek Historical Writing: A Historiographical Essay Based on Xenophon's Hellenica* (Chicago: Argonaut, 1967); Bodil Due, *The Cyropaedia: Xenophon's Aims and Methods* (Aarhus: Aarhus University Press, 1989); Vivienne J. Gray, *The Character of Xenophon's Hellenica* (Baltimore: Johns Hopkins University Press, 1989); John Dillery, *Xenophon and the History of his Times* (London: Routledge, 1995); Christopher Nadon, *Xenophon's Prince: Republic and Empire in the Cyropaedia* (Berkeley: University of California Press, 2001); the essays collected in *The Long March: Xenophon and the Ten Thousand:*, ed. Robin Lane Fox (New Haven, CT: Yale University Press, 2004), and in *Xenophon and his World*; Vivienne J. Gray, "Le Socrate de Xénophon et la Démocratie," tr. Louis-André Dorion and G. Mosquera, *Les EPh* 69:2 (May 2004): 141–76; Pownall, *Lessons from the Past*, 65–112; John W. I. Lee, *A Greek Army on the March: Soldiers and Survival in Xenophon's Anabasis* (Cambridge: Cambridge University Press, 2007); the essays collected in *Xenophon: Oxford Readings in the Classical Studies*, ed. Vivienne J. Gray (Oxford: Oxford University Press, 2010); Michael A. Flower, *Xenophon's Anabasis, or the Expedition of Cyrus* (Oxford University Press, 2012); the essays collected in *Xenophon: Ethical Principles and Historical Inquiry*; Eric Buzzetti, *Xenophon the Socratic Prince: The Argument of the Anabasis of Cyrus* (London: Palgrave MacMillan, 2014); James Tatum, *Xenophon's Imperial Fiction: On the Education of Cyrus* (Princeton, NJ: Princeton University Press, 2016); the essays collected in *The Cambridge Companion to Xenophon* and in *Plato and Xenophon: Comparative Studies*, ed. Gabriel Danzig, David Johnson, and Donald Morrison (Leiden: Brill, 2018); Thomas L. Pangle, *The Socratic Way of Life: Xenophon's "Memorabilia"* (Chicago: University of Chicago Press, 2018), and *Socrates' Founding: Political Philosophy in Xenophon's "Economist," "Symposium," and "Apology"* (Chicago: University of Chicago Press, 2020); the essays collected in *Xenophon and Sparta*; and Matthew R. Christ, *Xenophon and the Athenian Democracy* (Cambridge: Cambridge University Press, 2021).

classify the son of Gryllus as a fully proper successor to Olorus' son, for such was not his aim. He is best understood as an admiring critic.

The key fact, explaining Xenophon's lack of the astonishing diligence displayed by Thucydides, is that he did not think the study of history a pursuit as serious and weighty as did his predecessor. Theopompus of Chios—another continuator of Thucydides—took the son of Olorus as his model because he shared the man's estimation of the importance of history; and so, like his model, he aimed at precision and accuracy and prided himself on his conscientiousness and diligence. To the period stretching from 411/10 to 395/4, he devoted twelve books of his *Hellenica*—which is to say, twelve papyrus rolls.[15] By way of contrast, for that same sixteen-year span, Xenophon thought four books sufficient. If the latter's *Hellenica* begins with the words *metà dè taûta*—"after these things"; if it ends, pointedly, on the very same note; if there is nothing within it comparable to the defense of history as an aid to statesmanship that Thucydides limns in the twenty-second paragraph of the first book of his great work, it is because the younger Athenian doubted that events in the future would closely resemble those in the past.

Moreover, there is no evidence that, like Herodotus and

---

[15] Diodorus on the period covered by the *Hellenica* of Theopompus of Chios and on the number of books he devoted to that period: 13.42.5, 14.84.7. Exceptional diligence and accuracy: Theopompus of Chios *FGrH* 115 F26, T28a with Michael Attyah Flower, *Theopompus of Chios: History and Rhetoric in the Fourth Century BC* (Oxford: Clarendon Press, 1994), passim (esp.17–19, 63–66, 184–210). See also, from the postscript added to the paperback edition published in 2006, 257–58, and Riccardo Vattuone, "Looking for the Invisible: Theopompus and the Roots of Historiography," in *Between Thucydides and Polybius: The Golden Age of Greek Historiography*, ed. Giovanni Parmeggiani (Washington, DC: Harvard University Press, 2014), 7–37.

Thucydides both, Xenophon supposed that an event, such as a great war, could give structure to a particular period. He seems, instead, to have doubted whether such structures really exist and to have regarded the overall course of events—except on those rare occasions when a leader endowed with an extraordinary capacity for persuasion and a comprehensive strategic intelligence intervenes—as one damned thing after another. It is as if the son of Gryllus deemed history to a very considerable degree irrational—an unending chronicle of occurrences that frequently defy the laws of probability and that lie largely beyond rational comprehension. In short, it is as if Xenophon anticipated the sharp criticism that Aristotle, a student of his fellow Socratic Plato, would later direct at Thucydides when, without mentioning that historian by name, the peripatetic argued that historical works are less philosophical than works of poetry in that they do not relate what is apt to take place but what actually happened—and then, to illustrate his contention, pointedly singled out a Thucydidean theme: "what Alcibiades did and what happened to him."[16]

Xenophon nonetheless regarded his *Hellenica* and his other works as "a possession for all times" rather than as a mere "contest piece to be heard straightaway." As he puts it himself in a

---

[16] Xenophon and history: cf. Thuc. 1.21–22 (esp. 22.4) with Arist. *Poet.* 1451b1–12, and ponder the significance of Xen. *Hell.* 1.1.1 and 7.4.27 in light of the brief remarks of Leo Strauss, "Greek Historians," *RMeta* 21:4 (June 1968): 656–66 (esp. 660–63); Proietti, *Xenophon's Sparta*, ix–xxii (esp. xvi-xviii); John Marincola, "Genre Convention, and Innovation in Greco-Roman Historiography," in *The Limits of Historiography: Genre and Narrative in Ancient Historical Texts*, ed. Christina Shuttleworth Kraus (Leiden: Brill, 1999), 281–324 (esp. 311); and Aggelos Kapellos, *Xenophon's Peloponnesian War* (Berlin: Walter de Gruyter, 2019). For another view, well argued and highly informative but, on this crucial point, I think wrong-headed, cf. Tim Rood, "Xenophon and Diodorus: Continuing Thucydides," in *Xenophon and his World*, 341–95.

passage, squirreled away in a minor work, in which he deliberately appropriates the language deployed by his predecessor, his "purpose in writing" was not to inculcate sophistry and mere sophistication and to make men "*sophistikoí*—both cunning and clever." His aim was to render his readers "wise and good." In that sense, he wanted his work to be, and not simply to seem, "useful [*chrēsima*]" so that it would "in all times be unquestioned and beyond reproach [*anexélegkta eaeí*]."[17] If he thought that he could rival Thucydides in his quest for literary immortality, it was not because of the universal patterns and propensities that he thought he had uncovered in the course of his research. It was, rather, because of the insight that he as an author brought to the task of telling what were, he did not deny, rip-roaring stories. It is this that explains why the entertaining account he provides in his *Hellenica* is far less precise, detailed, and accurate than Thucydides' monumental work; and it is why, in what might be thought a cavalier fashion, he leaves out so much that an historian on the Thucydidean, or even the modern, model would think of prime importance and very much like to know.[18]

In short, if at times Xenophon seems careless, it is because he could not care less...about the matters that most concerned Thucydides and still concern modern political historians. In consequence, his *Hellenica* is a lot like his *Anabasis* and his *Memorabilia*. None of these is from our perspective a proper history. As one classical scholar noted nearly fifty years ago, Xenophon's *Hellenica* more nearly resembles what we would call a memoir. It records the author's impressions, what he witnessed, and what, he thought, he had learned from his conversations with others—and most important, at least for our purposes here, it

---

[17] Xenophon's programmatic statement: *Cyn.* 13.7.

[18] For a list of Xenophon's omissions, see George E. Underhill, *A Commentary with Introduction and Appendix on the Hellenica of Xenophon* (Oxford: Clarendon Press, 1900), xxi–xxxv

presumes on the part of its readers an overall familiarity with events in the period that it covers.[19]

In consequence, when we study Xenophon, we should not expect to find a systematic analysis of the course of events. We should, instead, look for his judgment of particular political regimes and of the character, skill, discernment, and tactical and strategic competence of particular individuals as well as for his assessment of the significance of developments for those caught up in them. In short, what he produced was not a chronicle. It was what we would now call a running commentary.

A Two-Part Book

There are two parts to Xenophon's *Hellenica*. The first of these is dedicated to completing Thucydides' account of the *War between the Peloponnesians and the Athenians*. It picks up where Thucydides' narrative peters out, and it takes the story down to the moment when the Long Walls at Athens were torn down. It is distinguished from what follows by its focus on Athens, by the degree to which it takes for granted the reader's familiarity with Thucydides' narrative, by the presence of chronological

---

[19] Memoir: see Cawkwell, "Introduction," 22–46. Note also C. H. Grayson, "Did Xenophon Intend to Write History?" in *The Ancient Historian and his Materials: Essays in Honour of C. E. Stevens on his Seventieth Birthday*, ed. Barbara Levick (Westmead, Farnborough, Hants: Gregg International, 1975), 31–43; Gray, *The Character of Xenophon's Hellenica* , passim; Edmond Lévy, "L'Art de la déformation historique dans les *Helléniques* de Xénophon," in *Purposes of History: Studies in Greek Historiography from the 4th to the 2nd Centuries B.C.*, ed. Herman Verdin, Guido Schepens, and Eugénie de Keyser (Louvain: The Catholic University, 1990), 125–57; and Jean-Claude Riedinger, *Étude sur les Helléniques de Xénophon et l'histoire* (Paris: Les Belles Lettres, 1991). Although these last four scholars are perceptive and pay close attention to Xenophon's subtlety as a writer, they are too prone to suppose that an author cannot display literary skill without engaging in mendacity. For a corrective, see the works cited in note 12, above.

indicators specifying the end of one year and the beginning of a new campaigning season, and by the presence of interpolations indicative of the keen interest it attracted in and after the Hellenistic period. Stylistically, it is also distinct, at least in the deployment of particles; and this has led to speculation that it was written well before the book's second part.[20]

The latter part of the book picks up the story of Hellenic affairs and carries it down to the second battle of Mantineia in 362. In it, Athens recedes for the most part into the background; Persia and Thebes loom large; and Lacedaemon is the focus.

By way of contrast, within Thucydides' great work, Lacedaemon and the policy she pursued had been a matter of secondary concern—for he did not believe that Sparta's victory was due to the brilliance of her commanders or to any particular geopolitical or military advantage that she possessed. It was his view that Athens had vanquished herself. So, his book is an attempt to explain how it was that a political community—which he had expected to emerge triumphant in the war—had squandered the tremendous advantages it had possessed and had, in fact, snatched defeat from the jaws of victory.[21] In the first part of his *Hellenica*, Xenophon fills out that story. In that work's second part, he examines how the Lacedaemonians did the like.

If, in the latter part of his book, Xenophon ignores the foundation of the Second Athenian League, if he has nothing to say about Epaminondas' role at Leuctra, if he does not mention the foundation of Megalopolis and highlight Epaminondas' liberation of Messenia, it is because, in his estimation, Sparta's failure was due to Spartan incapacity and not primarily

[20] The first part of Xenophon's narrative: *Hell.*1.1.1–2.2.23. Use of particles in the two parts: Malcolm Maclaren, Jr., "On the Composition of Xenophon's *Hellenica*, Parts I and II," *AJPh* 55: 2 and 3 (1934): 122–39, 249–62.

[21] Thucydides supposes that Athens had defeated itself: 2.65.7–12 (esp. 12).

to the resurgence of Athens and to the signal accomplishments of the Thebans Pelopidas and Epaminondas. He knew about these developments. He alludes to them in passing. But he does not highlight them—for he regarded them as a byproduct of Lacedaemonian fecklessness and thought them for the most part epiphenomenal. The frustration that modern historians feel when confronted with Xenophon's omissions is of a piece with what they feel when they express a regret that Thucydides has so little to say about governance at Corinth, policy-making in Boeotia, factions at Lacedaemon, the operations of the Spartan constitution, and developments within the Persian empire. There is, of course, this difference. Thucydides' narrative is generally ample and detailed while that of Xenophon tends to be spare.

Athens

Thucydides admired Athens, as did Xenophon. It was impossible not to do so. The city responsible for the Hellenic victories over the Mede at Salamis, Mycale, Eurymedon, and Cypriot Salamis was a marvel, and there was grandeur also in the catastrophic losses that she suffered in Egypt in the 450s and in Sicily in 413. Pericles spoke the truth when he told his compatriots,

> We inspire wonder now, and we shall in the future. We have need neither for the panegyrics of a Homer nor for the praises of anyone to whose conjecture of events the truth will do harm. For we have forced every sea and every land to give access to our daring; and we have in all places established everlasting memorials of evils [inflicted on enemies] and of good [done to friends].[22]

Xenophon testifies to its veracity when he displays the

---

[22] Thuc. 2.41.4.

134

astonishing resistance that the Athenians put up against the Spartan-Persian alliance in their time of gravest adversity in the aftermath of the Sicilian catastrophe when, despite their lack of the requisite financial resources, they managed to deploy fleet after fleet and to eke out two naval victories in the Hellespont; to destroy the entire enemy fleet at Cyzicus; and to win back Perinthos, Chalcedon, Selymbria, and Byzantium. He also shows them, in a moment of desperation, dispatching a rag-tag fleet – manned largely by landlubbers, resident aliens, and slaves – and winning at Arginusae, by the sheer brilliance of their generalship and by their unexcelled grit, a great battle against a battle-tested fleet of nearly the same size.[23]

It was Thucydides' claim that Athens' demise stemmed from the very qualities produced by the Athenian regime that were responsible for her successes. On the eve of the war, he reports, the Corinthians juxtaposed the Athenians with the Spartans in the following way:

> The Athenians are innovators, keen in forming plans, and quick to accomplish in deed what they have contrived in thought. You Spartans are intent on saving what you now possess; you are always indecisive, and you leave even what is needed undone. They are daring beyond their strength, they are risk-takers against all judgment, and in the midst of terrors they remain of good hope—while you accomplish less than is in your power, mistrust your judgment in matters most firm, and think not how to release yourselves from the terrors you face. In addition, they are unhesitant where you are inclined to delay, and they are always out and about in the larger world while you stay at home. For they think to acquire something by being away while you think that by proceeding abroad you will harm what lies ready to hand. In victory over the enemy, they sally farthest forth; in

---

[23] Xen. *Hell.* 1.6.24–34.

defeat, they give the least ground. For their city's sake, they use their bodies as if they were not their own; their intelligence they dedicate to political action on her behalf. And if they fail to accomplish what they have resolved to do, they suppose themselves deprived of that which is their own— while what they have accomplished and have now acquired they judge to be little in comparison with what they will do in the time to come. If they trip up in an endeavor, they are soon full of hope with regard to yet another goal. For they alone possess something at the moment at which they come to hope for it: so swiftly do they contrive to attempt what has been resolved. And on all these things they exert themselves in toil and danger through all the days of their lives, enjoying least of all what they already possess because they are ever intent on further acquisition. They look on a holiday as nothing but an opportunity to do what needs doing, and they regard peace and quiet free from political business as a greater misfortune than a laborious want of leisure. So that, if someone were to sum them up by saying that they are by nature capable neither of being at rest nor of allowing other human beings to be so, he would speak the truth.[24]

In his view, what the well-being of Athens required was restraint, and the one man in his time capable of reining in his compatriots was Pericles, who had a stature, an intelligence, and a justified reputation for incorruptibility that enabled him to hold the people in check without flattering them or depriving them of their liberty.[25]

Although Thucydides does not convey this in so many words, he elsewhere implies that Pericles bore considerable responsibility for the blunders his compatriots later made. In his Funeral Oration, for example, he encouraged in them a patriotism rooted in an eros he shows to be incompatible with rational

---

[24] Corinthian depiction of the Athenians and the Spartans: Thuc. 1.70.
[25] Periclean restraint: Thuc. 2.65.5–12.

deliberation. In the last speech that he delivered before he died, he instilled in them a dream of universal dominion over the sea, extending well beyond the bounds of the empire they currently held; and at this time, he exhorted them:

> Remember that this city has the greatest name among all mankind because she has never yielded to adversity, but has spent more lives in war and has endured severer hardships than any other city. She has held the greatest power known to men up to our time, and the memory of her power will be laid up forever for those who come after. Even if we now have to yield (since all things that grow also decay), the memory shall remain that, of all the Greeks, we held sway over the greatest number of Hellenes; that we stood against our foes, both when they were united and when each was alone, in the greatest wars; and that we inhabited a city wealthier and greater than all. The splendor of the present is the glory of the future laid up as a memory for all time. Take possession of both, zealously choosing honor for the future and avoiding disgrace in the present.

It is no wonder that they engaged in over-reaching after his death. As Thucydides makes clear, Pericles' political legacy was the eros and the megalomania that later led his compatriots to undertake the Sicilian Expedition.[26]

---

[26] Thucydides' judgment of Pericles' statesmanship: consider 6.24.3–4 in light of Diodotus' analysis of the impact of political eros on the human capacity for rational deliberation at 3.45; ponder the implications of 2.37–46 (esp. 41.4, 43.1–2); and see Paul Rahe, *Sparta's Second Attic War: The Grand Strategy of Classical Sparta, 446–418 B. C.* (New Haven: Yale University Press, 2020), 137–62. See also Paul A. Rahe, "Thucydides' Critique of *Realpolitik*," *Security Studies* 5:2 (Winter, 1995): 105–41; Paul W. Ludwig, *Eros and Polis: Desire and Community in Greek Political Theory* (Cambridge: Cambridge University Press, 2002), esp. 121–69; and Matteo Zaccarini, "What's Love Got to Do with It? *Eros*, Democracy, and Pericles' Rhetoric," *GRBS* 58:4 (2018): 473–89.

There was also another dimension to Pericles' failure. His Funeral Oration is noteworthy for its silence regarding the gods and for its treatment of the games put on and the sacrifices performed in honor of the gods as nothing more than species of entertainment, and in it he praises his compatriots in a fashion consistent with the supposition that his aim was to wean them from their ancestral gods and redirect their devotion to the city itself. "We philosophize [*philosophoûmen*]," he told them, "without becoming soft," and he implied that they knew the score. It was he, we know from other sources, who encouraged Protagoras and the other sophists to settle in Athens.

The consequence in due course was a reactive religious hysteria that tore Athens apart and prepared the way for civil strife. What Thucydides depicts when he discusses the Herms and Mysteries Scandals Xenophon reviews when he describes the trial to which the generals of Athens were subject when they returned from their victory at Arginusae.[27]

Within the last three books of Thucydides' history, Alcibiades, the ward of Pericles, looms large. In reading about him, we come to appreciate his strategic insight, his charm, and his persuasive capacity. But we also come to understand how his propensity for self-indulgence and arrogance tripped him up and helped occasion Athens' defeat in Sicily. Xenophon does much the same. He takes for granted his readers' familiarity with Thucydides' narrative and the attendant analysis. Then, he invites us to watch this remarkable man charm, bamboozle, and then enrage the Spartans, the satrap Tissaphernes, and once again in turn his compatriots back home. We are witness to his tactical

---

[27] Pericles, philosophy, and religious hysteria: consider Thuc. 6.27.29, 53–61 in light of 2.35–46 (esp. 2.38.1, 40.1–4), and see Alexander Rubel, *Fear and Loathing in Ancient Athens: Religion and Politics during the Peloponnesian War*, tr. Michael Vickers and Alina Piftor (Durham: Acumen Publishing, 2014). The Arginusae trial: Xen. *Hell.* 1.7.1–34.

brilliance, his courage, his audacity, and his unexcelled ability to see and seize an opportunity, and we look on as his defects bring him down.

Sparta

Thucydides was also an admirer of Lacedaemon, as was Xenophon. It was difficult, if not impossible, for a Greek to forget Thermopylae and Plataea. All that it took to defeat the Athenians in Sicily was the arrival of a single Spartiate, and the Lacedaemonians did, in fact, win the Peloponnesian War.[28] Moreover, Sparta was in one other particular a wonder. The members of every Greek community thought of their own *pólis* as an educational, character-forming polity, and they all supposed that the quality of a city was to be assessed in light of the quality of the citizens it produced. Nowhere, however, was this imperative taken as seriously as it was in Lacedaemon—where the citizens were supposed to be not only brave but possessed of *sophrosúnē*—moderation. It was said that the Delphic admonition—"nothing too much"—was coined by a Lacedaemonian.[29]

Thucydides uses the term *sophrosúnē* to describe the Spartans, and from him we learn that they took pride in its possession. But he intimates that it was not a product of their education and not in them a quality of character. It was, he lets us see, a function of the presence within their borders of an enormous and restive class of subject laborers. In the absence of that threat,

---

[28] See Paul A. Rahe, *Sparta's Sicilian Proxy War: The Grand Strategy of Classical Sparta, 418–413 B.C.* (New York: Encounter Books, 2023), and *Sparta's Third Attic War: The Grand Strategy of Classical Sparta, 413–404 B.C.* (New York: Encounter Books, 2024).

[29] See Paul A. Rahe, *The Spartan Regime: Its Character, Origins, and Grand Strategy* (New Haven: Yale University Press, 2016), 23–32, 117–20, 161.

he implies, it would dissolve.[30] Moreover, in quoting the Athenians' response to the Corinthian description of their character, he includes a brief but telling remark regarding Spartan propensities. "If you were to overcome us and to take up an empire," they observed,

> you would swiftly lose all the goodwill which you have secured because of the fear we inspire—that is, if you hold to the pattern of conduct that you evidenced in the brief span when you were the leaders against the Mede. You have institutions, customs, and laws that do not mix well with those of others; and, in addition, when one of you goes abroad he follows neither his own customs and laws nor those employed in the rest of Hellas.[31]

There is nothing comparable to this in the pages of Xenophon's *Hellenica*. In that work, he was even more reticent than Thucydides was wont to be. Therein, he was happy to show, but for the most part he chose not to tell. Moreover, his silence in one particular spoke louder than words. Never, in that work or any other, did he ever attribute *sophrosúnē* to the Lacedaemonians.[32] That they were defective in this particular was evident from their conduct.

Telling was a function that Xenophon reserved for the most part for his brief treatise on the Spartan *politeía*. There he interrupts what seems to the unsuspecting glance like a highly appreciative discourse on the education that the Lacedaemonians gave their young and on their mode of governance and way of

---

[30] Spartan *sophrosúnē* rooted in a fear of the helots: consider Thuc. 8.24.4 in light of 40.2.

[31] Athenians issue warning at Sparta in 432: Thuc. 1.77.6.

[32] The point was made by Leo Strauss, "The Spirit of Sparta or the Taste of Xenophon," 512–21 (esp. 512–15), and is forcefully reiterated by Noreen Humble, "*Sophrosyne* and the Spartans in Xenophon," 339–53, and "Was Sōphrosynē Ever a Spartan Virtue?" 85–109.

life more generally, and this he does with what one can only describe as a savage critique of what the Lacedaemonians had become as a consequence of their acquisition of an empire:

> I am aware that in earlier times the Lacedaemonians chose to live with one another at home having modest possessions rather than to serve as harmosts in the cities and to court corruption by subjecting themselves to flattery. I am also aware that back then they feared it being discovered that they were in possession of gold while now there are those who actually make a display of its possession. To prevent this, I know, there were back then acts dictating the expulsion of foreigners [*xenelasíai*]; and to travel abroad was prohibited lest the citizens ingest *hrądiourgíai*—a species of slackness and sloth apt to eventuate in recklessness and crime. Now I know that those deemed first [*prôtoi*] among them are zealous that they never cease serving as harmosts in foreign parts. There was a time when they took care to be worthy of leadership. Now they exert themselves much more to exercise rule than to be worthy of doing so. Accordingly, while in former times the Hellenes would journey to Lacedaemon and ask her to lead them against those regarded as malefactors, many are now rallying one another to prevent the Spartans from regaining dominion. There is no need to wonder why these censures are directed at them, since it is clear that they obey neither god nor the laws of Lycurgus.[33]

To suppose Xenophon a partisan of Lacedaemon, one would

---

[33] Xenophon on the corruption of Spartiates dispatched abroad: *Lac. Pol.* 14.2–7 with Humble, "The Author, Date and Purpose of Chapter 14 of the *Lakedaimonion Politeia*," 215–28, and *Xenophon of Athens*, 52–69, who shows that the harsh critique of Lacedaemon articulated in this particular chapter follows naturally from the analysis and understated critique of the Lycurgan regime presented in the chapters preceding. See, in this connection, the other secondary literature cited in note 12, above.

have to avert one's gaze from this passage or simply treat it as an interpolated text drawn from another author, as a great many scholars have done. In fact, however, it is an especially blunt restatement of what was the Thucydidean as well as a standard Socratic critique of the education accorded her citizens by Sparta—to wit, that, as a form of *paideía*, it was defective because it relied entirely on oversight and the power of shame and never had any impact on character. Thereby, moreover, it produced citizens far more unfit for hegemony than the Athenians, with all of their defects, had ever been.[34] As the narrative of Xenophon's *Hellenica* demonstrates, the Spartans, when free from oversight and situated beyond the purview of their compatriots, tended to conduct themselves in a disgraceful and counterproductive manner.

The Unity of Xenophon's *Hellenica*

Although there are two parts to the *Hellenica*, which may well have been composed at different times, the book is an organic whole. Xenophon stitches the two parts together so unobtrusively that no seam can be discerned.[35] This he does by two expedients.

He completes the narrative that Thucydides intended to write by describing in dramatic detail what transpired at the end of the war on the 16th of Mounichion in the Athenian year 405/4. Then, without missing a beat, he pivots immediately to what followed. First, he reports, "Lysander sailed into the

---

[34] See Noreen Humble, "Xenophon, Aristotle, and Plutarch on Sparta," in *The Contribution of Ancient Sparta to Political Thought and Practice*, ed. Nikos Birgalias, Kostas Buraselis, and Paul A. Cartledge (Athens: Alexandria Publications, 2007), 291–301; "Isocrates and Xenophon on Sparta," *Trends in Classics* 10:1 (2018): 56–74; and "Sparta in Xenophon and Plato," in *Plato and Xenophon*, 547–75, as well as *Xenophon of Athens*, 40–202.

[35] On the work's unity, see Henry, *Greek Historical Writing*, passim.

Peiraeus, the exiles returned; and, with music supplied by flute girls, the victors began with great eagerness to raze the walls, regarding that day as the beginning of freedom for Greece." Then, he undercuts the illusion of finality so powerfully in evidence at that moment by listing disturbing developments that took place at about the same time. In Thessaly, he reports, Lycophron was mounting an attempt to make himself tyrant. In Sicily, Dionysius, after having established himself as tyrant in Syracusa, was battling with the Carthaginians for control of the island; and, on Samos, Lysander was about to install in power a junta of the sort that the Greeks called a *dunasteía*—one made up of ten men. In this fashion, Xenophon paid his dues to his predecessor by finishing the tale that figure had set out to tell and then intimated that the great *kinēsis* that Thucydides had identified at the very beginning of his *War between the Peloponnesians and the Athenians* had not come to an end and that freedom would not be in the offing for Hellas.[36]

To the same end, Xenophon also sketches out the events in the last two years of Thucydides' war in such a manner as to lay the groundwork for his account of the struggle that followed. The end of the war did not mark rupture with the past. There was, he shows, continuity. In these chapters, Xenophon brings the Lacedaemonians to the fore, and thereby he introduces his readers to the conflicts over public policy that will continue to beset Sparta after Athens' defeat. This he does by way of juxtaposing Lysander son of Aristocritus with another Spartiate named Callicratidas. Given the importance of what these two men did Thucydides would surely have dealt with their appearance on the geopolitical stage with the same care with which he

---

[36] Razing of walls: Xen. *Hell.* 2.2.23. Projected endpoint for Thucydides' narrative: 5.26.1. Immediate aftermath of the war: Xen. *Hell.* 2.3.3–6. *Kinēsis*: Thuc. 1.1.1–2.

had earlier treated the exploits of Brasidas. But he would not have done what Xenophon does. He would not have used them to highlight the divisions within Lacedaemon that would again erupt in the aftermath of the war. The confrontation between the two men that Xenophon reports is a dramatic foreshadowing of troubles to come.

In telling this story, the son of Gryllus attends to a principle of rhetoric, frequently observed by his predecessors, that Aristotle's student Theophrastus would later fully articulate:

> It is not essential to speak at length and with precision on everything, but some things should be left also for the listener—to be understood and sorted out by himself—so that, in coming to understand that which has been left by you for him, he will become not just your listener but also your witness, and a witness quite well disposed as well. For he will think himself a man of understanding because you have afforded him an occasion for showing his capacity for understanding. By the same token, whoever tells his listener everything accuses him of being mindless.[37]

In keeping with his adoption of this *modus operandi*, Xenophon treats Lysander and Callicratidas in a manner both dispassionate and subtle.[38]

When the former appears on the scene as the Spartan navarch, this historian tells us, he concentrates the Lacedaemonian forces present in Ionia and stations them in Ephesus—the

---

[37] Theophrastus of Eresus F696 (Fortenbaugh).

[38] For an analysis at odds with my own of what Xenophon is up to in this juxtaposition, see Gray, *The Character of Xenophon's Hellenica*, 22–23, 81–83. See also ibid., 14–19, 146–49. In my judgment, leadership is only one of the foci of Xenophon's narrative. For interpretations more sensitive to the political context and to Xenophon's broader view, see John L. Moles, "Xenophon and Callicratidas," *JHS* 114 (1994): 70–84, and Kapellos, *Xenophon's Peloponnesian War*, 98–132.

coastal city in Anatolia that was the closest to the Persians' satrapal center at Sardis. When Cyrus, the younger son of the Great King, reaches that capital, the Spartiate journeys inland and charms the man, inducing him to promise to the mariners in the Spartan fleet a wage one-third greater than that the Athenians could offer—more than sufficient, as Xenophon apparently felt no need to spell out, to encourage desertion on the part of the non-Athenians rowing in their fleet. And so, we are left to contemplate Lysander repairing and drying out the triremes in what is evidently—thanks to the assembly lines in operation at Lacedaemon, Antandrus, and, we can assume, elsewhere—a growing fleet. Finally, however, if fleetingly, we see the man in action. When the helmsman left in charge of the Athenian fleet at Notium in the absence of its commander Alcibiades attempts to lure a squadron of the Peloponnesian fleet at Ephesus into an ambush, the Spartan navarch perceives an opportunity. With a force upon which he has evidently imposed a salutary discipline, he manages to stage a battle in which he wins a signal, if incomplete, victory fatal to the ambitions of Athens' absent supreme commander.[39]

It is only when Lysander's statutory year as a navarch has come to an end and when his successor Callicratidas arrives in Ionia that we are led to suspect that his tenure may have been less salutary for Lacedaemon than we have thus far assumed. To begin with, the departing navarch evidences resentment and boasts that he is the master of the sea; and, when his successor disputes the claim and invites him to prove it by conducting the Peloponnesian fleet from Ephesus to Miletus past the Athenian base at Samos, he dodges the challenge. This unveils Lysander's vanity but it proves nothing more. Soon, however, we learn that his erstwhile subordinates are doing everything within their

---

[39] Lysander's navarchy: Xen. *Hell.* 1.5.1–16.

power to subvert Callicratidas' efforts, and we are led to wonder whether Lysander had himself engineered obstruction and even civil strife [*stásis*] on the part of those characterized in the text as his "friends." What begins as a sneaking suspicion becomes a near certainty when we discover that, shortly before his own withdrawal, Lysander had returned to Cyrus the Persian funds in his possession as yet unspent.

Xenophon felt no need to spell out the implications. In this regard, as in others, he simply states the facts and leaves it to his readers to draw the proper conclusion themselves. For, however frustrated and resentful he might be, no departing commander who was a genuine patriot intent on securing victory for his *pólis* in a war would have deliberately attempted to cripple his successor and render his tenure in office a disaster. Lysander does not want Lacedaemon to win the war on someone else's watch.

Xenophon is similarly reticent in his treatment of Callicratidas. When his predecessor descended to boasting, the newcomer forcefully drew attention to its emptiness. When that man's subordinates deliberately made trouble for him, he met the challenge head on, asking whether they would prefer that he do the job he was assigned by the authorities at home or return home to report on their conduct. The threat was sufficient to force them into line.

Then, Callicratidas journeyed to Sardis in search of funds. When he was denied an audience with Cyrus, told to wait, and forced to dance attendance at the Persian prince's gates in a manner evidently intended as a humiliation, he returned to Ephesus empty-handed, shifted the fleet back to Miletus, and voiced his regret that Lacedaemon was so dependent on the barbarians—remarking that, if he survived and made it back home, he would move heaven and earth to reconcile the Athenians and his compatriots. From the Milesians and, a bit later, the Chians, he then raised the requisite money. Even those at Miletus who were associated with Lysander and hostile to his successor were made to think it prudent that they contribute.[40]

By this time, the Peloponnesian fleet amounted to 140 triremes. Lysander's force, which had been seventy in number at the time of his arrival at Ephesus, had grown to ninety. To it Callicratidas had added a contingent of fifty triremes supplied by Chios and Rhodes. Then, with this great armada, he set off for Methymna on the northern shore of Lesbos. There, when the Methymnians and the Athenian garrison lodged in that town refused to surrender, he took it by storm. The Athenians and the slaves captured he sold as slaves, as was the norm. The citizens he released, explaining to those within his force who objected that, while he was in charge, no Greeks would be enslaved. Although Xenophon does not spell out his rationale, we can easily see that his aim was to intimidate those in Athens' other garrisons and to encourage surrender on the part of the citizens of the *póleis* hitherto allied with that *pólis*.

We are told nothing by Xenophon concerning the Athenian response. His subject is, one must conclude, Callicratidas, his qualities as a commander, and the political stance he represented. All that is said is that the Spartiate sent an emissary to Conon, who had succeeded Alcibiades as commander of the Athenian fleet, ordering him to stop "fornicating" with the sea. The implication, not made explicit, is that Conon was to be found in the vicinity of Methymna—where, in fact, he is placed by sources dependent upon the *Hellenica Oxyrhynchia*. In the event, we are told, Conon set forth with the triremes in his fleet and fled down the channel between Lesbos and the mainland. There, with the Peloponnesian fleet in hot pursuit, he lost thirty of the seventy ships he had managed to man, and he successfully

---

[40] Callicratidas copes with the attempts of Lysander's allies to hobble his efforts: Xen. *Hell.* 1.6.2–12.

sought refuge with the rest at Mytilene, where he soon found himself besieged both by sea and by land. At this point, as if to acknowledge that he had erred, Cyrus sent to Callicratidas the funds he had hitherto denied the man.[41]

From there, despite Callicratidas' efforts to prevent communication, Conon managed to get word to Athens. The Athenians responded by deploying 110 triremes, manned by a general mobilization of the citizens (including those who served in the cavalry) and by the city's able-bodied slaves. To this fleet, when it reached Samos, they added forty triremes supplied by their allies, and with a force of 150 triremes they rowed up the Anatolian coast to the Arginusae isles, which lay opposite the southeasternmost point on Lesbos. Callicratidas, whose fleet had grown in numbers, responded by leaving a force of fifty triremes to keep Conon's force bottled up in the harbor at Mytilene and by fielding a fleet of 120 triremes.

Xenophon does not tell us the relief fleet thrown together by the Athenians was a rag-tag force manned to a considerable degree by landlubbers, but the details he supplies are sufficient for us to draw that conclusion ourselves. The Athenians turned cavalrymen and slaves into mariners only when they were scraping the bottom of the barrel. Nor does he mention the fact that Callicratidas' crews were men of experience, who had been serving on triremes of one side or the other for a number of years. But this, too, is obvious. All that Xenophon indicates is that the Athenian triremes were slower and less maneuverable than those of the Peloponnesians and that, with this in mind, the Athenian commanders deployed them in two lines—so that the enemy could not easily outflank them or slip through their line, turnabout, and strike them in the stern where triremes were vulnerable.

---

[41] Callicratidas at Methymna, Conon's force chased to Mytilene, besieged: Xen. *Hell.* 1.6.13–18.

Outnumbered and faced with this defensive formation, Callicratidas chose to fight, and in the process he lost the battle and his own life. In describing the Spartan navarch's decision, Xenophon is appropriately laconic. He mentions merely that his helmsman had urged him not to seek a decisions in these circumstances, and he reports Callicratidas' response—that Sparta would not be worse off if he died and that it would be shameful to flee. He does not tell us that, with Conon's flotilla bottled up in Mytilene, the Athenians were in a bind and that Callicratidas was in a position to dictate the terms on which the battle would take place. He leaves it to us to figure out for ourselves the degree to which the Lacedaemonian navarch's impatience and sense of honor got in the way of his strategic judgment.[42]

In the aftermath, Xenophon tells us, the Spartans gave way to pressure from the Chians and their other Greek allies and from Cyrus, who demanded that Lysander be sent out again. As the Athenian historian points out, there was a law ruling out iteration in office as navarch that precluded their placing him in that post. So they got around the law by naming another man navarch, by dispatching Lysander as his second-in-command, and by instructing the former to do what the latter told him to do.[43]

Xenophon does not tell us that this set a dangerous precedent and that Lysander might well emerge as an overmighty subject. But he does supply evidence sufficient to justify a suspicion that, in his time in Ionia, the victor in the battle of Notium had put together a coalition of men prominent in the eastern Aegean and in Anatolia prepared to use their leverage to force the Spartans to incur such a risk. So it comes as no surprise that, in the wake of his great victory at Aegospotami, Lysander

---

[42] Athenian relief fleet, battle at Arginusae: Xen. *Hell.* 1.6.24–34.
[43] Successful clamor for Lysander's return: Xen. *Hell.* 2.1.6–7.

emerged as the figure dominant at Lacedaemon and that he articulated for that city a postwar hegemonic policy favorable to his "friends," which was noteworthy for its tyrannical character, its ruthlessness, and its propensity for introducing corruption at Lacedaemon. What Xenophon says bluntly in the fourteenth chapter of his treatise on the Spartan *politeía* he conveys in his *Hellenica* by indirection of the sort later described and prescribed by Theophrastus.

7

A SOCRATIC MIDDLE ROAD
BETWEEN VIRTUE AND VICE

(Xenophon, *Memorabilia*, 2.1)

Richard S. Ruderman

Respect for continence or simple self-control has fallen on hard times. The very word, once thought to be the foundation of a serious human life, sounds altogether archaic. And its reverse (incontinence) is nothing but a concern for makers of adult diapers. In dismissing all thought about continence, however, we might be driven to assume that there are no human longings or appetites that need to be controlled at all—unless perhaps, as John Stuart Mill teaches, they present a harm to others. As Plato's Socrates puts it in the *Republic*, we have become advocates for "a certain equality of pleasures" (560b)—and reject, accordingly, all efforts to limit any passion as repressive or "Victorian."[1] Xenophon and his Socrates bring clarity to the situation by attempting to isolate the specific passion (or hopes) that, for our own good, need to be controlled—so that we can better pursue the highest or best life. More important, they urge—and

---

[1] The one area in which our world has rediscovered a need for continence—in fact, for enforcing continence—is in the realm of speech. As we shall see, this places those seeking to restrict speech in a kind of ironic agreement with Socrates who also practiced continence chiefly in the realm of speech. But whereas Socrates' continent speech served the purpose of "turning" people toward a dialectical consideration of virtue, ours more or less forbids dialectic.

practice—a certain continence in speech, especially regarding speech critical of the political life. Finally, we must solve the puzzling fact that, insofar as Xenophon's Socrates does offer a muted critique of the political life, he does not critique it for making demands on our continence.

Socrates, concerned as ever to examine the best way of life, insists on raising, quietly, the question: For what purpose ought the desires be contained? And are there desires other than for food, drink, and sex to be contained? After all, self-control can be exercised by both the just and the unjust: a good safe-cracker must practice self-control. Are the desires in and of themselves distractions from "what ought to be done" (2.1.33), demanding a life of austerity or self-denial?[2] Or are the desires compatible with a life of virtue, being something like a reward for the continent? Are the pleasures more enjoyable to those who wait to indulge them until the need to do so provides a spice to their enjoyment unknown to routine hedonists? Are they more enjoyable to those who have made earlier sacrifices? And, finally (the question with which Socrates begins his conversation), does the desire to rule or to engage in politics at the highest level presuppose the need for self-control with respect to the pleasures or is a higher form of continence to be found in controlling or overcoming one's desire to rule itself?

At all events, continence would seem only to be necessary if there exist robust desires (or perhaps the excessive hopes that egg them on) in the first place that require taming. And Socrates, the subject of Xenophon's "memoirs," appears, at least to

---

[2] All citations, unless otherwise stated, are to Xenophon's *Memorabilia*. I mostly use the Bonnette 1994 translation, though I occasionally (as here) alter it for greater literalness. As we shall see, Xenophon's consideration of "what ought to be done"—namely whether to pursue a life of political action (ruling) or a life of pleasure or a life of contemplation (science)—replaces the question of becoming continent or virtuous.

some of his closest students, to be so devoid of robust desires that he lives the life of a stone, a life so grim that they would rather die than live it (1.2.16). Easy for him to preach continence! Whence, then, Socrates' own continence? Xenophon begins his defense of Socrates against the charge of "corrupting the young" on the grounds that he was "the most continent of all human beings in matters of appetite and sex" (1.2.1). While this might seem to imply that Socrates had the most robust desires for food, drink, and sex—and somehow successfully tamed them—Xenophon immediately goes on to say that, rather than exercise brute self-control, "he had *educated* himself to have such measured needs that, although he possessed very little, he quite easily had what was enough for him" (1.2.1; emphasis added). If this mysterious self-education (a kind of intellectual virtue, apparently devoted to analyzing what we ultimately desire in, say, having sex or being virtuous) resulted in the drying up or minimizing of the "needs" that drive the desires, then it would seem to undercut any need for continence (understood as a moral virtue) at all. Socrates might then appear to be the most continent human being, but in truth, he was a human being least in need of continence. Moreover, Socrates' clear-sighted desire to possess the good things went along with a simple indifference to the less-than-good ones: he needed no continence to "resist" drinking the poor wine he could afford when he knew he would get the good stuff at Critias' next party.

Xenophon, accordingly, revises his defense of Socrates. Perhaps he was—whether in need himself of continence or not—a great teacher of continence to those who did indeed need it. Xenophon assures us that Socrates "rid many individuals of these things [viz., impiety, lawbreaking, gluttonousness, incontinence with regard to sex, and softness with regard to labor], after making them desire virtue and providing them with hopes that if they attended to themselves they would be gentlemen [noble and good]" (1.2.2). This would make Socrates a "teacher of continence" only insofar as continence prepared one for virtue or was the "foundation" of virtue (1.5.4). He simply modeled good behavior (without giving a hint of the "self-education" that enabled him to engage in it—and without even being the "most continent human being" with regard to impiety, lawbreaking, and softness with regard to labor) so as to give "those who spent time with him" the "hope" that, by imitating him, they would "come to be of the same sort" (1.2.2). Xenophon's subsequent remark, then ("he never promised at any time to be a teacher of *this*" [1.2.3; emphasis added]), introduces a new problem. Did Socrates, even after teaching continence, never promise to be a teacher of "gentlemanliness" or even of virtue itself (the goals for which continence is a preparation)? We know from the *Oeconomicus* that Socrates was not a teacher, but a student, of gentlemanliness. And in our chapter (2.1), we find some evidence that, despite Socrates' ability to "converse most nobly *about* virtue and the other human things" (1.2.18; emph. added), he does not teach virtue either. Could "attending to virtue" indeed be a kind of corruption (1.2.8)—at least to the extent of turning one away from virtue and toward the "other human things," presumably the "beneficial" and "most serious" things that make them "better"? To what end, then, and in control of which specific behaviors and hopes did Socrates teach continence? And what explains his "continent" refusal to promise to teach virtue? Did he not understand virtue? Or did he understand it all-too-well?

Missing from the above cited list of areas in which Socrates appears to have taught continence is "engaging in political life" and, in particular, the desire to rule. In fact, rather than tell the likes of "the most incontinent" Alcibiades (1.2.12) that he should control his longing to rule, Socrates (convinced that "no one receives any education from someone who does not please him"; 1.2.39) instead presented himself to the young Alcibiades as an ally of his deepest longing, the "desire for honor" (1.2.8). Now, Socrates and his education eventually "did not please" Alcibiades (and Critias) and they broke away from him (1.2.47). What accounts for Alcibiades' initially having been pleased with Socrates? If Alcibiades' debate with his god-parent Pericles is any indication (1.2.40–46), Alcibiades learned that democratic rule is no more just or noble than tyrannical rule: every form of political rule requires "force" or a non-rational component of "persuading without convincing" the ruled.[3] And while Socrates appears to have intended eventually to develop this insight into a critique of engaging in political life *tout court*,[4] he allowed the young Alcibiades to entertain the thought that he might, in good conscience, transcend the confusion of the ruling life of Pericles and live the fulfilling (because unqualified) life of grand rule.[5]

The Setting of *Memorabilia* 2.1

Our chapter (2.1) of the *Memorabilia* constitutes the culmination of a five-chapter section of the work, commencing with 1.4. The theme of that section is Xenophon's effort to meet the widespread objection to Socrates, according to which he may "turn" people toward virtue (in the sense of making them enthusiastic for it), but he cannot or does not "lead" them to it (1.4.1). Now,

---

[3] The formulation "persuade without convincing" is Rousseau's characterization of the fundamental task of the statesman (*Social Contract*, 2.7).

[4] The only critique leveled against Alcibiades in the *Memorabilia* is that, by engaging in the political life, he "neglected himself" (1.2.24). We will consider this problem—and the inability of either continence or virtue to address it—at the end of this chapter.

[5] Plato too suggests that Socrates, when Alcibiades was even younger, far from discouraging his desire to rule, sought to promote it, and even inflated it until Alcibiades considered ruling the whole world (*Alcibiades I*, 120c1–2, 124b4–6).

"leading" people to virtue turns out to be rather ambiguous and its meaning is never directly explained. The simplest implication would appear to be "making people virtuous." But the verb translated "to lead to" [*proagagein*] implies "to lead toward" rather than "to lead into." And this would imply that Socrates not only failed to make people virtuous, he did not even bring them to the cusp of being able to choose it for themselves. And this difficulty leads, in turn, to a further ambiguity. For Xenophon retrenches yet again and asserts only that he will prove that Socrates did make others, or at any rate his "companions," "better" (1.4.1). How can one become "better" without becoming more virtuous? Is there something about virtue itself—especially about coming to understand what virtue is—that reduces one's enthusiasm for embracing or engaging in it? Or must one be "continent" with respect to one's expectations of virtue no less than to those of vice? Our chapter (2.1) not only introduces the reader to Virtue herself—and thereby to the precise nature and extent of her attractiveness—but does so in the context of a specific aspect, seemingly the peak aspect, of virtue, namely "political virtue" understood either as "ruling" or as "laboring" to serve others, such as the "gods," one's "friends," one's "city" or even "all of Greece" (cf. 2.1.1 and 2.1.28).

By the end of Book One, we have learned that continence is itself not a virtue and that Socrates did not bother even to condemn incontinence in some of his more promising associates. (He does ostentatiously denounce Xenophon's "incontinence" in defending the kissing of a beautiful person; 1.3. We will return to this later.) Continence is merely a trait, allegedly providing the conditions necessary to develop or engage in virtues. Socrates has not yet specified what virtue continence aids in achieving. Moreover, in providing the self-discipline needed to achieve any goal, continence can also provide the condition to succeed at vice. Accordingly, Xenophon first presents

Socrates giving a "nondialogical" or merely rhetorical[6] exhortation to continence (1.5). There, beginning from the hypothetical "*if*…continence…is both a noble and good possession for a man [*aner*]" (1.5.1, emphasis added), Socrates asks whether those "believing" that continence is "the foundation of virtue" should not wish to have it "first" in their souls (1.5.4). Socrates interrogates that belief, that wish, and that initial hypothetical properly, that is dialectically, only in 2.1. Our puzzle, in attempting to understand *Memorabilia* 2.1, is that continence is at first presented as though it were necessary only for those wishing to rule—whether that be in controlling one's desires *while ruling* or in controlling one's desire to put oneself forward to rule in the first place—and Socrates makes this case to the hedonist Aristippus, who has no desire to rule or to engage in politics at all. And, while we might expect Socrates to then shift gears and urge Aristippus to control his passions, he does no such thing, outsourcing that task to Virtue herself. And while Xenophon, for his part, does praise Socrates for making his companions more "moderate" (4.3.2, 18), he nowhere offers an example of making them continent. Does a person such as Aristippus (or others, like Socrates,[7] who also avoid ruling) then need continence at all? If so, for the control of what urge or desire exactly? And for what positive purpose? For Socratic continence certainly controls something other than the targets of regular

---

[6] Leo Strauss, *Xenophon's Socrates* (Ithaca: Cornell University Press, 1972): 26.

[7] Xenophon says Socrates "displayed himself" to be "still more continent in his deeds than in his speeches" (1.5.6). Recalling that Socrates distinguished "what is said, what is done, and what is silently deliberated" (1.1.19), we are forced to complete the pattern by assuming Socrates was still *less* continent or even not continent at all in his silent deliberations. Unlimited or incontinent thinking, however, seems compatible with and may even rely upon—or lead to—continence in speech and deed.

continence, namely unrestrained[8] sexual and monetary urges.

Xenophon's Socrates is presented in 2.1 as making the case for continence to a well-known hedonist, Aristippus. But he does so only because he had heard that one of his "companions" (evidently listening in to the discussion) was "undisciplined in such respects" (2.1.1). Moreover, he presents, as the conclusion of his argument, a (highly modified) retelling of the famous Choice of Hercules, in which Hercules must choose between a life of Virtue or of Vice. Accordingly, Xenophon leaves the impression, to a cursory reader, that Socrates was something of a moralistic scold who encouraged others to pull their socks up, resist temptation, and prepare for a life of virtue, which appears to mean or culminate in a life of dedication to others.

Certain features of the chapter, however, undermine this first impression. We begin by noting the absences of some expected components of the argument for continence. Most striking, of course, is Socrates' or Xenophon's failure to present the choice Hercules ultimately makes between Virtue and Vice. Such discretion can be explained by the fact that Hercules became notorious for his almost unlimited incontinence (see Aristophanes, *Frogs*, 503–522). This becomes a matter of greater or more general concern when we recall that Xenophon had earlier stated "Socrates conversed most nobly [or beautifully] about virtue" (1.2.18): is there something inherently ugly or off-putting about virtue that Socratic rhetoric seeks to counter? Does conversing about virtue (or even to Virtue herself!) make us virtuous—or does it "nobly" attract us to it, only to elevate us above

---

[8] Thomas L. Pangle, *The Socratic Way of Life: Xenophon's Memorabilia* (Chicago: University of Chicago Press, 2018), 47 shows that Xenophon, in the earlier chapters discussing Socrates' "regimen" for self-control, reveals him to have been "abstemious, but not ascetic," that is, he indulged in his passions in a measured or reasonable way.

and beyond virtue?[9] In the language of the chapter: can Socrates make his companions—can he make himself—"better" by some means other than making them more virtuous? Moreover, while Vice promotes the very pleasures that, in leading to happiness, can be expected to appeal to Aristippus, Virtue does not quite make the case for ruling nobly (that we have been expecting from the start). Virtue urges a life of the "good worker" for the "noble and high" things (2.1.27) but leaves it as provisional whether this requires one "to desire to be honored by *some* city" (apparently permitting one to live as an Aristippean "stranger" to one's own or indeed any city)[10]—and even then, says only that one must "benefit" that city somehow, without specifying that one must rule to do so (2.1.28; emphasis added). But, in addition and upon closer inspection, Socrates never suggests that there is anything *unjust* about Aristippus' dedicating his life to pleasure or to the apolitical life of the "stranger." He does warn him, at some length, of the dangers and risks he faces as a stranger, above all in his presumed inability to "ward off those who are unjust" (2.1.14). That is, while there appears (to Socrates) to be nothing unjust about living the life of the stranger—the "middle road" that travels "neither through rule nor through slavery, but through freedom" leading ultimately to "happiness" (11)[11]—there is little, save the acquisition of "arms" (14), that

---

[9] In a later chapter (addressed to "someone" who had been elected cavalry commander), Socrates argued that one might then have to transcend even the noble things (at least those "learned…according to law") in the direction of the "most serious things" (3.3.11). At no point does Socrates equate the most serious things with the noble or virtue (much less continence).

[10] Did Xenophon adopt this understanding of virtue when, during his retreat with the Ten Thousand, he considered founding a city "in some barbaric place" (*Anabasis* 5.6.15–16)?

[11] Xenophon tells us that Socrates arranged his life so that he could enjoy "freedom" (1.2.6) and that Socrates was "a most good and happy man"

can protect such "strangers" *from* injustice. And it may well appear to "those who are unjust" that Aristippus and his ilk, lacking all patriotism, are *themselves* unjust (and thus fair prey for them). The chief lesson in continence that Socrates here teaches is to "arm" oneself by hiding or suppressing any words or deeds that imply a disdain for politics. This appears to be how he "benefited" the city. Let us attempt to unravel these two mysteries.

The fact that we are not told what choice Hercules makes might seem to mean that it is so obvious that he would choose Virtue as to relieve Xenophon of the burden of having to state it. But is it, in the context of the *Memorabilia*, so obvious? After all, earlier in the work, in the part most openly devoted to defending Socrates against the charges made against him—of corrupting the youth and not believing in the gods of Athens—Xenophon suggests that the teaching and even the meaning of virtue are somewhat ambiguous. In fact, right after denying that Socrates even "professed" to teach "anything of the sort," Xenophon says that Socrates sought to make his students "friends to himself and to one another"—and not, that is, either to the gods or to their cities (1.2.8). Let us then turn to the beginning of the dialogue in order to see what exactly Socrates is arguing, not only about continence but also the relative merits of the lives of virtue and of vice, and of political and of private lives.

The Opening

The chapter opens with Xenophon stating he wishes to show how Socrates "turned his companions toward training themselves to be continent" in their desires for (or to avoid) seven

---

(4.8.11). And, like Aristippus, he lived a life that involved neither rule nor slavery. What then distinguishes the two men's respective ways of life? Are philosophic pleasures more solid? Is Socrates simply more continent than Aristippus? And is Socratic continence, especially in speech, somehow a "benefit" to the city?

things: "meat and drink, and in regard to lust, sleep, cold, heat, and labor" (2.1.1).[12] Continence appears to have two faces: while one must, presumably, resist the temptation to *enjoy* food, drink, lust, and sleep, one must resist the desire to *evade* (excess) cold, heat, or labor. Just as Socrates merely "turned" his companions toward virtue without successfully leading them to it, likewise he "turned" them toward continence. Xenophon then says that when Socrates recognized that "one of his companions" was "too" undisciplined "in this regard," he engaged Aristippus in a conversation about continence, virtue, and more. Since Aristippus was not a "companion" of Socrates (consider 3.8.1), the conversation must have chiefly been for the benefit of the companion who, presumably, was overhearing it.[13]

Xenophon then presents Socrates asking Aristippus a question purporting to show the need for continence:

> Tell me, Aristippus, if you should have to take and educate two youths, one so that he would be competent to rule, and the other so that he would not even lay a claim to rule,[14] how would you educate each? (2.1.1)

Rather than turn Aristippus toward continence in any direct way, Socrates sets a puzzle for him. First, he puts him in the position of having to educate others in continence, not in becoming so himself. Second, he implies without ever stating openly what the nature of the passion to be controlled by continence is, which appears to be "desiring so strongly to rule that

---

[12] Strikingly omitted from this list are "impiety" and "lawbreaking" (see again 1.2.2). Does Socrates agree with Machiavelli who taught that political rule (the topic he immediately turns to) always requires impiety and lawbreaking?

[13] Pangle (2018, 64) suggests convincingly that the companion was Xenophon himself.

[14] Socrates, in his subsequent education of the woefully ill-prepared Glaucon, shows these two educations could be combined into one (3.6).

one overlooks the need to become competent at it." And he then leads Aristippus to equate "competence" to rule with first developing the ability to be continent. (It is only later, in a discussion with Glaucon, that Socrates speaks of the far more important areas requiring competence, namely knowing finances, the extent of one's land and sea power, and so on [3.6].) In doing this, Socrates leaves Aristippus (and the reader) with the impression that the alternative of "not putting oneself forward to rule" entails restraining one's desire to rule until one becomes continent over one's sub-political desires. But, re-examining Socrates' initial question, we see it may not be presenting the simple dichotomy it appears to do. That is, someone could be competent to rule and yet not "lay a claim" to it. And there is a further ambiguity in the phrase "not lay a claim" to rule. Someone might not lay a claim to rule simply because they do not wish to rule, despite being competent to do so. But someone might not "lay a claim" to rule—in the sense of arguing that they deserve to rule—because they do not think that justice can identify anyone as deserving to rule, however competent and willing they may be. To clarify, there may be three quite distinct types of people who would not even "lay a claim to rule": (1) those who, aware that they lack continence, come to realize that they should not put themselves forward to rule until they have "trained" themselves in continence (these are the recipients of the "first" education that Aristippus and Socrates discuss); (2) those who are both continent and competent to rule, but do not wish to do so (Socrates might seem—and does seem to Aristippus—to be of this sort); and (3) those who are both competent and willing to rule but have learned (perhaps from this very conversation) not to "lay a claim" to rule (in the sense of claiming they deserve to rule, by right). Knowing his subsequent career, it would seem Xenophon himself could be of this type. For, as we learn from his *Anabasis*, Xenophon was exceptionally competent to rule and was willing, under unusually compelling circumstances, to do so but never "laid a claim" to rule.[15] But how could it not be just for the wise and competent to rule?

Without being aware of this question, Aristippus implicitly answers at least a part of it in explaining to Socrates why he does not have any wish to rule at all: ruling is a burden, undertaken moreover not for one's own benefit but for the city's. In response, Socrates never claims that it is just—that there is a duty—to rule (if one is competent to do so), but only that it is unwise or unsafe to lead a wholly apolitical life. With this, Socrates turns the conversation not to what one might want "first" to have in one's soul, but to the question of what the best way of life is. Is there, accordingly, a role for continence in the making of a more fundamental choice (which foreshadows but is not the same as the one Hercules is presented with later), namely the choice of whether or not to rule simply? Pangle puts the presumed choice this way: "joining those who become self-disciplined so as to seek to become competent rulers, or joining those who, *lacking* self-discipline, make no claim to rule."[16] But Pangle merely infers that all members of the latter group lack self-discipline. Might their not putting themselves forward to rule be instead an instance of self-discipline? Now, Socrates surely stresses that self-denial, especially with respect to food, drink, and sex, coupled with working hard (labor) is the ticket

---

[15] We note that Xenophon begins the *Anabasis* accepting Cyrus the Younger as ruler of the Ten Thousand and seems to praise him as a superior ruler to his brother (whom Cyrus seeks to supplant). And yet, in the crucial confrontation, Cyrus loses his life—putting in motion the circumstances that result in Xenophon's becoming ruler—precisely because he lacked continence (*Anabasis*, 1.8.26). Xenophon never loses his life, in large part because he learned Socratic continence.

[16] Pangle, *Socratic Way of Life*, 65, emphasis added.

to political domination or at least survival.[17] But Pangle's formulation (that those who recognize that they lack self-discipline, especially in food, drink, and sex and so withdraw themselves from politics) overlooks the possibility that some of those who refrain from entering politics are (if there is a primordial urge to dominate and avoid being dominated) themselves *exercising* self-discipline in holding back from entering the contest. After all, Socrates presents both alternatives as fulfilling Aristippus' imputed education in continence (if in different ways).

Now, insofar as both forms of continence are premised on the assumption that it is somehow needed either to make competent one's political urge or to restrain it, Socrates is guilty of "excluding the middle"—or rather of excluding the other half of what might be called a decision-matrix. In particular, he excludes (1) those who may not seek or wish to rule at all, as well as (2) those who wish to rule and are competent to do so (perhaps even possessing, in addition to self-control regarding the carnal pleasures, the "art of ruling" itself) and yet do not "make a claim" to rule. Do those in the first category—into which Aristippus places himself—require any form of continence at all? And on behalf of what non-political way of life do those in the latter category—into which Aristippus seems to place Socrates—exercise the self-control of not engaging in politics? For it would seem that the alternatives Socrates directly asks Aristippus to explore are not really relevant to either of the two of them. Who are the respective audiences, however, of Socrates' continued discussion (after the initial alternatives prove irrelevant for them) of the implied but not stated alternatives just sketched? Socrates' teaching on the kind of continence required

---

[17] Consider Octavius Caesar's denunciation of Mark Antony for having lost his once admirable ability to live "with patience more/ than savages could suffer," eating whatever was available (perhaps engaging in cannibalism) during a particularly bad retreat (*Antony and Cleopatra*, 1.4.57–70).

for non-political pleasure seekers would seem to be directed at both Aristippus and the un-named "companion" of Socrates whose incontinence occasioned the conversation in the first place. But how would Socrates' teaching on giving up politics to live the Socratic way of life be of benefit for Aristippus—whose capacity for philosophy Socrates shows no signs of recognizing or encouraging? And while the conversation might amount to a mini-apology for Socrates' way of life, how would that benefit Socrates himself? Might this (buried twice-over) alternative be presented for the sake of one particular companion listening in, namely Xenophon himself?

Socrates, who claims elsewhere to possess the "art of rule" (more so than acting Athenian rulers such as Pericles; Plato, *Gorgias* 515e) and is thought by Aristippus to possess the "kingly art" (2.1.17) while not in fact ruling or ever seeking to rule, is aware of and even exemplifies this possibility. And while Aristippus, in the course of the subsequent dialogue, falls into Socrates' trap by accepting continence as the necessary prerequisite for a ruler (which leads in turn to Aristippus' rejection of the life of politics altogether for being incompatible with happiness), he overlooks another possible response to Socrates' question: might continence be more or even most prominently on display in those who control their desire to "lay a claim to rule" either by ruling without advancing a "claim" to do so or declining to enter a life of politics altogether? Might this, in fact, be the type of continence that Socrates sought—apparently only partially successfully—to recommend to Xenophon?

Aristippus appears to overlook this alternative response because, as it turns out, he has no desire to enter politics in the first place and thus cannot see a need for overcoming it. If, however, Aristippus neither needs continence (instrumentally) to become a ruler, nor ever felt the need for it to control a desire to rule he never had, Socrates' question seems ill-advised or pointless. But if continence is also—and perhaps best—revealed in not advancing claims of deserving to rule, then Socrates' might indeed have reason to continue speaking to Aristippus. For though Aristippus seems to reject justice as nothing but a city's belief that it "deserves" to treat its rulers as servants, he immediately pivots and claims he "deserves" to have servants who provide him with goods (2.1.9). Aristippus, that is, relies on justice, chiefly in the sense that he is "deserving" of having others who free him from "troubles" (here labor) by putting his good ahead of their own. If Socrates could teach Aristippus continence with regard to making such claims of justice and de-serving—continence here meaning simply the application to himself of doubts Aristippus already entertains with regard to the city—it might perhaps benefit Aristippus' servants as well as him. At any rate, Socrates continues to avoid urging Aristip-pus to develop political ambition, even without laying a claim to rule.

Upon being asked by Socrates if control over the "belly" is necessary for "both" (that is, for ruling and for not putting one-self forward for rule), Aristippus replies "it is likely"—but he goes on merely to explain its necessity for those ruling. And, according to Aristippus, those who rule must, in fact, deny more than just the pleasures of the belly. The ruler is to be concerned exclusively with "the city's affairs" (2.1.2): his own needs must simply be sacrificed to those of the city. His later claim that such self-denial is required for Socrates' "kingly art"—and that Soc-rates would equate such self-denial with "happiness"—is chal-lenged, not in the course of this conversation, but later in one of Socrates' conversations with the none-too-promising Euthyde-mos. There, Socrates asks:

> Do you not, Euthydemos, desire that virtue through which people become fit for political affairs, fit to manage

households, competent to rule, and beneficial to human beings *as well as themselves?* (4.2.11; emphasis added)

On one hand, Socrates here stresses "fitness" or "competence" to
engage in politics, clothed as a "virtue," without ever suggesting
one should or could put forward a just claim to engage in it. On
the other, Socrates here seems to admit a kind of political rule
that could benefit oneself as well as others. In short, Socrates
permits Aristippus, throughout their conversation, to maintain
the hedonist's (negative) view of politics, without ever recognizing the possibility of a more genuinely beneficial (both to oneself and others) attitude toward or understanding of politics. If
Socrates is then talking past Aristippus throughout their discussion, what education in politics does Socrates have in mind
for those listening in on it (including us readers)?

One might object that this line of argument—that becoming continent in one's desire for or expectations from justice is
one of Socrates' ways of benefiting others[18]—is paradoxical or
even confused. Isn't continence, especially when completed by
justice, the best way to ensure that our relations with others are
at their best or most just? Socrates' own brand of continence
suggests otherwise. How, precisely, does Socrates' own vaunted
continence (with regard to food, drink, sex, material goods) affect his relations to his fellows, both his companions and his
fellow citizens? Insofar as he has minimal needs, he might be
expected to engage less in stealing or otherwise taking things
from others. In this way, he can surely be understood as treating
his fellow citizens more justly. Is not the virtue to which continence prepares one, then, justice? Only if Hobbes, who

---

[18] Owing to his Socratic education, Xenophon, in stark contrast to Cyrus the Younger, "never let zeal to avenge a wrong overcome his prudence,
even for a moment." Christopher Bruell, "Xenophon," in *History of Political
Philosophy*, 3rd ed., Leo Strauss and Joseph Cropsey, eds. (Chicago: University of Chicago Press, 1987), 113.

understands justice as "not doing unto others" or leaving others and their goods alone, is correct (*Leviathan*, 14.5). But Xenophon takes the preliberal view that justice entails also the positive or proactive benefiting or helping of others. And, he asserts, Socrates did act justly in this manner—but only toward those who "associated" with him (4.8.11). This suggests he did not particularly benefit his fellow citizens as such. And this makes sense, insofar as a chief motive for benefiting others is to incentivize them to benefit you in return (see 2.3.11–14). Needing fewer benefits—and not expecting the vast majority of his fellow citizens to be capable of conferring those that mattered to him (namely teaching him something)—Socrates' justice toward his fellow citizens may have mostly consisted in his not harming them.

Now Socrates did benefit his "companions."[19] To understand how, we would have to consider the entire *Memorabilia* and each of the companions benefited by Socrates in it. This is clearly beyond the scope of this paper. But how might he have benefited the audience of companions listening in to his conversation with Aristippus (who, to repeat, is not included among his "companions")? Socrates indicates, in his opening question to Aristippus, that one chief benefit was to learn continence with respect to ruling. Now, neither Socrates nor Virtue explicitly calls ruling a virtue. It might then not require the sort of continence Socrates is discussing to engage in. Does Socratic continence require one to abstain from politics in order to live the philosophic life?

Restraining our desires or our hopes?

While Xenophon (as narrator of 2.1) lists 7 desires as calling

---

[19] Socrates is described only once in the *Memorabilia* as "wishing" to benefit his companions (3.8.1).

out for continence, Socrates (as he begins his conversation with Aristippus) modifies that list in a few important ways. Xenophon, we recall, lists continence with regard to "meat, drink,… lust, sleep, cold, heat, and labor" (2.1.1). We desire, generally, to have the first 4 and to avoid (at least extremes of) the last three. All seven examples appear to be purely bodily, though Socratic "labor" may differ (in being purely a labor of the mind or the soul) from the general view of labor (shared by Aristippus).[20] And continence is presented here as a means to accomplishing various (unstated) goals. In his series of questions to Aristippus, however, Socrates makes some changes to the topics listed in Xenophon's introduction. After asking about "food" and "drink," Socrates then asks about "sleep" before "sex" (which now becomes the central topic), then turns to "labors," adds "learning" (especially about how to "overpower one's adversaries") and concludes with the need to stand against "cold and heat" (now combined into one topic) (2.1.2–6).

In addition to making "sex" now the central topic, Socrates speaks of it (as was common among Greeks) as "the things of Aphrodite" rather than as "lust" (or even "screwing" [*lagneias*]) as Xenophon had initially. Xenophon, that is, in writing the introduction (long after the conversation in question had taken place), can be understood as having undergone the Socratic education with regard to continence in "sex." While continence with regard to lust is necessary only so as to avoid "risky situations," continence with regard to sex ("*ta Aphroditē*") appears to have to do with controlling both "the desire *and the hope [for]* sex" (2.1.5; emphasis added). I have taken the liberty of placing

---

[20] Socrates later jokes "about his own lack of busyness" to Theodote by saying that "it is not easy for me to find leisure" (3.11.16). Socrates does avoid labor as most people conceive it, but only by laboring incessantly at philosophy. Does Xenophon, by contrast, exercise some continence in his practice of philosophy to pursue other ends?

"for" in square brackets because it does not appear in the Greek text itself, and is being assumed from the grammar of the surrounding words. The phrase could also—and more plausibly—be translated as "the hopes associated with [or with the things of] the divine goddess Aphrodite." That is, while all animals (including humans) desire to have physical intercourse ("lust") and may conceive hopes to obtain it, humans generate additional hopes from the having of intercourse, namely that it might overcome our mortal nature, enabling us to share a taste of divine immortality. (Consider Heidegger's analysis of the word *ekstasy*, which he takes to mean giving the illusion that we are outside of time and its inevitable effects on us.) Continence with regard to "sex," then, entails a resolution of the theo-sexual problem: we must learn, as Xenophon the narrator evidently has, not to invest additional and unsupportable hopes for things beyond sex into our natural "lust" (which, to repeat, requires some continence to restrict it as well).

In addition to replacing "lust" with "sex," Socrates adds something new, immediately after "labor," to his list: "learning," in particular "whatever is serviceable for overpowering one's adversaries" (2.1.3). And these two latter themes both stick out on the list. For while one must be continent in the sense of not allowing (too much) food, drink, sleep, lust, and heat and cold to interfere with what one ought to do, one must be "continent" in the sense of being ready to labor and to learn endlessly (even in the face of the other temptations on the list). That is, one must be *incontinent* in one's labors and one's learning. Moreover, these two themes are personified in the conversation: Hercules is famous for his twelve labors and Socrates for his learning. And while there was a limit to Hercules' labors, Socrates, we are later told, "*never* ceased examining with his companions what each of the beings is" (4.6.1; emphasis added).

Now, Aristippus places both "labors" and "learning" in the

category of things one seeking to rule must do. And he stresses the importance of learning how to overpower one's adversaries in the top rank: "there is no benefit from the other things without such learning" (2.1.3). What then are the implications for those in the other category, the ones not "making a claim" to rule? Just as the ones not even wishing to rule (such as Aristippus) can, it seems, enjoy unlimited food, drink, lust, warmth (when it's cold) and cool air (when it's hot), so (he implies) they need not labor or learn how to overpower their adversaries. They, Aristippus has implied, need not be "educated" (per Socrates' initial question) at all. But while Aristippus concedes there is plenty of labor involved in living his private life of pleasure (so much that he sees no sense in adding the much greater labors entailed in ruling to it; 2.1.8), he does not see or concede the need for learning. That may be because he sees no "adversaries" in his chosen way of life. On the grounds that only cities have enemies—and Aristippus intends to live the life of a "stranger everywhere" (2.1.13)—he does not foresee having any adversaries to speak of. And, unlike those concerned with continence, Aristippus does not consider the pleasures themselves to be adversaries to his own good at all. At this point, the role of educator passes from Aristippus to Socrates. Rather than educate Aristippus to learn continence and put himself forward to rule, however, Socrates educates him on how more intelligently or at any rate safely to live a private life. For, Socrates argues, he will indeed have adversaries. And Socrates goes on, in his *Aristippupedia*, to reveal the reason he does not foresee having adversaries. Not only does Aristippus feel he "deserves" to have servants who will work for his good instead of their own (2.1.9), he also (as Socrates divines) thinks he "deserves" neither to rule nor be ruled (2.1.12). Aristippus, that is, has incontinent hopes for or from justice: because he doesn't deserve to be treated unjustly, he will not be treated unjustly. Socrates spends a considerable amount of time explaining to Aristippus that this is not so. Not only are there no protections "on the highways" for the free cosmopolitan (Socrates mentions the "unjust" behaviors of Sinis, Sciron, and Procrustes to travelers at 2.1.14), Aristippus should not expect each city's arrangement to protect its own citizens from injustice to extend to him. Aristippus expects transpolitical justice itself—or his just desserts—to protect him. But injustice is more universal. And even within the "cities" that seek to carve out islands of justice in this harsh world, those very cities think they owe justice only to their own citizens, or to those who "labor" for its good (consider 2.1.15). Cities will no more "take heart" from Aristippus'implicit declaration that he is no one's enemy than he should "take heart" when cities "announce" that "it is safe to come and go" (2.1.15).

Socrates then turns to methods by which masters "deal with" their servants (16). He speaks of preventing them from engaging in sex, stealing, running away, and being lazy. Household servants, that is (not unlike Aristippus) long for sex, possessions, freedom, and leisure from working. And their masters utilize harsh measures—withholding food from them, removing them from comforts, placing them in bonds, and even beating them—to bring them to a state of continence. In stark contrast, we recall, those who would be rulers impose every manner of continence on themselves, their ambition seeming to achieve self-mastery without recourse to the harsh "compulsions" needed for the servants.

Despite or because of the resemblance of his longings to those of these servants, Aristippus is asked by Socrates how he, as master, deals with his servants (16). In the course of his answer, Aristippus instead sees a greater similarity between his servants and the rulers who "willingly" endure the deprivations he forcibly imposes on his servants (17). As though correcting Hegel's understanding of the Master/Slave relationship,

172

Aristippus sees both political ruler and slave as being denied all happiness in life, the slave through compulsion, the ruler through self-mastery.

But how, according to Socrates, might Aristippus better protect himself from injustice? Must he labor harder in some way? Socrates uses the word "labor" seven times in the chapter; Virtue uses it six times; and Vice once. Socrates, we have seen, promotes the "labor" of the soul, namely learning "how to overcome adversaries," where "adversaries" are to be understood—by the bystanders such as Xenophon, if not by Aristippus himself—as false or misleading views, especially of justice and deserving. The position of Vice toward labor is clear: "have no fear that I might lead you to procure these [pleasant] things for yourself by means of labor and hardship of body and soul" (2.1.25). Aristippus, seeking the most easy and pleasant life, might indeed be tempted by this thought. But he has already stressed to Socrates that "a lot of work" is required to live his hedonistic life (2.1.8). While Xenophon does not report Aristippus' response to Vice (or to Virtue), it would seem that, by accepting the need to work hard for that life, he can comfort himself that he is not really vicious at all. This is not to say that he would accept Virtue's blandishments—we will see that that is also unlikely—but that he feels he is worthy of traveling his path of (an excluded) "middle." Is his synthesis of the best that both Vice and Virtue have to offer, however, coherent?

Virtue's attitude toward labor is somewhat more complicated. After confessing to Hercules her "hope" that he will become "an exceedingly good worker of what is noble and august" (2.1.27), she reveals that (1) "*if* [he] wishes the gods to be gracious" to him, he should know that "without labor and attentiveness, the gods give humans none of the things that are good and noble" (2.1.28); (2) "*if*" he wishes to become "powerful" in body, he must "train with labors and sweat"; (3) laboring gives a purpose to, and presumably greater enjoyment of, sleep (2.1.30); (4) those who are "without labor" when young are destined to pass "a miserable and laborious old age" (2.1.31); and finally (5) that while she herself is "honored most of all among gods and among those human beings by whom it is fitting to be honored," she is a "cherished co-worker" for, among other things, being a "good helper for the labors of peace" (2.1.32). She concludes her long speech to Hercules with the admonition "When you have worked hard at such things, Hercules, child of blessed parents, it is possible to possess the most blessed happiness" (2.1.33).

Socrates, then—who concedes he is revising somewhat Prodicus' "treatise" of Hercules (2.1.21)—ends the chapter by replacing the emphasis on "continence" with an emphasis on "labors." If "labor and sweat," that is, makes one "strong in body," there would seem to be relatively little need for "continence" regarding food and drink.[21] Indeed, in responding to Vice's defense of pleasure, Virtue pivots from (initially) having critiqued pleasure to allowing as how, for her "friends" (presumably the virtuous), "the enjoyment of food and drink is pleasant and trouble-free" (2.1.33). This concession to pleasure is more than merely rhetorical (for the purpose of seducing Hercules): there is nothing wrong with pleasure, from Virtue's point of view, if one is (as Kant too says) "worthy" of it.

While we know that Hercules (and perforce Aristippus?) did not choose continence, did he (and perforce Aristippus?) choose Virtue or at least some aspect of it? Did Socrates? As we have already seen, Aristippus chooses a middle way that, we have argued, turns out to consist in an uneasy synthesis of Vice's pleasures with Virtue's worthiness to enjoy them. Socrates reveals this sense of deserving as the core of virtue when

---

[21] Virtue, in fact, never once speaks of continence. She uses the word "labor" six times (and the word for "having worked hard" once; 2.1.33).

recounting (again, in his revision) Virtue's opening case for the life of virtue. Amid her list of things that Hercules might "wish" or "desire" to obtain (and what he would need to do to obtain them), Virtue singles out one thing that Hercules might think he "deserve[s]" to have on account of his "virtue" (the only time Virtue uses the word): being admired (or "being wondered at" [*thoumazdesai*]) by "all Greece" (2.1.28). The possession of virtue, then, confers on us the belief or hope that we "deserve" what we might otherwise idly or simply desire to have. But there are some grave problems here. First, Virtue says that one must "attempt" to "do good [or 'well']" for Greece to be worthy of her admiration (or wonder). If one seeks Greece's admiration, however, one must do what Greece as a whole thinks is good for her. And "the many seem to define as good those who benefit them" (*Hellenika* 7.3.12).[22] Second, seeking widespread admiration—permitting "the many," that is, to be the judges of one's worth—is clearly not Socrates' standard: unlike Virtue, he had characterized the "rewards for one's labors" (he does not call them virtues) as being "self-admiration" (2.1.19; translation modified). Third, while seeking the admiration of competent judges (those formed by a Socratic education) is something to be labored for, Virtue speaks, everywhere else in her speech, only of garnering praise or honor. And while one is admired for being good, one is praised or honored chiefly for giving up the pursuit of one's good.

The Socratic Middle Way and the Continent Pursuit of Pleasure

We recall that *Memorabilia* 1.4–2.1 is devoted to responding to

---

[22] Insofar as they understand these good individuals to have benefited them at a cost to themselves, they might indeed "wonder at" (and not merely admire) them.

the charge that Socrates merely "turned" people toward virtue but did not "lead" them to it. The unresolved ending of our chapter—we are not given any indication that either Hercules or Aristippus were led to (choosing) virtue by Socrates' account of Virtue's blandishments—leaves us with the uncomfortable suspicion that these particular critics of Socrates were right. And indeed, Xenophon almost concludes the *Memorabilia* by saying that Socrates could "turn" those who dealt with him "toward virtue and gentlemanliness" (without saying a word about his leading them to it). And yet, immediately prior to this remark, Xenophon says "all who desired virtue even now still continue to long for him most of all, on the grounds that he was most beneficial with regard to attending to virtue" (4.8.11). It was, then, Socrates' "attending" to virtue—thinking it through— and assisting those who desired it to think it through as well that most benefited them. Throughout the work, Socrates' speech regarding virtue was so continent that he leaves most readers with the impression that he tried to lead his companions to virtue rather than reveal that he was in fact "testing" and "refuting" the claims of virtue.

Socrates does, however, show Vice "refuting" a part of Virtue's argument. In the one part of the tale said to be "as Prodicus tells it," Vice says "Reflect, Heracles, how hard and long is the road to the delights that this woman describes for you. But I shall lead you to an easy and short road to happiness" (2.1.29). Vice here both urges Hercules to "reflect" on or think through the situation and reveals that, at the end of the hard road of self-denial urged by Virtue lie "delights." Despite being angered (now calling Vice "Wretch!"), Virtue instead of condemning Vice's endorsement of pleasure, proposes better ones. And while, in an echo of the initial list Socrates made of things requiring self-control over, she suggests that "eating," "drinking," "sleep," and "sex" are all more enjoyable when done in response to a real felt need, she endorses "labor" as a prerequisite only for the enjoyment of "sleep" (2.1.30). Moreover, in her concluding statement (promising "the most blessed happiness"), Virtue repeats the prospect of enjoying food, drink, and sleep, but omits "sex." In its place, she substitutes the pleasures of "praise" (granted to the young) and "honors" (granted to the old, who also enjoy reminiscing over past accomplishments), becoming "dear to gods, cherished by friends, and honored by fatherlands" and, above all, "when their allotted end comes," those who befriended Virtue "do not lie without honor and forgotten, but thrive remembered in hymns sung through all time" (2.1.33). In short, Virtue greatly de-emphasizes the having of "good things" (which require no praise or honors to enjoy and are best enjoyed in the having as opposed to in one's recollections), and correspondingly elevates the importance of earning the attachment of gods, friends, and fatherlands so as not to be forgotten in death. "Recall[ing]" fondly one's own "ancient" deeds (33, using translation from Bonnette's endnote)—the chief or at any rate final pleasure to be enjoyed by the virtuous—seems, in this context, to be less an exercise in nostalgia than an effort at modelling the behavior expected of—or hoped for in—others who will (reciprocally) "sing hymns [about the virtuous] throughout all time" after they are dead.

Are these posthumous honors, then, the reward for one's (virtuous) labors? If they are, it seems that Hercules' almost unique experience of visiting Hades while still alive may shed light on the ultimate value of that incentive to virtue. It was only Hercules' final labor that required him to visit the afterlife (the only person, until Odysseus, able to do so while alive). Is the absence of a record of any additional labors performed by Hercules a sign that, upon learning in the afterlife what Odysseus learned—namely that the dead do not appear to know about or thereby enjoy honors or praise and, moreover, would trade them in an instant to regain the meanest sort of life[23]—he elected to perform no more? Xenophon—by withholding from the reader the decision made by the young Hercules—seems to be suggesting that, while Hercules may have initially chosen Virtue, he might well have, upon fulfilling the regimen set out by her (or the gods), reversed or undone his choice.

What benefits, then, did Socrates confer on Xenophon, the true addressee of the conversation we have examined? We consider here only the two topics of the conversation with Aristippus: continence and engaging in a life of politics. First, Socrates taught him that "easy and immediate pleasures" are indeed to be resisted, but only on the grounds that they "produce [no science] worth mentioning in the soul" (2.1.20, translation altered). Only by pursuing the higher pleasures—the things of Aphrodite— and thinking them through can one achieve a measure of knowledge. Having gained that knowledge, however, chiefly knowledge of the limits of what we can reasonably expect from our devotion to the higher pleasures, might Xenophon then not be able to enjoy the easy and immediate pleasures for what they are (recall his substitution of "lust" for Socrates' "the things of Aphrodite")?

Xenophon's own continence indeed appears to differ from that of Socrates, who effortlessly gave up all such pleasures for the most pleasant "delight in thinking" (2.1.18; cf. 1.3.11 and 1.6.8). That is, Xenophon made more of an effort to combine other pleasures, in particular that of ruling the Ten Thousand, with the life of the mind. Second, Xenophon learned that Socrates exercised genuine continence chiefly with respect to speech. In speaking to Aristippus, Socrates spoke as though

---

[23] So says the shade of Achilles upon greeting Odysseus in Hades, rejecting as mere "shiny words" Odysseus' reminder that Achilles had been treated "as a god" while alive (*Odyssey*, 11.477–491).

praising—while in fact restraining his praise of—the political life. As perhaps the most ironic writer among philosophers, Xenophon exercised continence in his accounts of Socrates. Yet Xenophon, again resisting Socrates (*Anabasis* 3.1.5–7), later did enter—and excelled at—the life of politics. Socrates appears to have taught him, through the conversation under consideration, how to enter and rise in political life "continently," that is, without "even lay[ing] a claim to rule" (2.1.1).

In conclusion, we need to examine what became of the initial, implicit suggestion made by Socrates to Aristippus that, should one develop the capacity for continence, one could then contemplate engaging in political life or rule. For, in the subsequent discussion, Socrates limited himself to encouraging Aristippus merely to take political life more seriously, at least to the extent of taking the benefits of citizenship (namely security) more seriously. And even Virtue, speaking through Socrates, does no more than offer Hercules the prospect of being honored by "some city" or being admired by all of "Greece" (2.1.28), of becoming an "artisan" or a "trusted guardian of masters of households" (32), culminating in becoming "honored by fatherlands" (33). One need not, as the silence on it implies, become a ruler of a city to "benefit" it in any of these myriad ways. But when we recall that the entire conversation, including the debate between Virtue and Vice, was conducted, not for the sake of Aristippus but for the "companion ... too undisciplined" in the areas of "food, drink, sex, and labors" (2.1.1), whom we have identified as Xenophon himself, the possibility arises of a Socratic form of rule. Only a full account of the *Anabasis* (for which, see Buzzetti 2014) could explain and ground this possibility. But one who desired to rule and was competent to do so, without needing to become "too" disciplined with regard to the pleasures attendant on ruling—and even to be found in ruling itself—and without relying on the expectation that his efforts would be rewarded or even honored might be able to enjoy the labors of the body and the soul alluded to in *Memorabilia* 2.1.

Bibliography

Buzzetti, Eric. Xenophon the Socratic Prince: The Argument of the Anabasis of Cyrus. New York: Palgrave Macmillan, 2014.

Bruell, Christopher "Xenophon," in *History of Political Philosophy*, 3rd ed., Leo Strauss and Joseph Cropsey, eds. Chicago: University of Chicago Press, 1987.

Pangle, Thomas L. The Socratic Way of Life: Xenophon's Memorabilia. Chicago: University of Chicago Press, 2018.

Strauss, Leo. Xenophon's Socrates. Ithaca: Cornell University Press, 1972.

Xenophon. Memorabilia. Translated by Amy L. Bonnette. Ithaca: Cornell University Press, 1994.

8

SNIFFING OUT SWEET SMELLS OF FREEDOM IN XENOPHON'S *SYMPOSIUM*

Thomas R. Martin

"Smells are evocative, perhaps the most instantly evocative of all our human sense impressions ..."—Reginald Hill, *Dialogues of the Dead* (2001), p. 330

Soon after the start of Xenophon's *Symposium*, Socrates discusses smells that socially elite men emit and what those odors signify (2.3–7). He concludes his remarks by linking these smells to "being fine and good" (*kalokagathia*), without commenting further on what that designation indicates. Scholars have not paid much attention to the question why Socrates chooses human smells to introduce this ethical and socio-political concept that figures so prominently in the dialogue.[1] My

---

[1] On *Symp.* 2.3–7, see Bernard Huss, *Xenophons Symposion. Ein Kommentar* (Stuttgart: B. G. Teubner, 1999), 127–131; Gabriel Danzig, "Xenophon's *Symposium*," in Michael Flower, ed., *The Cambridge Companion to Xenophon* (Cambridge: Cambridge University Press, 2017), 136–137; David M. Johnson, *Xenophon's Socratic Works* (London: Routledge, 2021), 209–210, who does not mention the passage on smells in his summary of *Symposium* (192). The abstract noun *kalokagathia* that I render as "being fine and good" is related to the adjectival phrase *kalos kagathos* ("fine and good"). Johnson, *Xenophon's Socratic Works*, discusses the definition of these terms and translates the latter as "noble and good" (26, n. 44); O. J. Todd, *Xenophon IV. Memorabilia and Oeconomicus, Symposium and Apology* (Cambridge: Harvard University Press, 1923), uses "great and good men" (535); Jeffrey

argument here is that Xenophon introduces the subject of smells early on in his narrative to draw his audience's attention to a crucial theme of the *Symposium*: the ambiguities of freedom for Athenians who identify as "fine and good." These uncertainties inherent in freedom even for those whose positions in life render them privileged are revealed above all by the disastrous consequences later suffered in real life by prominent characters in Xenophon's *Symposium*—including above all Socrates—who are portrayed as attending a fancy party whose dramatic date falls near the end of the first decade of the Peloponnesian War (431–404 BCE).

The passage on smells is the first substantive conversation in the *Symposium*.[2] The passage's salience is emphasized by its being expressed in evocative but ambiguous terms that are neither fully contextualized nor explained. To summarize, Socrates proposes that, if his male colleagues at the party want to be all that they should be, they should aim to exude the right kind of smells, the ones that women find pleasing on men who train in a gymnasium while lubricating their muscles. That is, Socrates means the smells of body sweat and of the olive oil that men who have the time and money to work out every day smear on

---

Henderson, *Xenophon IV. Memorabilia, Oeconomicus, Symposium, Apology* (Cambridge, Mass.: Harvard University Press, 2013), revises this translation to "gentlemen" (565); Elisabetta Poddighe and Alberto Esu, "*Kalokagathia*" in Andrew Erskine, David B. Hollander, and Arietta Papaconstantinou, eds., *Encyclopedia of Ancient History* (John Wiley and Sons Online Library, 2021) use "honorable and good" (https://onlinelibrary.wiley.com/doi/book/10.1002/9781444338386). Xenophon's mention of body smells in this context in the *Symposium* is accentuated by their absence in *Mem.* 2.1.28, where Socrates says that Arete, in the story of Heracles' choice, states that, to be good, men need "fatiguing effort" (*ponos*) and "sweat" (*hidrôs*).

[2] The earlier section *Symposium* 1.8–10 on *sôphrôn Erôs* is a reflection by Xenophon as narrator, not a conversation among the symposiasts.

themselves during their training sessions.³ Socrates sums up his point about these odors by saying that men who devote themselves to these "toils of free men" and "activities that first of all are useful and extend over a long period of time" give off smells that are "sweet and free" (2.4).⁴ This is the first—and seemingly a unique—reference in ancient Greek literature to the idea that, for convenience of reference, I am calling "sweet smells of freedom."⁵

---

³ On athletes' use of olive oil, see Stephen G. Miller, *Ancient Greek Athletics* (New Haven: Yale University Press, 2004), 14–16.

⁴ The text here reads *hai d'apo tôn eleutheriôn mochthôn osmai epitêdeumatôn te prôton chrêstôn kai chronou pollou deontai, ei mellousin hêdeiai kai eleutherioi esesthai*. The adjective *hêdeiai* (feminine plural; the lexical entry is *hêdus*) means "sweet" but is also sometimes rendered in English as "pleasant/pleasing." The adverb *hêdeôs* and other adverbial forms of *hêdus* can also be translated as "gladly" (e. g., at *Symp.* 2.14, 16). On *eleutherios* in fourth-century BCE Greek, see Kurt Raaflaub, "Zum Freiheitsbegriff der Griechen. Materialien und Untersuchungen zur Bedeutungsentwicklung von *eleutheros/eleutheria* in der archaischen und klassischen Zeit," in Elisabeth Charlotte Welskopf, ed., *Soziale Typenbegriffe im alten Griechenland und ihr Fortleben in den Sprachen der Welt*, Vol. 4 (Berlin: Akademie-Verlag, 1981), 299–300. Raaflaub, "Democracy, Oligarchy, and the Concept of the 'Free Citizen' in Late Fifth-Century Athens," *Political Theory* 11 (1983): 517–544 says the phrases *eleutherioi technai* ("free skills") and *eleuthera erga* ("free deeds/works") "describe precisely those pursuits that are removed from the immediate and base necessities of life and, therefore, suitable for the truly free person" (531). The adjective *chrêstos* that I am here translating as "useful" is supplied in Xenophon's Greek text by modern editors from the explicit quotation of this passage by Athenaeus 15.686f. The nuances of this term are discussed below.

⁵ This observation is based on searches of the Greek texts in the Perseus Project and the Thesaurus Linguae Graecae databases. Plutarch, *Lysander* 11 ("a sweet drink of freedom," citing Theopompus, a comic author of the late fifth/early fourth centuries BCE) and Lucian, *On Salaried Posts in Great Houses* (*De Mercede*) 8 ("the sweet pleasure of freedom") associate the sensual perception of sweetness with freedom, but the only reference I have found specifically to "sweet freedom" (*eleutheria hêdeia*) is a metaphorical use in the

Elsewhere in Greek literature, sweet smells are said to come from wine, flowers, etc., but usually not from human bodies, in particular not from adult male bodies.[6] In fact, body odors are generally characterized as foul-smelling, especially the smell of sweat from the armpits, which is of course generated by physical activity such as sustained exercise.[7] This incongruity certainly makes Socrates' claim about bodily "sweet smells" noteworthy.

What then, in this passage whose emphasis on smells makes its references to freedom stand out, does Xenophon intend for his audience to think about by introducing this unexpected reference to sweet smells of freedom that emanate from human toils? And why in particular does the passage refer to sweet smells of body sweat and olive oil in relation to toils and useful activities? To provide context for my answer, I will start with relevant points in the *Symposium* that precede the smells passage.

The *Symposium* begins with Xenophon speaking in the first person as the unnamed narrator of the story (1.1). He states that not only the deeds done with "earnestness" by "fine and good

---

scholia to Pindar, *Olympian* 7 (Eugenius Ábel, *Scholia Recentia in Pindari Epinicia* [Budapest: Academia Litterarum Hungaricae, 1890] 273); this entry rephrases the poem's reference to the legendary Tlepolemus' "sweet requital/recompense" (*lutron gluku*, line 77 = 141) for a difficult situation that he had endured. Precise dates for Pindar scholia cannot be established, but the origins of these scholarly comments likely lie in the Hellenistic period, that is, after Xenophon's time. See Mary Lefkowitz, "The Pindar Scholia," *American Journal of Philology* 106 (1985): 269.

[6] See, for example Homer, *Ody.* 9.210 for wine; *Homeric Hymns* 2.13 for flowers, 4.131–2 for sacrificial meat. Kakia ("Vice") in Xenophon, *Mem.* 2.1.24 tells Heracles that she provides things that are enjoyable to smell, without naming them.

[7] Mireille M. Lee, *Body, Dress, and Identity in Ancient Greece* (Cambridge: Cambridge University Press, 2015), 65–66. On armpit odor, see Aristophanes, *Clouds* 852 and Theophrastus, *On Sweat* 9.

men" but also their "childish play activities" seem worth remembering. He then explains that he wants to make clear the identities of the people whose company allowed him to acquire this "knowing." These two sentences opening the dialogue seem to be a claim by Xenophon that he was present at this particular symposium, but it appears that in reality he was too young to have been a guest: the dramatic date of the party is 422 or 421 BCE, and Xenophon had been born probably less than a decade earlier.[8] Xenophon apparently composed his *Symposium* in the 370s or 360s BCE; whether his mid-fourth century BCE contemporaries would have grasped the likely anachronism of him intimating that he had been a guest at a gathering held when he

---

[8] The fictive date of the *Symposium* is derived from Xenophon saying that Callias is holding the party to celebrate a recent athletic victory at the Panathenaic Festival by the young man Autolycus, son of Lycon. On the date of this particular festival, see Donald G. Kyle, *Athletics in Ancient Athens* (Leiden: Brill, 1987), 198, A12 Autolykos; Debra Nails, *The People of Plato. A Prosopography of Plato and Other Socratics* (Indianapolis: Hackett Publishing, 2002), 62, 301; Fiona Hobden, *Xenophon* (London: Bloomsbury Academic, 2020), 5. On Xenophon's birth date, see Shane Brennan, "Introduction," in Shane Brennan and David Thomas, eds., *The Landmark Xenophon's Anabasis* (New York: Pantheon Books, 2021), xvii. Adolescent males could be invited to observe and assist at symposiums, but they needed at least to be in their early teens; see Marek Wecowski, *The Rise of the Greek Aristocratic Banquet* (Oxford: Oxford University Press, 2014), 34. Athenaeus 5.216d understands Xenophon as claiming to have been present at this symposium even though he was in fact not old enough to have done so. Todd, *Xenophon IV*, comments that it seems right "to suspect that we must not consider [this] work as an historical document (though possibly based on an actual occurrence)" (530). Leo Strauss, *Xenophon's Socrates* (Ithaca: Cornell University Press, 1972), concludes that Xenophon "presented himself in the *Symposium* as an invisible and inaudible participant ..." (144). Henderson, *Xenophon IV*, says Xenophon's statement "need not be a claim that he was present, but merely that he himself had attended symposia with [the named guests], which is both historically possible and likely" (561).

was still very young we cannot know.[9]

Whatever the case, the *Symposium*'s first sentences would surely have led Xenophon's audience to anticipate hearing from or about Xenophon as a guest later on in the course of the narrative once the narrative turned to the symposiasts' conversations.[10] Therefore, readers of the *Symposium* would have been surprised to discover that Xenophon nowhere speaks as a character in the dialogue and indeed is not even mentioned in it; he only functions as its anonymous narrator. As a result, the *Symposium*'s audience learned from the dialogue's opening that, in trying to understand the implications of Socrates' expression "sweet smells of freedom," they should reflect on what it means that Xenophon had begun the work by presenting implicit ambiguities: was he present at the party or not, and why does he never make the answer clear? How in this context of ambiguity, they would have wanted to know, did Xenophon actually acquire his "knowing"?

In sum, the *Symposium*'s first sentences set up Xenophon's audience, then and now, to realize that not everything in the dialogue can be taken at face value, that ambiguity hides

---

[9] On the complex question of the date of composition of Xenophon's *Symposium*, see Holger Thesleff, "The Interrelation and Date of the *Symposia* of Plato and Xenophon," *Bulletin of the Institute of Classical Studies* 25 (1978): 157–170; Huss, *Xenophons Symposion*, 13–18, 72; Gabriel Danzig, "Intra-Socratic Polemics: The *Symposia* of Plato and Xenophon," *Greek, Roman, and Byzantine Studies* 45 (2005): 331–357, and "Introduction to the Comparative Study of Plato and Xenophon," in Gabriel Danzig, David Johnson, and Donald Morrison, eds., *Plato and Xenophon: Comparative Studies* (Leiden: Brill, 2018), 1–30; Henderson, *Xenophon IV*, 560; Benjamin McCloskey, "Xenophon the Philosopher: *E Pluribus Plura*," *American Journal of Philology* 138 (2017): 605–640; Robin Waterfield, "Xenophon and Socrates," in *The Landmark Xenophon's* Anabasis (2021), 267–276.

[10] Gabriel Danzig, "Apologetic Elements in Xenophon's *Symposium*," *Classica et Mediaevalia* 55 (2004): 19.

beneath what scholars generally regard as its lighthearted, cordial, and prosperous surface.[11] In other words, the audience from the start learns that they need to find a way to discover the message concealed in Xenophon's narrative, to discover how —to use an expression apt for analysis of a passage on smells—to proceed in sniffing out his concealed meanings.[12]

An initial point to notice in this context is that Xenophon's contemporary Greek audience would have known that his reference to "fine and good men" in the dialogue's opening

---

[11] At the same time, they acknowledge that the dialogue concerns important philosophical points. See, e. g., W. E. Higgins, *Xenophon the Athenian: The Problem of the Individual and the Society of the* Polis (Albany: State University of New York Press, 1977),18; Robert C. Bartlett, *Xenophon. The Shorter Writings. "Apology of Socrates to the Jury," "Oeconomicus," and "Symposium"* (Ithaca: Cornell University Press, 1996), 173; Danzig 2004, 17; Mark J. Thomas, "The Playful and the Serious: A Reading of Xenophon's *Symposium*," *Epoché* 15 (2011): 263–278; Vivienne J. Gray, *Xenophon's Mirror of Princes. Reading the Reflections* (Oxford: Oxford University Press, 2011), 334; Danzig 2017, 135; Hobden, *Xenophon*, 45. Katarzyna Jazdzewska, "Laughter in Plato's and Xenophon's *Symposia*," in Danzig, *et al.*, eds., *Plato and Xenophon* (2018), 193–199 discusses the ambiguity of laughter in Xenophon's *Symposium*, judging Xenophon to be more light-hearted than Plato in his *Symposium*. On the issue of categorizing Xenophon's *Symposium* as a type of historical fiction, see Danzig 2004; Huss, *Xenophons Symposion*, 38–49; Noreen Humble, "Xenophon of Athens," in Koen De Temmerman, ed., *Oxford Handbook of Ancient Biography* (Oxford: Oxford University Press, 2020), 111–124; Irene Madreiter, "*Cyropaedia* and the Greek 'Novel' Again: History and Perspectives of a Supposed Generic Relationship," in Bruno Jacobs, ed., *Ancient Information on Persia Re-assessed: Xenophon's* Cyropaedia. *Proceedings of a Conference Held at Marburg in Honour of Christopher J. Tuplin, December 1–2, 2017* (Wiesbaden: Harrassowitz, 2020), 19–43. Athenaeus 5.187f-188d, 216c-217a criticizes Xenophon's *Symposium* as ambiguous for presenting an inconsistent portrayal of Socrates, as well as being anachronistic in its dramatic date.

[12] Higgins, *Xenophon the Athenian*, observes that "the *Symposium* builds upon a clear perception of a situation which is so described as to lead to the awareness that there is more to something than its surface" (19–20).

sentences points to a prominent ambiguity about social ranking and the responsibility of citizens at Athens during Xenophon's time. In his era, Athenians could and did disagree over who among them were entitled to the designation "fine and good" and what sort of activities those deserving that appellation were supposed to practice in order to live up to the implications of this special standing in Athenian society. So, Xenophon's audience knew that the focus in his *Symposium* on activities conducted by these so-called "fine and good" men creating "sweet smells of freedom" concerned the question how to define who qualified as elite in Athenian democracy and what vocabulary to use in describing this status.[13] Since Xenophon in his *Oeconomicus* has Ischomachus use the description of "fine and good" to categorize slaves who behave appropriately toward their master (14.1–10), Xenophon clearly recognized the ambiguities encompassed by the label "fine and good."[14]

The socio-political challenge of figuring out who and what exemplified "being fine and good" had in fact developed earlier in Athenian history and then continued to evolve in the fourth century BCE. Modern scholars have devoted many pages to discussing this subject.[15] All I can do here is stress that

---

[13] Matthew R. Christ, *Xenophon and the Athenian Democracy: The Education of an Elite Citizenry* (Cambridge: Cambridge University Press, 2020), discusses how the *Symposium* offers "evidence of Xenophon's communications with his elite Athenian readers concerning their proper role in the democratic city" (102–125). See also Johnson, *Xenophon's Socratic Works*, 233–234, 262.

[14] Ingomar Weiler, "Inverted *Kalokagathia*," *Slavery & Abolition. A Journal of Slave and Post-Slave Studies* 23 (2002): 9–28 discusses the reversal of the aesthetic aspect of *kalokagathia* in the representations of slaves' bodies.

[15] On *kalokagathia* and *kalokagathos* in Xenophon's *Symposium*, see Huss, *Xenophons Symposion*, 61–64; F. Roscalla, "*Kalokagathia* e *kalakagathoi* in Senfonte," in Christopher Tuplin, ed., *Xenophon and his World* (Stuttgart: Franz Steiner, 2004), 115–124; Fiona Hobden, "How to Be a Good

Xenophon's striking reference to "sweet smells of freedom" belongs to a fraught socio-political context in Athenian democracy, and that it emphasizes the ongoing effort needed for even elite citizens to "sniff out" the meanings of being fine, good, and free.

After his initial comments as narrator in the *Symposium*, Xenophon begins his story with Callias happening upon Socrates and four companions in the street and inviting them to join the symposium that he has already planned for later that day. Callias is an Athenian who claims the status of a "fine and good man," as will become clear from the wealth he expends on the quality and quantity of the provisions and entertainment he

---

Symposiast and Other Lessons from Xenophon's *Symposium*," *Proceedings of the Cambridge Philological Society* 50 (2004): 121–140; on the *Memorabilia*, see Christ, *Xenophon and the Athenian Democracy*, 65–71. For wider discussions of these designations for the socially elite, see, for example, Walter Donlan, "The Origins of *Kalos Kagathos*," *American Journal of Philology* 94 (1973): 365–374; Brigitte Johanna Schulz, "Bezeichnung und Selbstbezeichnung der Aristokraten und Oligarchen in der griechischen Literatur von Homer bis Aristoteles," in Elisabeth Charlotte Welskopf, ed., *Soziale Typenbegriffe im alten Griechenland und ihr Fortleben in den Sprachen der Welt.* Vol. 3. (Berlin: Akademie-Verlag, 1981), 67–155; John B. Weaver "The Noble and Good Heart: *Kalokagathia* in Luke's Parable of the Sower," in Patricia Gray and Gail R. O'Day, eds., *Scripture and Traditions: Essays in Early Judaism and Christianity in Honor of Carl R. Holladay* (Leiden: Brill, 2008), 151–171; Irena Martinkova, "How to Understand *Kalokagathia?*," *Telesna Kulturá* 35 (2012): 93–105; Poddighe and Esu, "*Kalokagathia*;" Noreen Humble, *Xenophon of Athens: A Socratic on Sparta* (Cambridge: Cambridge University Press, 2022), 154–158. On these concepts as applied to modernity, see Elena Nikityuk, "*Kalokagathia*: to a Question on Formation of an Image of the Ideal Person in Antiquity and During Modern Time," *Studia Antiqua et Archaeologia* 25 (2019): 429–442; Thomas L. Pangle, *The Socratic Way of Life: Xenophon's* Memorabilia (Cambridge: Cambridge University Press, 2018), and *Socrates Founding Political Philosophy in Xenophon's* Economist, Symposium, *and* Apology (Chicago: University of Chicago Press, 2020).

provides for his guests, as well as by his craving for status and respect.[16] He tells Socrates that he wants to add him and friends to his guest list for the party because he desires to heighten the gathering's "brightness" by inviting men "purified in their souls" and therefore seriously knowledgeable about philosophy (1.4).

These seemingly cordial comments elicit an indignant, almost hostile reply from Socrates. In what seems a remarkably incongruous response to a party invitation, Socrates calls out Callias for always looking down on him and his friends (1.5). Socrates explicitly accuses Callias of having previously disdained them because they had not been professionally trained in "wisdom" (*sophia*) by paid teachers, as had Callias, but instead were autodidacts in "philosophy" (*philosophia*).[17] Does Socrates' bristling and extended reply indicate that he knows Callias does not regard him and his colleagues as members of the self-asserting and exclusive fraternity of the "fine and good" to which Callias clearly sees himself as belonging? Xenophon's audience is not told.

Callias tries to lower the rhetorical heat of the encounter by proclaiming that he wants to demonstrate to his newly invited guests that he is worthy of their "earnestness" (1.6), a term repeated from the dialogue's opening sentence. He means that he wants them to take him seriously when he speaks about serious things. When Socrates and his companions now politely decline the invitation, Callias becomes visibly angry. In response to this escalation of emotion, Socrates and his friends agree to show up at the party; this reversal seems an odd reaction to an unwelcome behest by an irate non-friend who has no way to

---

[16] See Johnson, *Xenophon's Socratic Works*, on the "fine and good" being "motivated by praise and honor" (262).

[17] See Tazuko Angela van Berkel, "Socratic Economics and the Psychology of Money," in Danzig *et al.*, eds., *Plato and Xenophon* (2018), 391–430 on Xenophon's rejection of taking fees for teaching.

compel obedience to his wishes. Once again, however, Xenophon provides his audience with no explanation for this baffling outcome to the episode. It can only accentuate the audience's notice of the *Symposium*'s attention to ambiguity, spurring them to ponder why Socrates and his companions yield to Callias despite, according to Socrates, this rich Athenian having always scorned them.

The scene in the dialogue then shifts to the commencement of the symposium at Callias' house. The original invitees arrive, with the narrator adding the (at this point) seemingly unmotivated description of their previously having exercised in a gymnasium and having been smeared with olive oil, with some also having visited a bath (1.7). The motivation for including this uncontextualized information will be revealed subsequently when Socrates introduces the topic of smells.

Next, Xenophon mentions Autolycus, the youthful athlete who is the honorand of the symposium (1.8–10). The guests are said to appreciate Autolycus for his "beauty (*kallos*), modesty (*aidôs*), and self-control (*sôphrosyne*)." Xenophon as narrator adds that the symposiasts' gazing on the youth's possession of these qualities strongly affects everyone present in their souls, especially Callias, who is erotically fixated on the young athlete. Xenophon adds that the young man's attractiveness is created by the powerful effect of the god "Love with Self-Control" (*sôphrôn Erôs*), a category of love between men that Socrates in the penultimate section of the *Symposium* (8.1–43) will insist must mean love without physical sex, or at least not intercourse.

Next comes the unconventional entry to the gathering of the comic entertainer Philip when the invited guests are already eating (1.11–16). He presents himself as an uninvited addition to the party in search of a meal and demonstrates through his initial interchange with the guests his ability to fake an emotional response to attract the attention of his audience. The ambiguity of his behavior, this episode makes clear, is the key to his effectiveness as a performer. Next, the hired entertainers— two girls, a boy, and their Syracusan boss—enter the scene to begin their performance in front of the party-goers (2.1–2). This entertainment, too, will turn out to embody ambiguity, when at the end of the dialogue a supposedly performative scene of het-erosexual attraction appears to the audience to be a genuine demonstration of true love (9.2–7).

At this point, Socrates compliments Callias for having pro-vided his guests "a blameless dinner" and "the sweetest sights and sounds" (2.2). Socrates' choice of words here emphasizes the human senses and their ability to contribute to positive experi-ences. This emphasis connects his remarks to the following sec-tion of the dialogue (2.3–7) in which, as mentioned above, Soc-rates turns in notable detail to the topic of smells. The smells section begins when Callias, in response to Socrates' praise of his arrangements for food and entertainment, proposes to have perfumes now brought in to be applied to the (exclusively male) party-guests.[18] Callias says that this additional party favor would allow his guests, in addition to taking pleasure in tastes, sounds, and sights, to enjoy a "good smell" (euôdia).

Socrates immediately says "No way!" (Mêdamôs). In my opinion, Socrates' emotive reply to Callias' offer to provide per-fumes for his guests to increase their delight in the party's envi-ronment is an aggressively negative response to his host's appar-ently good-natured proposal.[19] Moreover, the force of Socrates' reply seems to resemble that of his earlier initially negative re-sponse to Callias' spur-of-the-moment invitation to the sympo-sium. In short, this interchange suggests a further ambiguity in

---

[18] See Lee, 61–65 on the role of perfumes in Greek society.

[19] The translation by Todd, *Xenophon IV*, ("No, indeed!") seems closer to the implied emotion of Socrates' response than Henderson, *Xenophon IV* ("Please don't!").

the atmosphere at the party—the potential for hostility to erupt at any point in an ostensibly relaxed, good-natured gathering.[20] Socrates then proceeds to elaborate his opposition to Callias' definition of "good smell." From what Socrates says next, Xenophon's audience can deduce that Socrates regards the nature of smells as embodying a crucial ambiguity: what are *good* smells? The answer, Socrates reveals, depends first on gender: women should have different smells from men. Accordingly, men certainly do not put on perfume to appeal to other men, Socrates says. He then adds that newly-wed women need apply no additional perfume, presumably implying that their smell is pleasant as a by-product of enjoyable exertions in married heterosexual sex. Women, Socrates adds, regard the smell of the olive oil smeared on men when they are exercising as sweeter than the smell of perfume.

He then proceeds to the crucially important point about the problem with the smells that come from perfume: they smell the same on slaves as on free men (2.4). The significance of this remark is that it presents a question about the ambiguous nature of freedom: how is the status of freedom to be identified? Perfume does not help because its odor, no matter how strong or pleasing, cannot resolve the ambiguity of whether an unknown person whom one encounters is enslaved or free.

It is important to note that Xenophon did not fabricate the existence at contemporary Athens of the importance, at least for the socially elite, of this issue of the ambiguity concerning how to determine whether someone is free or not. We know this from the anonymous work entitled *Constitution of the Athenians*,

---

[20] Danzig, "Xenophon's *Symposium*," 136 and Johnson, *Xenophon's Socratic Works*, 209–210 think that Socrates' response is not aggressive. I, however, conclude that it corresponds with the observation by Higgins, *Xenophon the Athenian* that "[d]inner at Kallias' … becomes more and more sinister" (17).

which erroneously became included among Xenophon's genuine literary products.[21] This political treatise was evidently composed in the latter portion of the fifth century BCE, the same general chronological context in which the dramatic date of Xenophon's *Symposium* falls. Overall, the *Constitution* criticizes Athenian democracy as unfair to the city-state's socially elite citizens, whom it calls the *chrêstoi* (sing. *chrêstos*), literally meaning "the useful" (on which term see below). In particular, Athens' constitution is said to be unjust because it is designed to satisfy the needs and wishes of the masses, the *dêmos*, who in this work are often labelled the *ponêroi* (sing. *ponêros*), "the wicked."[22] Nevertheless, the treatise explains, Athens' democratic constitution will endure despite its injustice because it favors the masses, and the Athenian elite should have no hope of democracy being replaced by an oligarchy simply as a result of their immoral treatment (as judged from their point of view) by the city-state's direct democracy.

The *Constitution* (1.10–11) explicitly documents the ambiguity about the concealed nature of the status of freedom in democratic Athens by explaining that, if at Athens it were legal to strike physically a slave (or ex-slave or legal immigrant), you would frequently hit a legitimate citizen by mistake on the assumption that this person was a slave. This is, the treatise claims, because at Athens the mass of free citizens—the "many"—not

---

[21] For introductions to this work, see G. W. Bowersock, trans., "Pseudo-Xenophon. Constitution of the Athenians," *Xenophon VII. Scripta Minora* (Cambridge, Mass.: Harvard University Press, 1968), 461–473; Robin Osborne, ed. and trans., *The Old Oligarch: Pseudo-Xenophon's Constitution of the Athenians* (London: The London Association of Classical Teachers, 2017), 1–17; Dominique Lenfant, ed. and trans., *Pseudo-Xénophon: Constitution des Athéniens* (Paris: Les Belles Lettres, 2018), I-CLIX.

[22] Osborne, *The Old Oligarch*, 18 lists all the terms in the *Constitution* referring to "oligarchs" and "democrats."

only wear the same clothing as slaves or immigrants and dress no better than they do, but they are also no better in their physiques than are slaves. Furthermore, Athenians even let some slaves live in luxury. These comments in the treatise reveal that the classical-era Athenian social elite could in fact be faced with the puzzle of how to distinguish slaves from free people based on their outer appearances. In other words, at Athens in Xenophon's time, people's status *vis-à-vis* freedom was visually ambiguous.

Socrates wraps up this section of the passage on smells by, as noted above at the start, specifying that men need to give off the smells of "the toils of free men" and "activities that first of all are useful and also are done for a long time" rather than smelling of perfume. Only by exhibiting these characteristics, Socrates concludes, can men give off smells that are "sweet and free" (2.4).

Xenophon's audience would have recognized that the words he employs in this context in the *Symposium* are meant to draw their attention to the question of what kind of life defines freedom and how to determine whether someone is free, at least in the sense of being free that would be acceptable to the socially elite characters in the dialogue. The word Xenophon uses that is here translated as "toil" (*mochthos*) is rare in prose before Xenophon's time.[23] It is also noteworthy for its emphasis on toils being exertions that are difficult, uncomfortable, and even dangerous.[24] For example, this word can designate the onerous and

---

[23] See Vivienne J. Gray, "Xenophon's Language and Expression," in Flower, ed., *The Cambridge Companion to Xenophon* (2017), 238 on Xenophon's use of rare words; cf. Huss, *Xenophons Symposion*, 127–128."

[24] For this reason, I think *mochthos* is a more salient word choice by Xenophon than the Greek word *ponos*, which is translated and discussed as "toil" by Steven Johnstone, "Virtuous Toil, Vicious Work: Xenophon on Aristocratic Style," *Classical Philology* 89 (1994): 219–240.

potentially fatal "labors" that were imposed on the famously un-willing super-hero Heracles (Sophocles, *Trachiniae* lines 1101, 1170). Moreover, Xenophon in the *Cyropaedia* (1.6.25) uses this word to indicate the type of painful situations that a leader needs to endure so that he can convincingly demonstrate that he will be successful in leading those whom he rules. In addi-tion, he makes clear that the toils necessary for effective leader-ship must often be conducted in contexts of exertion involving pain and suffering. As for the adjective that Xenophon uses in the *Symposium* to characterize toils as being those undertaken by a "free man" (*eleutherios*), it also stands out because it was an epithet applied to Zeus.[25]

Finally, Xenophon's term *chrêstos* that I am rendering as "useful" amounts to a virtual Venn diagram of multiple overlaps of meanings. In its literal meaning, it can be applied to tools. When applied to human beings, it can have a strong moral con-notation, leading to its often being translated into English as "good" or "honest." In fact, other passages from Xenophon's works show it sometimes used interchangeably with the Greek adjective most commonly translated as "good" (*agathos*). Espe-cially important for my argument is that by Xenophon's time this term "useful" had become a buzz word in the Athenian con-text referenced above in connection with the *Constitution of the Athenians*, namely the controversy over who counted as elite and who did not: the *Constitution* uses the term "useful" numerous times to indicate "the few, the well-born, the rich" at Athens."[26]

---

[25] See, for example, Xenophon, *Oec.* 7.1. On this adjective, see Raaflaub 1981.

[26] Schulz, 109–111 discusses this term in the *Constitution*. Elisabeth Charlotte Welskopf. ed., *Soziale Typenbegriffe im alten Griechenland und ihr Fortleben in den Sprachen der Welt*. Vol. 2 (Berlin: Akademie-Verlag, 1985), cols. 1968–1978 cites the instances of *chrêstos* in classical-era Greek litera-ture.

The occurrences of this word in other works of Xenophon fully display its complex lexical spectrum, that is, the ambiguities of interpretation arising from the implications of its possible meanings. Perhaps most strikingly, Xenophon can apply this word to characterize both slaves as "useful = good" (*Oec.* 9.5, 12.19). In the context of the social status of free men, in his *Memorabilia* Xenophon uses this term multiple times in discussion of the issue of who is "fine and good" and how these elite individuals should behave.[27] In sum, it appears that Xenophon's conjunction of the prominent but multivalent terms "toils" and "useful activities" in the *Symposium*'s passage on smells gives his audience reason to ponder what these terms would mean in the context of freedom.

In fact, by doing this, Xenophon was perhaps building on this thought-provoking wording by implicitly drawing his audience's attention to a drama by a renowned and remembered author. In 409 BCE when Xenophon was a young adult, the famous playwright Sophocles had his tragedy *Philoctetes* presented to a mass audience at Athens. Xenophon could have seen the play in person and remembered it for its success—it won first prize in the theatrical competition—and perhaps also for its daunting political implications for leading citizens during what had become a prolonged period of political crisis for Athenian democracy as the Peloponnesian War lurched on into its third decade and conflict erupted between pro-oligarchical and pro-democratic Athenians.[28]

In Sophocles' play, the tragic hero Philoctetes begs the

---

[27] See 1.2.20, 1.3.3, 2.3.17, 2.4.5, 2.5.5, 2.6.14, 2.6.20, 2.6.28, and 2.9.8.

[28] On possible political implications of this play, see Michael H. Jameson, "Politics and the *Philoctetes*," *Classical Philology* 51 (1956): 221–227, and Osborne, "Sophocles and Contemporary Politics," in Kirk Ormand, ed., *A Companion to Sophocles* (Malden, Mass.: Wiley-Blackwell, 2012), 270–286.

young warrior Neoptolemus to free him from his solitary exile on a desert island that the Greek leader Odysseus had forced on Philoctetes at the time of the Trojan War. Philoctetes tells Neoptolemus that he knows that liberating him would take "toil," but that it would be worthwhile for Neoptolemus to endure this painful exertion because rescuing him from his miserable state of non-freedom would be to do something "useful" that would become well-known and therefore add to the youth's reputation (ll. 476–480). That Sophocles intertwined these terms to create a sense of urgency about Philoctetes' plight underlines how meaningful the implications of these particular words could be in the context of the significance of freedom as a contested status in Xenophon's Athens.

To return to the *Symposium*: immediately after Socrates proposes that "sweet smells of freedom" are created by "toils of free men" and their "useful" activities, the discussion moves to a further characteristic of the significance of smells (2.4). Lycon, the father of Autolycus, asks Socrates what smells men can have when, like Lycon himself, they are too old to exercise as younger men can. Lycon's point is that older men can no longer acquire the smells of sweat and olive oil that men in the physical prime of their life earn by working out hard and long, with the goal of becoming physically attractive and gaining the strength and conditioning necessary to serve in Athens' citizen militia.[29]

Socrates succinctly replies to Lycon that older men should smell of the quality of "being fine and good." Like Xenophon with his reference at the very start of the dialogue to "fine and good men," Socrates says absolutely nothing here about the specific meaning of this concept. Pressed by Lycon on how a man

---

[29] See David M. Pritchard, *Athenian Democracy at War* (Cambridge: Cambridge University Press, 2019), 193–196 on the close connection between strenuous athletics and war for the social elite.

can acquire what Lycon calls "the ointment" that brings this smell of "being fine and good," Socrates says it cannot come from buying perfumes. He then quotes the sixth-century BCE poet Theognis on the need to spend time in the company of men who are "noble" (*esthlos*) rather than "bad" (*kakos*). Lycon (2.5) takes this advice to refer to the company that his son ought to keep. Socrates replies that the young man is certainly doing this correctly, at least so far as his training in martial arts is concerned.

Unfortunately, a significant gap in the preserved Greek text has almost totally obscured Socrates' culminating remarks in this section of the dialogue. All we can say is that this poorly preserved fragment does appear to include a word meaning "to look carefully for or at, to examine thoroughly" (*skeptomai*). When we again have a continuous text (2.6), the party-goers are starting to discuss yet another ambiguity: is it possible to be taught, or even to learn, the (to us missing) knowledge that Socrates had just expressed about how Autolykus should act? At this point, the remarkable passage on smells comes to an abrupt halt when Socrates flatly says this "ambiguous" (*amphilogos*) topic should be left for another time. He cuts off any further discussion of the apparently obvious ambiguity of human smells by calling for the entertainment to resume with a performance by a female acrobat/dancer (2.7).

This brusque termination of the passage on "sweet smells of freedom" reinforces the thematic prominence of the ambiguity of what that phrase actually signifies. That is, Socrates' audience, then and now, is left wondering what could be the deep meaning(s) of what I am calling "sweet smells of freedom." To smell like that, exactly what are men supposed to do throughout their lives besides high-level physical training? And if they do engage in the proper "useful" activities throughout their lives, what will that commitment indicate about them socially and politically?

Finally, what can they expect to be the benefit of going to such lengths to exert themselves so as to have "sweet and free" smells by engaging in "the toils of free men" and continuously engaging in "useful pursuits"? No explicit answers have been provided so far in the dialogue—and neither will they be in the subsequent sections of the dialogue, as it turns out.

In sum, Xenophon in his *Symposium* presents his audience with a number of questions for which clear answers are not forthcoming. In the specific context of the possible meaning(s) of freedom, in particular as applied to the "fine and good," Xenophon indicates the existence of ambiguities that the "fine and good" need to detect and then contemplate how to address. This emphasis on the necessity to explore ambiguities of freedom explains why Xenophon introduces the topic of smells early on in the *Symposium* with such prominence.

Passages in other works of Xenophon support this interpretation by stressing the value of smells both as effective signs of status and also as guides in uncovering prizes well worth acquiring.[30] In his *Memorabilia* (1.4.5–6), Xenophon makes this importance of smells for human beings unmistakable by having Socrates explain that we gain the "benefit" of our senses, including that of smell, as a result of the "foresight" of "he who from the start creates human beings." In other words, our ability to smell has a premediated divine origin. It should also be noted that Xenophon is not alone in attributing special value to the human sense of smell: Hippocrates, Plato, and Aristotle in

---

[30] This is a point memorably made by Herodotus, whose history was probably published when Xenophon was a young man: smell is the sense that allows the Pythia to answer Croesus' question about what he was doing at the moment when she was fielding his question (1.47), and it is smell that allows giant ants in the East who mine gold to detect humans trying to steal their treasure (3.105).

different ways make the same point about sniffing out smells.[31] In short, the sense of smell is valuably salient for human beings in their interactions with the natural world, especially with other people.[32]

In Xenophon's *Oeconomicus*, the strong significance of the ethical benefit that human beings can derive from this particular sense emerges clearly in an extended episode in which Socrates gives advice to Critobulus. (4.1–25). When Critobulus asks what are the best types of knowledge for him to learn in order to improve his management of his household and property, Socrates begins his lengthy explanation by scorning the kinds of knowledge that "banausic workers" possess. This judgment is particularly relevant to Xenophon's *Symposium* because Antisthenes there (3.4) contrasts "banausic skill" (*banusanikê technê*) with "being fine and good." Banausic labor, Socrates archly comments in the *Oeconomicus*, requires men to work indoors in manufacturing, thereby feminizing their bodies and weakening their souls. Moreover, these men's occupations take

---

[31] Jin Yin Tan, "From Hippocrates to COVID-19: sniffing out the disease," *ENT & Audiology News* July 2021 (https://www.entandaudiologynews.com/features/history-of-ent/post/from-hippocrates-to-covid-19-sniffing-out-the-disease); Mark A. Johnstone, "Aristotle on Odour and Smell," in Brad Inwood, ed., *Oxford Studies in Ancient Philosophy* Vol. 43 (Oxford: Oxford University Press, 2012), 143–183.

[32] As one example, magic featured very prominently in ancient thought and life, and, as Britta K. Ager remarks, "smells [provided] a uniquely appropriate mental model for understanding what magic was and how it worked" (*The Scent of Ancient* Magic [Ann Arbor, Michigan: University of Michigan Press, 2022], 3). A particularly lamentable example of the significance of the human sense of smell in the context of interactions with other people is the history of its use in making invidious distinctions among groups. In the words of Steven Kruger, "Race and Sexuality," in Thomas Hahn, ed., *A Cultural History of Race. In the Middle Ages. Vol. 2* (London: Bloomsbury Academic, 2021), "Racialization also operates around the sense of smell [as well as the other senses]" (163).

up so much time that it makes them bad friends and also bad defenders of their homelands. Socrates then tells Critobulus that in choosing good kinds of knowledge, he should imitate the king of the Persians by focusing on farming and the "science of war." Critobulus responds incredulously to Socrates' report that the Persian king takes part in farming.[33] Socrates responds that the king's concern for national flourishing and defense in fact motivates him to oversee agriculture in his territories.

Smells then enter the conversation when Socrates informs Critobulus that the king indeed spends a great deal of his time in a way that, through its attention to fostering domesticated plant life, is also related to farming. That context is a "paradise" (*paradeisos*), an enormous and luxurious private garden and hunting reserve created for the enjoyment of the Persian royal family (*Oec.* 4.13).[34] Socrates then elaborates his point about Persian kings and farming by telling Critobulus the story of a meeting between the Spartan general Lysander and Cyrus the Younger (d. 401 BCE). Xenophon of course knew Cyrus personally from having served in his expedition seeking to seize the throne in Persia at the end of the fifth century and indeed describes the meeting between Cyrus and Lycurgus (*Hell.* 1.5.1–7).

Xenophon has Socrates report that Cyrus informs Lysander that he—a prospective king of a giant empire—in fact performed physical labor to help with the planting of his own paradise. In his description of this retreat's attractions, Cyrus

---

[33] Johnson, *Xenophon's Socratic Works*, discusses "Socrates' motivational speech on farming" (242–247) and also the discussion of farming attributed to Socrates in *Oec.* 15–20 (262–266).

[34] Xenophon in *Anab.* 1.2.7, *Hell.* 4.1.15, and *Oec.* 4.13–17, 20–24 is the first Greek author to use the word "paradise." See Bruce Lincoln, *'Happiness for Mankind.' Achaemenian Religion and the Imperial Project* (Leuven: Peters, 2012) 7, 66–68.

includes the sweet smells of its plants as contributing to its fabulous ambience of pleasure (4.21). Cyrus then concludes his revelation about his exertions as a horticultural laborer outdoors by adding that he never has dinner without previously having "worked up a sweat" (*hidrôsai*) in activities related to war, agriculture, or competition (4.24).[35] Lysander's reply concludes the story: Cyrus deserves to be "fortunate/happy" because he is a "good" man.[36]

So, Xenophon's story proclaims, Cyrus prides himself not only on the smells of the flowers in his royal paradise but also on the sweat and therefore the body odor that he generates by exerting himself in physical activities specifically related to his exalted socio-political ranking in his world. For Cyrus, these smells would be sweet smells of monarchic dominance, not of the freedom of a citizen in a democracy. But through this striking tale that surprises Socrates' Athenian interlocutor, Xenophon does mark out "sweet smells" as signals of an elite individual's personal commitment to non-banausic activities and therefore elevated social status. In Xenophon's *Symposium*, sweet smells of freedom correspondingly indicate the valued status of being an elite-level free "fine and good" citizen in Athenian democracy.

Other passages in Xenophon's works underline the specific benefit of smell in helping people discover hidden things of value. Just as the smell of Cyrus' flowers and sweat can reveal his special status, so, too, the central role of smells in successful hunting proves their high value for locating and acquiring

---

[35] Thanassis Samaras, "Leisured Aristocrats or Warrior-Farmers? Leisure in Plato's *Laws*," *Classical Philology* 107 (2012): 5–6 discusses this episode.

[36] Vivienne J. Gray, *The Character of Xenophon's* Hellenica (Baltimore: The Johns Hopkins University Press, 1989), 14–22 considers the wider context of this meeting.

concealed prizes. In the *Cyropaedia,* the father of Cyrus the Great (*ca.* 600–530 BCE), the future founder of the Persian Empire, tells his young son that he can improve his chances for inventing successful stratagems for prevailing over their enemies in war if he applies techniques that he can learn from hunting wild game (1.6.39–41). One of those techniques is to breed dogs specialized to discover the location of rabbits by detecting their smells even when the prey is concealed by the darkness of night (1.6.40).[37] Xenophon also makes this same point in the *Memorabilia* (3.11.8), a repetition that indicates the importance he places on the significance of smells for gaining desirable but elusive knowledge and its concrete payoffs.

Xenophon's work *On Hunting* further develops this point about the value of smells. This essay devotes considerable space to the practical details of preparing for and executing successful hunts, in particular by fielding dogs trained to employ their senses, especially that of smell, to detect their elusive quarries. Xenophon is explicit, however, that his overall goal in the work is to set forth the educational and moral values to be gained from learning how to hunt.[38] That this seemingly technical guide about a practical skill in fact has this wider, non-technical purpose is made clear near its end (13.7), where Xenophon explicitly states that he is writing to make people "wise and good"—and, it is important to note here, because he wants his writings thereby to be "useful" (*chrêsima*). It can hardly be an

---

[37] A. A. Phillips and M. M. Wilcock, *Xenophon and Arrian On Hunting (KYNEGETIKOS)* (Warminster: Aris and Phillips, 1999), 140–146 discuss "The theory of scent and the nature of the hare."

[38] Stephen Kidd, "Xenophon's *Cynegeticus* and its Defense of Liberal Education," *Philologus* 58 (2014): 76–96. In the *Memorabilia,* Xenophon's Socrates employs the metaphor of hunting to explain how best to find genuine friends. See Tazuko Angela van Berkel, *The Economics of Friendship: Conceptions of Reciprocity in Classical Greece* (Brill: Leiden, 2020), 354–370.

accident that Xenophon here uses a term that is directly related to the adjective (*chrêstos*) that, as documented above, he uses to describe the appropriate activities of free men in the *Symposium*'s passage on smells. The intellectual connection between the contents of Xenophon's *Symposium* and *On Hunting* is also indicated by *Sym.* 4.63 having what seems to be his only metaphorical use of the verb "to hunt," in this case for friends "hunting" to discover where each other happens to be located.

Given that Xenophon expresses an explicit ethical goal for *On Hunting*, it is not surprising that from the start of the treatise (1.1) he stresses the exceptional significance of its subject by stating that wild game and hunting dogs are the "discovery/invention" of the gods Apollo and Artemis. This claim is reminiscent of his statement in the *Memorabilia* cited above about our sense of smell as a benefit conferred by the divine. Moreover, learning how to hunt well is the first education that a young man should receive because hunting is one of "the forms of education by which one becomes good in war and in everything else that necessarily conduces to thinking, speaking, and acting finely" (1.18–2.1).

In *On Hunting* Xenophon also encourages his audience to reflect on how the sniffing out is very difficult, yet necessary, for successful discovery The rabbits' elusive behaviors, aided by challenging seasonal and climate conditions, make detecting this quarry very challenging (5.1–12; 6.2, 4; 8.2). Xenophon stresses the value of learning how to be successful in this particular example of sniffing out hard-to-find prizes with his extensive closing remarks: hunting provides great benefits for educating young men in truth, excellence, and supporting their family, friends, fellow-citizens, and their entire city-state (12.1–13.17).[39]

---

[39] As David Thomas says, "The Enemies of Hunting in Xenophon's

As Xenophon is concluding that those men who love hunting are thereby in fact "good," he ends the treatise with the surprising because uncontextualized statement that not only men who love hunting are good, but so also are women to whom Artemis has given this same characteristic (13.18). The implication seems to be that women, too, can recognize smells of freedom. Could it also be possible that they are able to produce those same sweet smells through "useful" exertions? No answer to this ambiguity is offered. This open-ended close to a non-Socratic work seems to parallel the ambiguity about sweet smells of freedom in the *Symposium*, emphasizing that there is still more to sniff out, in this case concerning gender, in the hunt for knowledge through education and what it means to be free, fine, and good.

A final point to make about the importance of smells in hunting according to Xenophon is that the ability to sniff out rabbits (hares) who are in hiding requires the skills of special dogs, animals whose selective breeding and training by humans has given them an innate ability to discover the concealed goals of their olfactory detection. That is, it takes a special nature and a special education to excel in the task of resolving difficult ambiguity. In his narratives of these dogs' success in locating their highly desirable but hard-to-locate prey, Xenophon uses the same verb meaning "to discover/find out" (*aneuriskô*) that he employs in non-hunting stories to describe acts of discovery by human beings that have crucially important consequences.[40] In

---

Cynegeticus," in Danzig, *et al.*, eds., *Plato and Xenophon* (2018), [Xenophon aims] "to put his audience on their toes about the targets of [his] attack [on the detractors of the value of hunting], leading [his audience] to tease out Xenophon's quarry for themselves (613).

[40] This theme offers a link between Xenophon's Socratic and non-Socratic works, a lingering question in scholarship on Xenophon, as Tom Rood, *Bryn Mawr Classical Review* 2022.02.06, remarks at the end of his

the *Anabasis* (7.4.14), the leaders of a people under attack use their local knowledge to "discover/find out" the locations of the buildings that they desperately need to reach at a moment when these structures are obscured by the darkness of the night and high fencing. In the *Memorabilia* (2.9), Socrates helps Crito, who is plagued by false accusations being brought against him by corrupt liars, "discover/find out" a fellow Athenian named Archedemus, who is poor but "loves being useful" (*philochrêstos*). Archedemus can be useful in this instance because he is adept at finding out the weak spots in the biographies of such con men. Sure enough, Archedemus soon "discovers/finds out" wrong doing by the false accusers; this discovery in turn compels them to abandon their attacks on Socrates' friend, keeping him free from bribery and from conviction for spurious crimes. Xenophon's use of the same word for "discover/find out" in these non-smells stories as in his hunting-smells stories speaks to his presentation of the significance of smells as a source of agency for human beings in general, especially in dealing with ambiguity, at least if they have been fortunate enough to have received the special breeding and training required to maximize their ability to sniff out hidden prizes.

If this supposition is correct, then Socrates' remarkable comments on smells near the start of the *Symposium* are meant to motivate his audience to focus on the philosophical goal of sniffing out the ambiguities of the concept of "being fine and good" for members of the social elite, the quality that Socrates told Lycon he should maintain in the context of "sweet smells of freedom." Since the question of the development of the social and moral meaning(s) of "being fine and good" in classical-era Greek thought is too extensive a topic to investigate here, all I can do is point out that Xenophon in the majority of the

---

review of Johnson, *Xenophon's Socratic Works*.

Symposium presents question and answer sessions related to what this concept might mean. Significantly, however, these sections offer lingering ambiguities rather than clear resolutions (3.1–8.43).

For example, Socrates' interchanges with other guests in this context embody ambiguities in which, for example, wealth can turn out to mean poverty, and poverty wealth. And as for freedom, Charmides in his contribution to the conversation says that everyone agrees it is better to be free than to be a slave, but he then adds that the rich at Athens are slaves to the people of its direct democracy because they have to make large contributions toward the city-state's public expenses (4.29–32).[41] A bit later on, however, Callias expresses the opposite view: being rich at Athens means the city-state cannot give you orders or treat you as a slave (4.45). As before in the dialogue, the ambiguities that these contradictory comments implicitly raise are left standing.

The only apparent exception to this narrative procedure comes in the long section *Symposium* 8.1–43 in which the conversation turns to defining "Love with Self-Control" (*sôphrôn Erôs*). There, Socrates makes it clear—at least to the extent that he ever makes anything clear in the *Symposium*—that full sexual intercourse between men cannot be part of the personal "excellence" (*aretê*) that must be a goal of those aspiring to be fine and good. In fact, Socrates adds, being the companion of a man who loves the body rather than the soul is "contrary to what a free man does" (*aneleutheros*, 8.23).[42] So, the question whether

---

[41] See Nails, *The People of Plato*, 90–94 for the sources and questions related to Charmides' identity and career at Athens.

[42] Félix Buffière, *EROS adolescent: la pédérastie dans la Grèce antique* (Paris: Les Belles Lettres, 1980), 575–580 discusses "pederasty" in Xenophon's *Symposium*; Clifford Hindley, "Xenophon on Male Love," *Classical Quarterly* 49 (1999): 74–99 surveys the topic in Xenophon's works; Johnson,

passionate love between men should include sexual relations ends up being the only one that Socrates appears to answer in Xenophon's *Symposium*.

In fact, however, not even this overtly blanket statement turns out to offer a full resolution to the question under discussion because it fails to clarify precisely which sexual activities short of intercourse are or are not allowed between male lovers. And this vagueness seems positively pellucid compared to what then follows in the context of "being fine and good." Immediately after Socrates has closed the conversation on male erotic relationships without addressing all their possible ambiguities, Lycon, Autolycus' father, gets up to leave the party with his son to go for an after-dinner walk. As he departs, Lycon spontaneously remarks "By the goddess Hera, Socrates you seem to me to be a fine and good person" (9.1). No response to this remarkable statement is forthcoming from Socrates, any other character in the dialogue, or Xenophon the narrator as the dialogue quickly comes to an end (9.7). The question is therefore left completely open how it is possible for the designation "fine and good" to apply to Socrates, who is neither rich, nor politically prominent, nor, as the dialogue's conversations have previously established (2.16–20, 5.2–8), distinguished by a handsome face and a physique sculpted by the sweat and olive oil of the gymnasium.

In sum, then, the series of conversations in the *Symposium*

Xenophon's Socratic Works, 210–227 discusses *Symposium* 8, with references to previous scholarship on the issue of sex. See Francesca Pentassuglio, "Socrates *Erotikos*: Mutuality, Role Reversal, and Erotic *Paideia* in Xenophon's and Plato's *Symposia*," in Danzig *et al.*, eds., *Plato and Xenophon* (2018), 365–390 for comparison with Plato's *Symposium*. Humble, "Xenophon of Athens," 105–107 refers to the "chaste pederasty" of the *Symposium* in her discussion of Xenophon's *Constitution of the Spartans* on the topic of love between adult men and adolescent boys.

about "being fine and good" is on the whole indirect and multi-faceted—and in the end offers no clear definition of this ambiguous and controversial concept that the symposiasts are investigating. As Socrates himself puts it, the topic remains "being fine and good, whatever that is" (8.3). Simply put, this ambiguity remains persistent. The same is true of the theme "sweet smells of freedom." This expression does not recur in the *Symposium* after the early passage on smells. Therefore, the uncertainty that it raises about freedom and social status in Athens' democracy never gets resolved. Any answers remain hidden for Xenophon's audience to sniff out as a prize for hunting down their desired quarry. They therefore need to realize that the hunt to uncover the nature of freedom for the fine and good will be arduous and perhaps even treacherous.

Just how high the stakes are in this hunt becomes clear to Xenophon's audience when they contemplate the actual fates of main characters in the *Symposium*.[43] Like Plato in his *Symposium*, Xenophon as narrator does not mention later sad personal histories suffered by main characters in his narrative, even though he of course knew these stories well, as did anyone who experienced, heard, or read about the dismal consequences for Athenians of the Peloponnesian War and its aftermath.[44] This designation certainly included every educated person coeval with Xenophon, and no doubt countless others as well in a society so thoroughly infused with oral gossip about well-known

---

[43] As Gray, *Xenophon's Mirror of Princes*, remarks, "*Symposium* has been considered ironic overall because of the later careers of some of the characters ..." (334, n. 8). Johnson, *Xenophon's Socratic Works*, 225–227 discusses the *Symposium's* "irony."

[44] Except for Aristophanes, main characters in Plato' dialogue either suffer disastrously (Alcibiades, Eryximachus, Phaedrus, Pausanias, and Socrates), or leave Athens for the court of the Macedonian king (Agathon and Pausanias). Nails, *The People of Plato*, provides source references.

individuals and families.[45] The life lesson to be learned was the troubling truth that there is no guaranteed benefit from the status designated by emitting "sweet smells of freedom."

I can here only briefly summarize this historical information so crucial for sniffing out hidden and potentially disturbing meanings implied by Xenophon's narrative of a "light-hearted" party. Callias' continuing extravagances of the expensive type on display at his symposium later reduced him to humiliating poverty.[46] Far worse was the fate of Niceratus, son of the famous Athenian general Nicias. First, he suffered a drastic diminution of the vast riches that he had inherited from his father (d. 413 BCE), and then, soon after the end the Peloponnesian War, he was treacherously killed by the murderous oligarchic faction from the Athenian social elite labelled "The Thirty (Tyrants)," who ruled Athens in 404/3 BCE.[47] Equally horrible was the fate of Autolycus, whose victory provided the

---

[45] See Alex Gottesman, *Politics and the Street in Democratic Athens* (Cambridge: Cambridge University Press, 2014) on the near ubiquity in Athens of informal discussion of political figures and issues, as vividly portrayed by Theophrastus, *Characters* 8. Gossip was such a hallmark of this discussion that speakers in court cases could identify it with the goddess *Phêmê* in their arguments to juries of randomly chosen citizens. See Nick Fisher, "Creating a Cultural Community: Aeschines and Demosthenes," in Andreas N. Michalopoulos *et al.*, eds., *The Rhetoric of Unity and Division in Ancient Literature* (Berlin: De Gruyter, 2021), 46, 48.

[46] Lysias 19.48; Aristotle, *Rhetoric* 3.2.10 (1405a); Athenaeus 4.169a, 12.537c. In addition, Xenophon, *Hell.* 6.3.2–6 in his description of the peace negotiations between Athens and Sparta in 371 BCE presents a speech by Callias as one of the Athenian representatives that outlines his personal character in a way that has raised controversy. See Gray, *The Character of Xenophon's* Hellenica, 123–131, especially 124–125, 129; Nails, *The People of Plato*, 68–74.

[47] Plutarch, *Nicias* 3; Lysias 18. 6, 19.47; Xenophon, *Hell.* 2.3.39; Diodorus 14.5.5; Plutarch, *Moralia* 998b; Nails, *The People of Plato*, 111–113 (on The Thirty), 211–212 (on Niceratus).

occasion for the *Symposium*: he was also brutally murdered by this regime of his fellow "fine and good" citizens.[48] Charmides was exiled and also lost his property in the aftermath of the impiety scandal of 415, but he recovered sufficiently to serve as a member of the board governing Athens' main port as part of the vicious rule of The Thirty; he then died in 403 BCE in the civil war against his fellow citizens who successfully fought to remove the Spartan-supported oligarchy at Athens and restore democracy.[49] And of course the most enduringly infamous consequence of the hatred polluting Athens in the aftermath of this bloody time was that Socrates himself was condemned to death in 399 BCE by vote of a jury of his citizen peers.[50] Socrates' other friends at the party—Antisthenes, Critobulus, and Hermogenes—were then present as Socrates' grieving supporters when he took the poison for his mandated execution.[51]

And above all there is the particularly startling connection between Socrates' trial and execution and the narrative of the congenial exchanges between Lycon and Socrates in the *Symposium*: Lycon actually joined in the prosecution of Socrates. Indeed, his participation in this process helped guarantee Socrates' condemnation, as Plato has Socrates say in his *Apology*, a work

---

[48] Diodorus 14.5.7; Plutarch, *Lysander* 15; Nails, *The People of Plato*, 62–63.

[49] Xenophon, *Hell.* 2.4.19, [Aristotle], *Athenaion Politeia* 35.1; Nails, *The People of Plato*, 90–94. Xenophon *Sym.* 4.30–32 anachronistically portrays Charmides as having been punished but not banished before the date of Callias' symposium.

[50] Nails, *The People of Plato*, 263–269; Thomas C. Brickhouse and Nicholas D. Smith, *The Trial and Execution of Socrates: Sources and Controversies* (New York: Oxford University Press, 2002).

[51] Plato, *Phaedo* 59b. Diogenes Laertius, *Antisthenes* 6.1.9–10 says Antisthenes agitated for the execution of Socrates' other two prosecutors; what, if anything, happened to Lycon is unknown. See Nails, *The People of Plato*, 189.

earlier than Xenophon' *Symposium* that his audience could well have read.[52] This is the same Lycon whom at the end of the *Symposium* Xenophon portrays as complimenting Socrates as being "fine and good" in front of all the other guests![53] This astonishing irony dramatically implies baffling issues of ambiguity left unanswered by Xenophon's narrative.[54]

The tragic histories of these characters in the *Symposium* create an ostensibly hidden but in fact unmistakable provocation to thought emerging from the dialogue's theme of "being fine and good": the necessity to reflect on the unsettling truth that the freedom of fine and good Athenian men—and women, too?—however that status is defined, cannot protect them from harm at the hands of fellow citizens. I believe this characteristic of Xenophon's *Symposium* points to a central theme of the dialogue: how challenging it is to recognize ambiguities of meaning in the human condition, and then to figure out ways to resolve these uncertainties when they embody potentially ultimate consequences for people's lives, whether socially,

---

[52] Plato, *Apology* 23e–24a, 36a; Nails, *The People of Plato*, 188–189. The date of Plato's *Apology* is uncertain but probably falls between 393 and 387 BCE, according to Charles Platter, "Plato's *Apology* of Socrates," *Oxford Bibliographies* https://www.oxfordbibliographies.com/view/document/obo-9780195389661/obo-9780195389661-0165.xml.

[53] Nails, *The People of Plato*, 189 refutes the suggestion that Xenophon cannot have meant that the Lycon in the *Symposium* was the same Lycon who joined the prosecution of Socrates.

[54] Another ambiguity not addressed by Xenophon is his likely role in the corps of cavalrymen that served as enforcers for The Thirty and the hard times that he experienced after being exiled from Athens in the 390s BCE, including in 371 losing the estate gifted to him by the Spartans that had supported him. See Brennan, "Introduction," xxi–xxv on these events. If Xenophon composed the *Symposium* in 360s, then its originally wealthy and prominent-in-Athens author was writing with some experience of a doleful fate, though admittedly one far less devastating than that of most of the leading characters in his dialogue.

financially, politically, or morally.

This characteristic presents Xenophon's audience with the challenge—which Xenophon leaves implicit—of having to sniff out what in the dialogue is meant to be taken seriously as philosophy and not just as bits of dramatic color and verve. The mixed-tone format of Xenophon's *Symposium* and its author's choice of historical figures as main characters who will later meet terrible ends emphasize the ambiguity of fundamental social, ethical, and political issues in late fifth/early fourth century BCE Athenian democracy: the ambiguities of what it means to be regarded as "fine and good" in Xenophon's time and place and how the "fine and good" can ultimately find it difficult and even deadly to live up to their special status.

Xenophon chooses to emphasize smells as a theme near the beginning of the *Symposium* to directly stress the nature and the challenge of these ambiguities about how to fulfill the social, political, and moral responsibilities of members of the free elite in society. Thinking about the meaning of smells in this context is relevant because the sense of smell metaphorically provides, as Xenophon's works reveal, a powerful, indeed divinely created method for sniffing out solutions to the huge puzzle of how to be free, fine, and good. The Socrates of the *Symposium* seems never to answer this question. Indeed, the last mention of "being free" (*eleutherios*) comes well before the dialogue's end, when Antisthenes, not Socrates, proclaims that what makes people free is keeping their desires and therefore their need for money modest (4.39).

If we today want to address this question of what it means to be free, fine, and good, I think that trying to sniff out the meaning(s) of the *Symposium*'s prominent passage on smells can help us to reflect on how we should define freedom as fine and good individuals living in society. Can sniffing out sweet smells of freedom motivate us to consider how to improve ourselves

and our own lives, how to define the philosophical, political, social, and moral meanings of freedom, and how to imagine improvements in our communities for everyone in the context of
that definition?[55] The prominence of the topic of smells in the
early part of the *Symposium* creates a dramatic context for this
theme of our sniffing out the best way to reach "fine and good"
goals if we enjoy the privilege of living as free people. Xenophon, I submit, can spur us on to regard our intellectual sense
of smell as a tool for interpreting meanings and answering questions about how best to handle significant uncertainties in life
as individuals and communities that value freedom.[56]

To be hopeful, our conclusion can be that where there is
ambiguity, there is the possibility of change and therefore
chances for improvement. Of course, the depressing fates of notable fine, good, and free characters in Xenophon's *Symposium*
remind us that freedom's ambiguity can also end in disaster.
What then should we be thinking about and doing if we are
fortunate enough to enjoy our own modern iterations of sweet
smells of freedom? Respecting what I see as the strongly open-
ended spirit of Xenophon's Socratic works, I end here with this
question that seems to me today ever more relevant to the state
of democracy in the United States.

---

[55] Vivienne J. Gray, *Xenophon on Government* (Cambridge: Cambridge
University Press, 2007), 56–7 remarks on how Xenophon is concerned with
the ambiguities of different systems of government and his interest in how
to improve them.

[56] Johnstone, "Aristotle on Odour and Smell," discusses Aristotle's view
on human beings' physical sense of smell as activating their capacity to perceive.